EMERGE

BE THE UNMISTAKABLE AUTHORITY IN YOUR FIELD

BRIAN TRACY, STEVE LOWELL, JAYNE LOWELL
AND OTHER EXPERTS FROM AROUND THE WORLD

Hasmark
PUBLISHING
INTERNATIONAL

Hasmark Publishing
www.hasmarkpublishing.com

Copyright © 2021 S & J Training Solutions Inc.
First Edition

No part of this book may be reproduced or transmitted in any form or by any means, electronic or mechanical, including photocopying, recording or by any information storage and retrieval system, without written permission from the author, except for the inclusion of brief quotations in a review.

Disclaimer
This book is designed to provide information and motivation to our readers. It is sold with the understanding that the publisher is not engaged to render any type of psychological, legal, or any other kind of professional advice. The content of each article is the sole expression and opinion of its author, and not necessarily that of the publisher. No warranties or guarantees are expressed or implied by the publisher's choice to include any of the content in this volume. Neither the publisher nor the individual author(s) shall be liable for any physical, psychological, emotional, financial, or commercial damages, including, but not limited to, special, incidental, consequential or other damages. Our views and rights are the same: You are responsible for your own choices, actions, and results.

Permission should be addressed in writing to
S & J Training Solutions Inc.
1180 River Road, Manotick, Ontario
K4M 1B4

Cover Design: Anne Karklins | anne@hasmarkpublishing.com
Book Design: Amit Dey | amit@hasmarkpublishing.com

ISBN 13: 978-1-77482-077-3
ISBN 10: 1774820773

To our incredible clients.
Not a single one of these pages would have ever been
written if it weren't for you.
Thank you for your willingness to be coached so you
truly can be "The Unmistakably Authority".

Brian Tracy's Endorsement

Congratulations on your investment in yourself and your business through this powerful book.

Through this book, multiple experts share with you their expert insights on everything from business to finances to personal growth. It's a profound collection of proven and tested wisdom to help you emerge stronger, more powerful and more profitable than ever.

If your goal is to grow your business, increase your wealth and create the lifestyle you desire, you'll find answers within these pages that could change your life.

This is truly a powerful book, filled with wisdom from experts from around the world who have earned that wisdom through success and failure. Aren't these the best teachers to have?

Thank you to Steve and Jayne Lowell and their team for their dedication to helping entrepreneurs around the world share their brilliance with you and me too.

To your success

Brian Tracy
Best-Selling Author and Professional Speaker

Acknowledgments

We are so grateful for those who have made this book a reality.

First and foremost, our thanks to our good friend, the legendary Brian Tracy, without whose influence, guidance, and friendship this book would not be possible.

Next, to each of our contributing authors who have not only shared their wisdom in these pages but worked tirelessly through a complicated and demanding process to make it so. To each one of you, we offer our gratitude, respect, and love. Your contribution and dedication to this project have been exemplary.

To our team; Amanda, Tara, Nim and Judy and her staff at Hasmark Publishing. Thank you for being there when we needed you, for steering the ship, avoiding some rocky shoals and bringing us safely to shore with the release of this book.

To our community of clients, colleagues and friends around the world who have shared with us, learned alongside us and worked with us to hone our craft, build our business and create the lifestyle we desire; we thank you for your contribution to the greater community.

And to you, the reader. Thank you for buying this book, for your trust in us and our experts within this book, and for stepping up to improve your own life so you can contribute to the lives of others through your own brilliance.

....and certainly last by not least, gratitude to God for without Him nothing would be possible.

With Love and Gratitude,

Steve and Jayne Lowell
Co-Founders S&J Trainings Solutions Inc.

Table of Contents

1

Leading from the Front
– Brian Tracy

You have more potential than you could use in one hundred years. Your primary job in life is not to become someone different, but to unlock the potential that you already have. Your job is to set big goals, make big plans, overcome obstacles, and achieve more than you ever thought possible.

In life, we usually start off at the bottom, as a junior employee, a worker, an hourly laborer. If you do a good job, and get more and better results, you begin to climb the ladder of success. You become a supervisor, responsible for helping others to get more and better results. And remember, in the world of work and success, results are everything.

Soon, with experience, hard work and continuous learning, you become a manager. You become responsible for getting results from more and more people. Finally, you become a leader. You are not only responsible for the results of large numbers of people, you are in charge of deciding exactly what is to be done, how it is to be done, when it is to be done, and who will be responsible for doing it. You move from being an addition sign to being a multiplication sign. And once you become a leader, there are no limits except for those limits you place on your own mind.

The Skills of Leadership

Your ability to negotiate, communicate, influence, and persuade others to do things is absolutely indispensable to everything you accomplish in life. The most effective men and women in every area are those who can quite competently organize the cooperation and assistance of more and more people toward the accomplishment of important goals and objectives.

Of course, everyone you meet has different values, opinions, attitudes, beliefs, cultural values, work habits, goals, ambitions, and dreams. Because of this incredible diversity of human resources, it has never been more difficult and yet more necessary for skilled leaders to emerge and form these people into high-performing teams.

Fortunately, leaders are made, not born. You learn to become a leader by doing what other excellent leaders have done before you. You become proficient in your job or skill, and then you become proficient at understanding the motivations and behaviors of other people. As a leader, you combine your personal competencies with the competencies of a variety of others into a smoothly functioning team that can out-play and out-perform all its competitors.

The Qualities of High-Performance Teams

When you become a team leader, even if your team only consists of one other person, you must immediately develop a whole new set of leadership skills. In order to determine what these skills are, you need to consider the progressive development of high-performing teams.

Teams usually go through four phases as they evolve toward high performance. These stages are called *forming, storming, norming,* and *performing.*

The *forming* stage is very important, perhaps even critical, to the success of the team. Your ability to select the proper team members in order to accomplish a particular task—personal or business—is the mark of the superior leader. It is estimated that 95% of your success as a manager, or leader, will be determined by the people you select in the first place. If you select the wrong people initially, it becomes almost impossible afterward to build a winning team, just as it would be impossible to win athletic championships with unskilled or ill-suited players.

In the forming stage, the team members come together and begin to get a feeling for each other. Or new people join the team and need to be introduced to the others and trained in their jobs. There is usually a good deal of discussion, argument, disagreement, personal expression of likes and dislikes, and the forming of friendly alliances between team members, as the team forms into a highly productive group.

This stage, especially the discussions and conversations that take place, may seem time consuming, but it is absolutely indispensable to the development of a high performing team of people that you can lead. One of the most important qualities of a leader is that of *patience.* And patience is never more necessary than when you are going through the early stages of assembling your team.

The second stage of team development is called *storming.* Storming is a shortened form of the word "brainstorming." It is during this stage when the group, whose members are now comfortable with each other, begins the hard work of setting goals and deadlines, dividing up the tasks, and getting on with the job.

During the storming phase, people learn about the contributions that each member can make to achieve the purposes of the team.

The third stage of team development is called *norming*. This is where norms and standards are established among the team members so that everyone feels secure and confident in his or her role. All members know what is expected of them and how it is to be measured. And all members are aware of their responsibilities and obligations, not only to getting the job done, but to each other as well. Your ability as a leader to promote the norming process is critical to the success of the team.

The fourth stage of team development is *performing*. In the final analysis, as we said, your ability to get results is all that really matters. Your lifestyle, your rate of promotion, your income and benefits, and the respect and esteem you receive from your co-workers and bosses will all be determined by your ability to perform and to get others to perform.

Five Qualities of Productive Work Teams

There are basically five qualities of the most productive work teams that you will need to foster throughout the stages of team development. The degree to which you accomplish these *before* you start working will determine your success as a team leader and the success of the team as a whole.

The first quality is the existence of *shared values*. You can foster this quality by asking the question, "What are our values?" or, "What do we stand for?" People will contribute the values they consider the most important. As they do, you or someone else can write them on a flipchart. The values will usually be something like: integrity, excellence, quality, caring about people, profitability, and harmony. Take the time to write them down and agree upon them right at the beginning.

The second quality of top teams is *shared objectives*. It is absolutely essential that everyone takes the time to discuss the actual reasons for forming the team and the chief results that are expected of them.

Leaders are those who can see the big picture. They are absolutely clear about what it is they want to accomplish and what it will look like. They have the ability to articulate this vision so that it is clear in the minds and hearts of others, and to get everyone, no matter what their background or personality, working together in harmony toward the realization of that vision.

My favorite word in business is "Clarity." People cannot hit a target they cannot see. Again, even though it may appear time consuming, everyone needs to have ample opportunity to discuss and agree on the ultimate goals desired *before* the work begins. The more thorough the discussion on goals and objectives, the more effective the team will be when it begins working, and the more it will get done, in less time.

The third quality of highly-productive teams is *shared activities*. Everyone knows what they are supposed to contribute to the achievement of the overall goals and objectives of the team. Everyone also knows what each of the other members is expected to do. All the work that has to be done is clearly divided up among the team members, and everyone knows their role in the process.

The fourth quality of high-performing teams is that the head of the team *leads the action*. You become the role model for everyone else. You go out in front. You set the example for how you want everyone else to perform. You continually look for ways to make it easier for your team members to do their jobs. You accept complete responsibility for the achievement of the overall goal.

You start a little earlier, you work a little harder, and you stay a little later. You set careful priorities on your time and you always work on your highest value tasks. You never ask anyone to do something that you wouldn't do yourself. You always put yourself out in front and go to bat for your people in every circumstance. You are a leader because you continually *lead*.

The fifth and final quality of high-performing teams is that individually, and as a group, they continually evaluate their progress toward their goals and values. They are always asking themselves, "How are we doing, and how can we do better?" When they manufacture or sell products in the marketplace, they ask their customers for continuous feedback and evaluation. Top teams set incredible standards of excellence and they are constantly striving to be better.

Continually Check Your Progress

Whenever you have problems, misunderstandings, or difficulties within your team, you call a "time out" and reexamine your values, your goals, their activities, their assignments, and their responsibilities. You should be more concerned with *what's* right than with *who's* right.

Three Great Questions

There are three questions that you can ask, especially when you are having problems. First you should ask, "What are we trying to do? Revisit your goals and objectives and make sure that everyone is clear about your goals.

The second question that you ask repeatedly is, "How are we trying to do it?" Is your current method of operation working for you? Are you getting the results you expected?

The third question you ask is, "Could there be a better way?" The fact is that there could *always* be a better way. As the leader, you must always be open to the possibility that you could be *wrong.* If you are wrong, if your current method is not working, what is your 'Plan B?" Remember, you are only as free as your well-developed options. What are yours?

Think About Winning

Excellent leaders are more concerned with *winning* than with not losing. High-Performing teams run by excellent leaders, are determined to perform in an excellent fashion, to get great results. All team members know that their ability to work together in harmony and cooperation is the key to the success of each person.

The wonderful thing about becoming a leader in your work and personal life is that you can continually practice the skills of influencing and persuading others toward a common objective. You can promote the principles of excellent teamwork by establishing your values and goals, determining your activities, and then leading the action. And you can improve yourself by continually evaluating your performance against your standards.

One of the marks of excellent people is that they never compare themselves with others. They only compare themselves with themselves and with their past accomplishments and future potential. You can become an even more excellent person by constantly setting higher and higher standards for yourself and then by doing everything possible to live up to those standards. The more proficient you become at getting the results for which you were hired, the more opportunities you will have to get results through others. And your ability to put together a team and then to lead that team to high performance will enable you to accelerate your career and fulfill your goals faster than ever before.

**Some of this chapter is based on the work of
Bruce Tuckman**

Brian Tracy

Brian Tracy is the Chairman and CEO of Brian Tracy International, a company specializing in training and development of individuals and organizations. He is among the top speakers, trainers and seminar leaders in the world today.

Brian Tracy has consulted for more than 1,000 companies and has addressed more than 5 million people in 5,000 talks and seminars throughout the US, Canada and 70 other countries worldwide.

He has studied, researched, written and spoke for 40 years in the fields of economics, history, business, philosophy and psychology. He is the top-selling author of over 80 books that have been translated into 42 languages.

2

The Thinking Big Delusion
– Steve Lowell

For over 35 years now, I have been hearing it. "You have to think BIGGER!" "You need BIG, SCARY GOALS!" "If you're going to think anyway, THINK BIG!" And for 30 of those years, I bought into the illusion that thinking big would help me grow my business and create wealth. I was wrong. I thought big; for my whole life. I have been studying personal development for my entire adult life. There's not much out there in the personal development space that I have not studied, practiced, and even taught. And all of it includes some form of advice around thinking big; but there was always something missing. It took me 30 years to figure out what it was.

The missing piece is a parcel of wisdom that comes from inside you called your Expert Insights™, which is found through a process called your Deep Thought Strategy™. With this preparation, when the time comes for you to think big, you'll be ready and properly equipped.

The problem with thinking big as a strategy is that it sets you up for near-certain failure. Thinking big by itself doesn't validate that whatever you're doing now is even possible in a bigger game. Through a deep thought strategy, you'll validate the scalability of your business before you make mission-critical decisions on a bigger scale and know how to position yourself for a much bigger game. Yes, there is a time for thinking big; but not before some preparatory work is done first. Thinking big can work. It can take you to levels you never knew were possible. But before you seriously begin thinking bigger, let me urge you to first prepare yourself by thinking deeper. Deeper precedes bigger every time. Deeper before bigger is what the deep thought strategy is all about.

What is a Deep Thought Strategy?™

Deep Thought Strategy™ is a framework by which we explore our business expertise and our clients' condition at the forensic level in search of what I call our Expert Insights™.

Expert Insights™ is a term I use to describe a perspective that comes from deep within your experience and of which only you can claim ownership. Your Expert Insights™ allow you to position yourself as being unique in your field by presenting to your prospects and audiences a snapshot of their world that they have never considered before, and then positioning yourself strategically and tactically as the only possible solution. It all starts with understanding where you currently land in the eyes of your highest-value prospects. You see, you need to have a high level of perceived authority for you to be able to stand out. Your deep thought strategy provides that perceived authority. Throughout my career, I have noticed that so many experts struggle to position themselves as unique in their field. Of course, the challenge is that very few of them actually ARE unique, even though most think they are – this is a big problem for those who try to think big.

I will often ask people the question; what makes you different? In almost every single case the answer contains one or more of these things:

- Tenure (I have been in the business 35 years)
- Service (We customize our service, spend more time with clients)
- Solution (I have a unique approach, my three pillars to this or my four secrets to that)

The problem is none of these three elements are differentiators. When you rely on any or all of these elements, all you are doing is making yourself look and sound exactly like everyone else who does what you do. Because of this, standing out can be a challenge. Nevertheless, standing out is what you must do on your way to thinking bigger and playing a bigger game. Based on my own experience of having gone through this myself, I can clearly see where so many others are going through the exact same thing; they just can't see it any more than I could when I was in the thick of it.

To help my audiences and clients better understand why they are getting stuck, I developed a grid to map out the various states that I went through. I can observe my clients going through these same states and know what causes them to move between the states. I thought if I could demonstrate that I understand what my prospects and audiences are going through, I might position myself as a good choice to help them. I didn't realize it at the time, but I was thinking deeper, not bigger. What I came up with was a description of the journey I experienced, and I represent it as the typical journey that I see most entrepreneurs go through. I have since validated this entire process with thousands of people all over the world. I call this grid, The Repumeter™.

The Repumeter™ is a tool that measures the state of your reputation. Looking back on my journey through the Repumeter lens, I can pinpoint every step I have made from one state to the next. Meanwhile, the Repumeter™ continues to evolve. I'm now known all over the world as "The Repumeter Guy." This is powerful. We have crashed through the 7-figure barrier by building a strategy around this information; that's the deep thought strategy. By understanding how you are placed in the minds of your target audience, you can develop a process to position yourself as the known expert in your field, whatever your field is, and then leverage that positioning by crafting your message strategically and delivering your message tactically. It's your deep thought strategy that gets you there.

The Four Repumeter™ Milestones

Through our professional journey, our reputation typically falls into one of four states. Some move from state to state; most just stay where they are.

Obscurity

The first state is what I call "Obscurity." Obscurity means people in your circles don't really know who you are or what you do.

This state can be somewhat deceptive because it's easy to confuse a large circle of connection for a large circle of influence. It's a common misconception that because you're connected to a lot of people, they all know what you do, when in fact, they don't.

You know you are in Obscurity when:

- The phone isn't ringing with referrals or prospective clients

- You go to networking groups or meetings and very few people, if anyone at all, knows who you are. People are not introducing you to others and you find it challenging to get noticed
- You're operating in your business from a standpoint of need; always trying to figure out where the next contract, or the next speaking gig, or the next customer is coming from
- Your energy and all your activities are all based on attracting business to you

In the state of Obscurity, you're always asking yourself these questions:

- Why am I not getting referrals?
- Why are people not calling and saying, "I want to work with you?"
- Why is it so hard to close sales?
- Why do I keep losing sales?
- Why are my books, products, or services not selling?

We can lock ourselves into the Obscurity state by doing the wrong things or by not doing the right things. Many people get stuck here and never make progress.

Competitive

When we stay in business long enough, and people start paying a little bit of attention to us, we come to the state that I call "Competitive." Competitive means people in your circles have a pretty good idea of what you do, but there's nothing that separates you from everybody else who does what you do. Even though it's certainly better than Obscurity, all it means is that now you're in the game. It doesn't mean that you're standing head and shoulders above anybody, and it doesn't mean that your business is building momentum. You know you're in the Competitive state when these things are happening:

- You're getting some business, but you're still working hard for it

- You find yourself negotiating your fees so you can get the business before your competitor gets the business

- You might include bonuses or freebies to sweeten the pot a little so you can win the business

- Your sales presentation always seems to come down to price

- Referrals start to come in from time to time, but most of them are exploring other options as well, and you go right back to competing on price or perceived value

- You have an "a" or "an" kind of identity. People refer to you as a noun. You're a coach, you're a speaker, you're a financial advisor, you're a trainer, you're a mortgage broker, you're a real estate agent, you're a consultant, you're a salesperson, you're "a" something. You're in what I call a category of many

- People you know hire your competitors to do what you do. If you're a coach, they hire somebody else to coach them. They hire other consultants, not you, even though they know you exist and you're in the game

- You may even be mis-branded. People may think they know what you do, but they may not be quite on the mark and pass you over when opportunities present themselves

The Competitive state is where most people stay forever. They do the same things everybody else does in exactly the same way.

Branded

The next state on the Repumeter™ is what I call "Branded." At the "Branded" stage, people in your circles know who you are and what you do, and there is beginning to be something noticeable about you, but they may not be able to define exactly what that is. At this stage, you begin to see an increase in referrals, though prospects will still be shopping around. You'll still need to compete with others for business, but your name comes up among the first recommendations by others. Typically, your referrals have some idea of what your fees might be, or at least what ballpark you play in regarding fees. They're not ready to sign on the dotted line until after they have done some checking, but you'll notice that they may attempt to negotiate a little less, and they may be ready to pay higher fees with a little convincing from you. You may still negotiate your terms, but you're not as concerned about survival, and you're at the point where you can be just a little more selective about your clientele.

Branded can be a tentative condition because your circles are starting to notice you a little more, which means they will watch you through a more critical lens. Their expectations will increase, they will evaluate what they see and hear more critically, and they'll seek to validate (or invalidate) your status. If the perceived reality does not match the expectations, your reputation can quickly drop back to Competitive, and this can be damaging because you can actually become known as one who was not able to measure up to the reputation.

This state on your Repumeter™ can also be a launching pad to bigger and better things. For that to happen, your name needs to be re-associated from your title to something else.

As previously mentioned, while navigating past Obscurity and into Competitive, your name is primarily associated with your title. You're known as "a" something or "an" something. This association pigeonholes you into a category of many. You become one of a larger population.

This makes thinking bigger dangerous because at these stages, all you have to offer, at least in the minds of your circles, is more of the same. Once you enter the Branded state, there's an opportunity for you to secure your position as an authority. This happens because of the increased scrutiny that occurs once you reach this status. For you to leverage your position at Branded, you'll need to make sure to reach or exceed expectations. The toughest part about all of this is that you won't even know it's happening.

THE One

The fourth state on the Repumeter™ is what I call "THE One." It's the ultimate. This is exactly where you want to be. At THE One, you are no longer in a category of many; you are no longer in a category of a few, you are now a category of one, the only logical choice. You know you're at this stage when these things are happening:

- You no longer have to compete for business. Clients come looking for you because they already know they want you

- You set whatever fees you like, and the only prospects who don't pay them are those who can't afford them, and you're okay with that

- You get to pick and choose with whom you work. You can turn away any business that doesn't meet your prerequisites

- You work from a position of passion instead of necessity
- People begin to emulate you. They look to you for answers because they want what you have
- Your work is recognized and implemented across your circles

In this state, your energy becomes more about working in your passion than about attracting business. You start to operate from a position of being creative and being of service. You don't have to worry about generating money as a full-time job. You don't need to work as hard to get new clients. Your reputation begins to spread quickly as others share with their own circles of influence the impact you have had, thus escalating the visibility of your reputation and your work. Before we move on, let me ask you these two questions:

1. Do you know where you are on your own Repumeter™?
2. Are you exactly where you want and need to be?

The Repumeter™ is part of my Expert Insights™ and has since become the foundation of my deep thought strategy, which now prepares me to think big. Thinking big is no longer an illusion for me; it is now part of a deep thought strategy that has taken and continues to take my wife, Jayne, and I all over the world. How would you like to know what your own Expert Insights™ are? Why not start with this… visit us at www.TheLowells.Global and join us as our personal guest at one of our monthly online events. We would love to see you there!

Steve Lowell

Steve Lowell, CSP has been speaking and performing on the live stage since the age of 6, that's over 50 years ago.

From Ottawa, Canada, Steve is an award-winning, global speaker and for over 30 years he has been training and mentoring executives, thought-leaders and professional speakers around the world to deliver high-impact keynote speeches, drive revenue from the platform and build wealth through speaking.

He's the 2021/2022 President of the Global Speakers Federation (GSF) and the past national President of the Canadian Association of Professional Speakers (CAPS).

He shares the stage with such greats as Jack Canfield (Chicken Soup for the Soul Series), Kevin Harrington (Shark Tank and "As Seen on TV"), and Brian Tracy (Author of over 70 books).

Together with his wife, Jayne he travels the world speaking, training, and mentoring those who have a message to monetize through the spoken word.

3

Your 7-Figure Mindset
– Jayne Lowell

I've been fortunate to see success early in my career, but just because I'd seen the summit, didn't mean I was always going to stay there. I soon found out that my biggest obstacle in my business and personal life, which became very interrelated, turned out to be my own mindset. On the journey back up, I've had to continue working towards my personal growth in order to achieve long term prosperity.

My Business Mindset

On November 29, 1991, I was sitting at my kitchen table, my week old baby in my lap, waiting for my husband to come home from work. I was really excited to see him because I was not used to being a stay-at-home mother.

Much to my surprise, he announced he'd been laid off. This wouldn't usually be a big deal, but I wasn't working since I'd just given birth. We had a tremendous amount of expenses and now no income.

Instead of looking for jobs in the same fields of our previous work, we decided to take the leap and start a clothing manufacturing business together. In our first year, we ended up making $1.2 million in sales. I also got pregnant with twins. So I had a business, a newborn, and two more on the way. What could possibly go wrong?

The business made several million in sales annually and remained stable for 15 years, until eventually I decided that the business needed to double in revenue. This was quite a bold goal as many retailers were closing at that time. I thought to myself, "How am I going to do that?" As I had never been formally trained in business, I decided to attend a conference in the United States to learn more about how to scale up.

Next, I hired a business coach to help me figure out how to run my business better. She said to me, "Oh no Jayne, you know how to run your business. I'm going to help you with your mindset. I'm going to help you understand what holds you back from doubling your sales."

I said to her, "I have an awesome mindset, what are you talking about?" I had lived and breathed the entrepreneur lifestyle since childhood. But I quickly came to realize that I did in fact have a mindset issue around trust; I just hadn't seen it up until that point.

In my head, I was the best salesperson. No one could do it better than me. I felt I couldn't trust any of my colleagues to do the same calibre of job that I did. I believed I was the one who had to do that type of work, and you couldn't tell me otherwise. When I finally realized I had to give that trust to others, I hired three different account managers, one for each of the major companies. In that year alone, we took our business from $5.5 million to $11.4 million in sales. Sales remained at that level until 2010, when we retired from that business.

This is where the story changes, and for a long time I wouldn't tell this part of the story, because I was ashamed and embarrassed. Things were unhappy in my marriage, and we ended up divorced. I couldn't believe it had actually happened to me. I'd had everything I had ever wanted: a beautiful home, three kids in private school, world travel — I'd been living the life I'd always dreamed. Suddenly, I found myself with absolutely nothing. For a long time, I'd blamed everyone else for my problems. But in 2012, I finally decided to take responsibility for the part that I played in my life.

Fast forward a little bit, and I end up meeting Steve. In the meantime, I worked with other people as a business coach. Yes, I loved making clothes and being good at what I did. But after a while, I didn't feel connected to what I was doing in the clothing industry anymore. Working with my business coach, I realized that my passion and my gift was helping other people the way she helped me. That was what I truly wanted to do with the rest of my life.

Soon after deciding that this new chapter of my life was what I was truly meant to do, my clients and I faced certain rifts in our business relationships. Time and time again, they would tell me that I didn't understand what they were going through. They didn't want to hear what I had to say because they thought that I couldn't see things from their perspective. To them, I was this person who had been making millions in sales in my past business, so how could I possibly understand the financial problems they were facing?

In the summer of 2016, someone came to our house for coaching. After spending the day together, he said to me, "so you're a millionaire?" I responded yes, because even though I wasn't, I had the mindset of a millionaire. But as a person who is highly authentic and integral, this left me conflicted. I had just told someone something that was no longer true. I then said to Steve, "2017 is the year that we make a million dollars, and I need to get on stage in 2018 to tell my story. People need to understand that it's okay to have it all, lose it, and then get it back."

Sure enough, 2017 was our first million-dollar year. That year, every time we made $250,000, we drank a bottle of Dom Perignon, and we kept those four bottles we acquired. They still sit in our family room to remind us what a million-dollar year looks like. In January of 2018, I was asked to speak on the Mo Monday stage in Ottawa because of our success.

A new person was running MoMondays – the same person who'd asked me if I was a millionaire in my living room back in 2016. He thought he knew exactly what I was going to say on stage, but I ended up telling the full story. I shared how I'd had it all, and when I lost everything, it wasn't just that I wasn't sure how I was going to pay my bills, it was that I had nothing. I sold my house and every piece of jewellery I had in order to pay the bills. I didn't tell them this to make them feel bad for me, but to show them that sometimes it takes a really big wakeup call in order to follow our passion.

My favorite piece of jewellery was an 8 carat princess-cut diamond and emerald tennis bracelet from my former life. I was broke and wanted to go to a specific business conference to learn how to monetize events. But I had no money in the bank. I called a jeweller in Washington, where the event was held, and told him that I had this bracelet worth $17,000. He told me that he would give me $1,500 for it.

That event was so important to me that I got on the plane with no money for a taxi when I landed and no money to give to the hotel for my stay. I took the subway to the jeweller, and he paid me the $1,500. That was enough money to pay for the rest of the trip. What I learned at that event allowed me to monetize an event in Montreal.

How to Change Your Business Mindset

I know the fears and overwhelm — and the sleepless nights — that come with having nothing. I know what it's like to have to put everything I possibly have into something and not be sure if it's going to work out. But I also know the joy that comes with the ability to manifest my thoughts into having the right mindset. That's my story.

From my many years of experience in business and with mindset work, I have created the **AFIRM**™ formula.

You need to **Acknowledge** that there is something in your life that needs to change for you to grow to where you want to be. Before you can grow as a person, that issue in your life needs to be identified.

You have to **Find** those life events — those stories — that have shaped who you are. They don't need to be traumatic; they just need to be true to yourself and to have played a role in the development of your life.

You need to **Identify** the limiting beliefs that are a result of those stories and life events.

You need to **Realize** that because of those circumstances, you decided on certain actions, and certain results came from those actions.

But because you're not in those circumstances anymore, you can **Move Forward**. You can learn from your prior experiences and actions and grow in order to become the person you desire.

My husband, Steve, is a prime example of how the AFIRM™ formula works. Twelve years ago, Steve's business existed, but he couldn't seem to get past a certain level. While attending an event in Las Vegas, a lady stopped him in the hall and said, "I can help you, I'm a psychic." Steve was puzzled because he had no idea at the time that anything was wrong or that he needed help. The lady said to him, "There is something from your childhood that you haven't dealt with, but I can't see it clearly."

Steve forgot about it until a couple of years later when he was at a dinner in Florida. A second psychic told him that they couldn't see what it was but that there was something he needed to deal with from his childhood. This caused him to remember what he had been told years before. Steve began to wonder if there really was something that he hadn't dealt with.

Some time later, Steve attended a conference in Dallas where a psychic was speaking on stage. After her talk, Steve approached the psychic. Before he even said anything, she said to him, "you want to ask me about your childhood, don't you?" As with the others, she could not see clearly what the issue from his childhood was. Three unconnected psychics had all said the exact same thing, years apart.

AFIRM™

After these three nearly identical conversations, Steve **Acknowledged** there was probably something that he needed to deal with, but he just couldn't figure it out. When I met him, he told me about the psychics, and I told him that he needed to tell me about his childhood. After an hour of talking to him about his life, I knew what he had to deal with.

Steve told me three very different but all connected stories about his life.

When Steve was five years old, he had eye surgery. He had to wear an eye patch all day, seven days a week. His parents told him not to touch the patch. When they weren't around, he tried to peek around the patch, but his caregivers always told him not to and pushed the patch back onto his eye. He remembers every minute detail about the patch.

The second story was that he tried to start a business at age eight. His mother commented, "Do you think it's fair that you're taking money for something you didn't pay for?" He stopped the whole enterprise because he figured his mom was right. But in fact there had been value in his time: curating content, arranging delivery, replenishing stock, etc.

The third story is from Steve's high school years. He hated everything about high school because he hated when someone in a position of authority told him what to do. He finished as soon as he was legally allowed to.

What I **Found** out from these stories was that anytime someone Steve perceived to be in authority told him what to do, he accepted what they said and didn't try to change what they told him. Steve did not attribute childhood trauma to any of these stories, but we were able to **Identify** that when someone told him that they didn't want him to raise his business fees, he just accepted it and moved on.

Steve **Realized** that the level of his business was dictated by others. It hadn't occurred to him that he could change it. Until then, Steve had never gone against his limiting belief that someone knew better than him. His acceptance of this false belief was holding him back from getting to the next position.

Steve values his freedom. When someone caused him to live a less emotionally free life, he was stressed but wasn't realizing it. Steve had to acknowledge these experiences and learn from them before he could **Move Forward**.

Develop Your Business Mindset

Steve's story is a very common story. You're in a business you are passionate about and that you love, and with which you want to make a difference in the world. But there is some limiting belief that doesn't allow you to be fully seen for your brilliance and for who you are in the world.

You may be scared to move forward. You may not be sure you deserve it. You may find it hard to be more successful than your family members. You may be trying to be a superhero and not let people know about your needs; you don't want to be like that needy person you know who asks for everything. Some of you may not even feel safe in the world.

As you grow, your limiting beliefs will come back to face you over time, and if you don't acknowledge them, there is little you can do about them. But, if you acknowledge these limiting beliefs, you can find what it is that is causing them and change them to better your life.

People in life are often not seen for who they truly are and don't feel heard as a result, whether it is in their personal or business life. Your limiting beliefs and your expert insights are tied together. You need to get rid of your limiting beliefs — not let them put a ceiling on what you can achieve — and get to your expert insights. This is a lifelong search for personal development.

In order to be seen for who you are, you need to acknowledge there is something that you want to shift so you can grow personally and determine how to overcome the problem. Life will always throw obstacles at you, but your mindset is the key difference between you failing or succeeding. Give your thoughts the energy they need. You can always buy another bracelet. But time is the only asset you cannot buy back.

Jayne Lowell

Jayne Lowell is an incredibly determined, confident, and goal-oriented person, who refuses to let any obstacles stand in her path to achieving the life she wants and knows she deserves. She is very intentional about where she wants to go and is willing to do what it takes (in alignment with her strong moral code) to get there.

Focused on her own continuous learning and improvement, Jayne inspires and encourages others to live their fullest life as their best self. She intuits what her clients need to know and bravely (but kindly) tells it like it is, even when they may not want to hear it. A non-conformist herself, her insights allow her to overcome their fears and objections and guide them on the path to their own destiny.

Jayne is the past-president of CAPS Ottawa. She is also Co-Founder and President of S & J Training Solutions Inc. She is a loving and supportive wife to Steve both personally and in business. Jayne is also a caring mother to their blended family of 4 children and 3 grand-children.

4

How My Shift to the Investor Mindset Helped Me Create Generational Wealth – Alfonso Cuadra

On my journey from childhood refugee and homeless teen to Canada-wide real estate investor and financial literacy mentor, I've taken control of my own circumstances. You can too.

I was born in Latin America and experienced two civil wars there. The government illegally detained my journalist mother for four years. When I was nine, we came to Canada as refugees. In this new and different country, I had trouble integrating into school. At 15, after several years of turmoil, I dropped out and became homeless, panhandling on the streets.

I didn't know much about money, except that I didn't have any and wanted to change that. My family didn't have much and didn't know how to teach me the skills I needed to create wealth.

My Pivotal Moment

The pivotal moment in my life was becoming a father at 17. My daughter, Thalia, is my guardian angel and the reason I worked so hard to change my life and financial circumstances. If not for her, I would be dead. Or in jail.

When I first held her, I started to take responsibility for my own actions and discovered my purpose. When your purpose is powerful enough, it makes you unstoppable.

As a result, I went back to high school and started selling clothing from my locker. Some of the people closest to me tried to warn me against starting a business, citing statistics about how many entrepreneurs fail and the need for a degree. But I stayed true to my purpose, graduated at 19, and turned my clothing business into a physical location. By the time I was 21, I had stores across Canada and loved being an entrepreneur.

At 25, I had a second daughter, Alicia. My girls are my purpose and the reason why I do this – to leave something behind for them.

Market Correction After 9/11

Shortly after the events of September 11, 2001, there was a market correction. Although I had a very successful business with multiple locations across the country, because I was not very financially literate, I almost lost everything.

I realized I needed to make another change. By reading and educating myself, I discovered the common thread between wealthy people: real estate. To create the secondary income I needed, the best choice was real estate.

I started with multi-family buildings, specifically apartments because the more people paying me rent, the more money I would have coming in. I learned to leverage the economy of scale by spreading the risk over more units.

The Investor Mindset

For my whole life my family has been in poverty, and I want to break that cycle. And the only way to break the cycle of poverty is by having the investor mindset.

Consumers make money and buy stuff; investors make money and buy assets that produce more income. With that income, they buy even more assets. Probably 96% of the people in the world are consumers. Many people think of real estate as buying a house, but a house is a consumer product.

But once you start thinking like an investor, everything changes.

I shifted to an investor mindset, reduced my expenses and started to collect assets – the apartment buildings. I now own apartment buildings across Canada.

The investor mindset is not just about wealth for right now; it's about acquiring long-term income-producing assets, which survive market corrections and political upheaval, and last for generations.

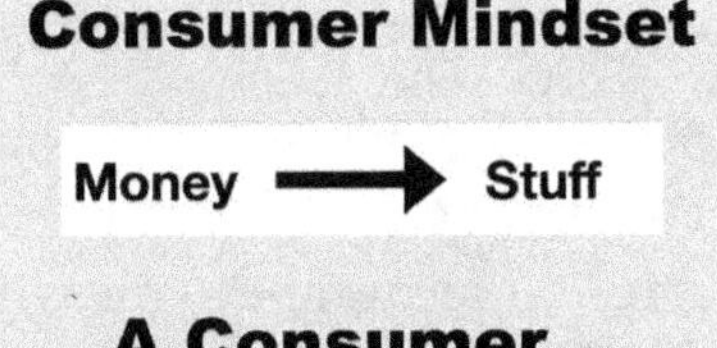

Teaching the Investor Mindset to Our Youth

I believe that the best investments we can make in this life are investments in ourselves, our families, and our communities. I've focused a lot on expanding my knowledge and improving my skills over the years – those are things no one can take away from me. I want to pass that knowledge and skill on to other people.

I still remember what it was like to be a young child with nothing, living in fear and not knowing how to change my circumstances. I was not taught financial literacy growing up, at home or school, which led me to being lost in the world.

No one teaches money management to young people. They find out the hard way. Instead, I want to see young people start out with the investor mindset. I want a better life for my two daughters and for everyone else. I take my two daughters out in the car, I drive them by all the properties we own, and I tell them, "These are not for you; these are for your children's children."

Growing up, my mom told me the most important things in life are getting good grades in school and getting a university degree. When I started buying apartment buildings, no one ever asked me for a university degree or what my grades were in high school. But they did ask me for my credit score.

I tell my kids, "Your credit score is the number you will be judged by when you get out into the real world. It doesn't say anything about your race, culture, background, gender, sexual orientation, or whether or not you're an immigrant. But your credit score says everything about your ability to manage money."

With my kids, I say, "These aren't credit cards; they're investment cards." The purpose of credit is to make more money — to create a business that will produce income to pay that debt.

What I'm teaching my kids is not what I was taught in school or at home. I'm completely breaking that cycle. I'm creating generational wealth, and I know that the wealth I'm going to hand down to my kids is going to continue on because I'm also handing down the investor mindset.

Combining my mission to increase generational wealth and my passion for teaching young people about financial literacy, I started the Cuadra Youth Foundation. Now I teach young people business, entrepreneurship, leadership, and financial literacy skills.

Combining Mindset, Team, and Influence

My goal has been to expand my circle of influence to become the undeniable expert in real estate. And the fact that I have made that goal a reality is the reason students want my coaching, investors want to invest with me, and I end up with very successful deals. People see me as the go-to person in real estate.

After a difficult divorce, I met Helene, who is now my partner in everything. Our strength and success together is based on finding love and being with someone who is on the same page. Helene is very detail oriented and I'm a visionary, so we balance each other well. Business has taken off because I trust her to take care of the operations while I focus on acquisitions, investor relations, teaching, and mentoring.

We started a property management company for both our own and other properties — a great decision since now we have the infrastructure in place to support our growth. We've built a multi-million-dollar portfolio of various apartment buildings all across Canada. And I've become successful by using my investor mindset, finding the right team, and expanding my circle of influence to become the undeniable authority in one thing.

I'm not a realtor; I'm not a mortgage broker. I'm the real estate investor and educator. People know me for that.

It's Never Too Late to Start Investing in Real Estate

I have a mentorship program to teach adults how to create wealth through real estate. To become an investor, you must educate yourself and shift your mindset. If you are still in the consumer mindset, you may see the best opportunity in the world and you won't recognize it because you're looking at it with the wrong mindset.

Once you understand what you're doing, you can look at a deal with the investor mindset and be able to recognize it. You'll quickly start to see opportunities everywhere. Then execute! The most powerful thing that you can do is take action.

Do you remember playing Monopoly as a kid? The object is to buy four green houses and level up to a red hotel. More units equal more money as people go around the board, landing on your property and paying you rent.

This is a hard concept to swallow. For example, when I was a kid, I remember my mom and other adults saying, "When you get older, you have to buy a house. You don't want to pay rent and make the landlord rich." Even though the message was coming from a good place, the message was actually wrong. The message should have been "become the landlord!"

We live in a consumer-based society. We need consumerism for the world to function. The government takes taxes from your paycheque first because they know if you leave money in the hands of consumers, they will spend it.

People who are living paycheque to paycheque are looking for instant gratification, often buying the most stuff and paying the most taxes. By contrast, the 4% of the population with the investor mindset buy nice stuff only after they've put their money to work.

Investors buy stuff with their passive income, not earned income. Earned income is taxed at the highest rate. Passive income, including income from real estate, is what creates freedom. We call it cash flow. And cash flow is sexy!

Investing in real estate is not for everyone. If you want to find a way to get into income-producing assets, but the management and operations side of the business is not for you, consider partnering with someone who is an investor.

If you are happy as a consumer, then buying a house is probably the best thing you can do because it is a form of forced savings, which benefits 96% of the people. But if you just know there's something better for you out there, investing in real estate to create generational wealth might be a good fit for you. Think about the movie *The Matrix*. They spend most of the movie searching for what they feel is missing from their lives.

Once you know that your life can change and you can better your circumstances, that's a big responsibility. Because now it's up to you to go out and make those changes happen. There are no longer any excuses. Investing in real estate is not for the weak or the faint of heart. You don't want to be like the character in *The Matrix* who wishes he could go back into the matrix because he would prefer to remain oblivious!

If you are unhappy as a consumer, make a change. Live on the uncomfortable side. Think about money working for you, not you working for the money. Focus on income-producing assets that will impact your life. Most people would be afraid of buying an apartment building, but that's exactly where you need to be because an apartment building is easier to buy and easier to manage. And it produces more profit.

When we shop at Costco and buy in bulk, we pay a reduced price per unit. It's exactly the same philosophy with real estate: the more units in a property, the lower the cost per unit, which makes the property more profitable. A good first investment is to buy either a triplex or a fourplex. Learn the mechanics of that and then level up as fast as possible.

With the increased profits, you can hire a property manager and focus on your next investment. I'm not talking about creating another job, I'm talking about creating freedom.

A Freedom Fighter

The most valuable asset we have is time. Now that I've created financial freedom for myself through my investor mindset, I can do what I want with my time. My passion is to create other millionaires. I see myself as a freedom fighter because I fight for other people's financial freedoms.

We're living through inflationary times. I believe we will see a change in the monetary system during our lifetime. It's not a matter of if; it's a matter of when. And no matter what happens to currency, that piece of real estate will always be there. If they introduced a new currency and, for example, that currency was chickens, someone could pay their rent with chickens and there's still value for both parties in that exchange.

People will always need to live somewhere. They don't always need brick and mortar to start a business, run a restaurant, or provide office spaces, but people will always have to live somewhere. Real estate is the key to financial freedom no matter what the monetary system is.

The impact I want to have on this world is to show others how to create generational wealth for themselves and their families. Ultimately, I want to be remembered for all the people I've helped.

Set Big Goals and Invest Forward

I keep photos of all my "ladies" (my apartment buildings) on my office wall to remind me, my students, and my clients of what's possible.

All of us have different goals. What makes a good goal? Well first, a good goal needs to excite you. It needs to scare the bejesus out of you. And it needs to be worthy of you. I've made my whole life about real estate and helping people get into real estate. I've set really big goals for myself, because it's fun.

Our goal is to get to 7500 apartments in the next five years. People ask me, why do you need that? And the answer is I don't. But I came from a war-torn country. We lived in poverty all our lives. When I came here as a refugee, my mom had $50 in her pocket. We struggled. I lived on the streets and panhandled for change. I think I owe it to myself and to my community to see how far we can take it.

I'm more interested to see the person I'm going to become on the way to achieving that goal than the actual goal itself. I'm more interested to see what my kids learn from me achieving that goal. I'm more interested to see the inspiration I'm going to create for my community. I want to show people from Latin America — immigrants — that yes, you can come to this country with $50 in your pocket, war torn, and you can definitely achieve anything you want. I'm more excited about all of that than the actual goal.

And if I can make you feel the same way I feel about real estate, I've done my job. Because now you are going to have the momentum to move forward. And my gift is that I can take anybody from any walk of life, as long as they're open-minded and coachable, and bring them through my process. By the end of it, they'll have built a significant portfolio for themselves.

Alfonso Cuadra

Alfonso Cuadra is the master at showing people how to change their lives and create freedom through Real Estate Investing. His revolutionary insights into how to create wealth and buy apartment buildings have made him "The North American Authority on Real Estate Investing."

Alfonso is a serial entrepreneur, award-winning real estate investor/educator, international speaker, real estate mentor, author of the 2012 book From the Ground Up!, and philanthropist who has been seen in Reader's Digest, The Huffington Post, and other international media. He is a TV Personality and host of the TV show "Success By Design."

Born in El Salvador during the revolution, his mother, the head of a newspaper, was illegally detained and thrown in prison for reporting the truth to all about the corrupt government in power. After escaping to Canada and being raised in poverty, he started a small company at 17 years old that quickly grew to multiple locations across Canada.

Now the President/CEO of the Cuadra Group of Companies, he has an extensive background in business and real estate management, investing, and development. A dynamic leader who has passionately shared his story with thousands of audiences around the world, Alfonso inspires others to create the life they want and to never give up on their dreams. He is truly in the business of changing lives and has a special gift in his ability to connect with people and move them forward to overcome their obstacles and become high performers.

Connect with Alfonso at http://alfonsocuadra.ca/

5

Enhanced Life Fulfillment Through Philanthropy: Creating A New Model For Giving – Betty-Anne Howard

In a world where most of us are striving for something better – for ourselves, our partners, our families, and our communities, wouldn't it be phenomenal to have a clear path towards the enhanced life fulfillment we all desire?

In my experience, philanthropy can be that clear path.

Unfortunately, I find most of us overlooking the opportunities we have right in front of us to make a real difference in the world because of misunderstandings and disparate viewpoints.

Depending on whose lens we are looking through, philanthropy can mean many different things, and this incongruity is keeping us from creating a world we can all be proud of.

Through philanthropy, we have the opportunity and ability to magnify our impact while at the same time meeting the needs of our own lives, our families, and our communities – the opportunity and ability to achieve enhanced life fulfillment.

We need to create a new framework or model for philanthropy that can demystify the process and embrace the perspective or lens used by everyone involved to create a holistic path forward. This means listening to and including the viewpoints of charities, donors, financial advisors, planned giving consultants, families, and our communities.

A New Model For Philanthropy

Let's open our minds to thinking about philanthropy differently.

People often find the term philanthropy confusing and equate it with donations given by the extremely wealthy or large corporations, and not something that you or I are involved in.

They feel more comfortable with the term charity or charitable donation, even when they are involved in philanthropy. This means that exploring how we think about philanthropy and the words that we use is a great place to begin our journey.

Words Create Worlds

Words like charitable giving, legacy planning, philanthropy, and estate planning mean different things to different people and professions.

For example, from a Financial Advisor's perspective, estate planning is defined as the accumulation and preservation of wealth and the distribution of wealth at your death. But we don't have an agreement or a common language when it comes to the definition of wealth, so many people think estate planning is not for them since they don't have "wealth."

I'm not saying we all have to agree on having the same definition however when we don't share a common language it makes communication difficult. For many people, the words we use when discussing philanthropy are intimidating and misunderstood, and rarely do we invite others to provide us with their definition. Even culturally we have many different ways of looking at the meaning behind the words we use.

Another example of how words can limit our conversation and behaviour relates to the idea of giving a charitable gift vs. being philanthropic. The difference is in the donor's intention.

Charitable donations can be seen as a response to an immediate situation where the giving usually occurs in the short term. Philanthropy, on the other hand, addresses the root cause of social issues with strategic long-term approaches that can include monetary donations or volunteering as well as advocacy work. Donating to a food bank is a charitable gift, while philanthropy is addressing the root cause of poverty.

Both are important and valuable to our society. One without the other is foolhardy. Which one we want to use depends on many different factors, but if we ask ourselves what approach or intentions best suit what we're trying to achieve most of us focus on the charitable gift because being philanthropic can feel intimidating or overwhelming.

Often we attach the idea of excess wealth and money to the word philanthropist. Sadly these preconceived notions keep us from exploring how we can direct our resources to become more philanthropic while also being charitable.

Opening ourselves up to other ways of defining words and approaching issues we have in our world helps us find solutions that we may not have considered. For example, Edgar Villanueva asserts that our current approach to philanthropy contains oppressive dynamics and that Native traditions for healing which emphasize connection, reciprocity, and a circular dynamic can open the floodgates for a rising tide that lifts all boats.

How we define a problem determines the solutions we seek and who does the defining determines how the definition unfolds. Many of us haven't taken the time to explore how we define the words we use or how we define the problems we are dealing with in our society, including the roots of these problems.

When we acknowledge that we need to stop taking for granted that we all speak the same language and open ourselves up to exploring and understanding what each of us means by the words we use we have taken a very important step forward in creating a new model for philanthropy.

Emotions Give Life To Intention

Another critical component for us to create a new model for philanthropy is to explore the emotions attached to legacy planning, philanthropy, and charitable giving.

Emotions are the glue that holds us and our charities together. Sadly, we live in a world that tells us that there is a time and place for our emotions – and no one has given us a handbook that tells us where and when that should be!

When I think about emotions in the context of philanthropy and legacy planning, much of what we call charitable giving can be seen as the relief of acute distress, whereas philanthropy, from an emotional point of view, can be seen as joy seeking, or pleasure activism.

In her book Pleasure Activism: The Politics of Feeling Good, adrienne maree brown suggests that pleasure needs to be at the core of our desire to make improvements in our society.

"Pleasure activists believe that by tapping into potential goodness in each of us we can generate justice and liberation, growing a healthy abundance where we have been socialized to believe only scarcity exists".

This perspective is also clearly aligned with cognitive psychology (how we think) and behavioural psychology (how we act). In other words, we primarily do things that make us feel good and give us pleasure. In addition, neuroscience tells us we release endorphins in our brain (the feel-good chemicals) when we give others a helping hand.

Very little focus has been placed on incorporating these concepts into philanthropy. And yet, we know that people talking to Financial Advisors welcome the opportunity to discuss how they want to make a difference in the world and the lives of others. More and more people are looking to their advisors to play a role, to help them with their charitable giving options. Philanthropic Financial Advisors can bridge the gap between vision, emotion, and making an impact.

Taking a deeper dive into the positive emotional aspects of philanthropy and legacy is worth pursuing within ourselves and in the work we do. Our emotions are on a continuum and further exploration into the psychological and societal benefits of philanthropy, legacy, and giving back will enhance our desire and therefore our ability to have an even greater impact in our lives, our communities, and the world.

That's enhanced life fulfillment through philanthropy in action!

Mindset Holds The Key

The words we use and the emotions that get stirred up add up to what we call our mindset. Our mindset determines to a large extent if we want to support a charity or charities, and when and how we wish to make a difference in the world and the lives of others.

Exploring our mindset unveils a lot of gems that will either stay buried or be brought out into the world as part of our legacy.

Carol Dweck's work on fixed vs. growth mindset shows us that those of us with a growth mindset view problems as something to solve using curiosity, embracing challenges, and persisting in the face of setbacks. This allows us to reach higher and higher levels of achievement – a perfect recipe for creating and building a new model for philanthropy.

Our family history, the beliefs and values we were taught in our community, schools, faith, and other societal factors have also all contributed to the way we see the world.

Codi Shewan in his book "Everyday Legacy: Lessons For Living With Purpose Right Now" is on the right track by encouraging us to live our values every day by being kind to others, and seeing how we can make a difference with our behaviour now – today – rather than thinking about legacy as something we leave behind.

Sadly, very few people think about and plan for what they intend to leave behind as a legacy. In our new model for philanthropy, we need to address the issue of legacy using our shared words, emotions, and mindset to find the right answers for ourselves.

So how do we do that?

In a recent conversation I had with Jenny Mitchell and Paul Nazareth, outstanding leaders in the field of philanthropy, they suggested we start by accepting our emotions and bringing together our heads and our hearts – with our hearts taking the lead. We can't fear the exploration of our emotions.

When I explore legacy and philanthropic possibilities with my clients by asking "who and what has made a difference in your life and how have they made a difference"? we often have an emotional conversation that includes stories about their lives.

I hear about the charity that was there when a child was born with a hole in their heart, or the wayward teen who was taken under the wing of mentors in the community, or the disadvantaged youth who found purpose in their life and now as an adult, having made their way up the ladder as an educator, says; "if it hadn't been for sports I wouldn't be here"!

Legacy questions need to be asked and stories need to be heard because they inspire the teller of the story as well as the listener to think about how they might like to give back to others in the same way that they received a helping hand.

If we aren't asking these questions and having these conversations, opportunities get lost. If we embrace a mindset of wanting to explore and discover more about each other from a curiosity perspective and tie that into what made a difference in our lives and the pleasure of making a difference in the lives of others, we achieve enhanced life fulfillment.

I've seen and experienced this many times in my own life and in the lives of others - what we focus on grows. When we focus and build on our own beliefs and values that coincide with building a world we can be proud of, the possibilities are endless!

On the other hand, a fixed mindset tells us that any focus or desire on helping others outside of our own families will take away from our family's inheritance or prosperity. This is a myth and misconception that needs to be addressed.

Leaving a gift in our will to our favorite charities can provide more money, in many cases, to our families. It doesn't have to be either-or, a choice between our families or charities. So why do so many of us come to believe that it has to be one or the other?

Misconceptions run rampant in the area of charitable giving and philanthropy. For too long the wealth management community has been an old boys club, underserving women and couples who want better choices, better communication, and a financial plan that lines up with their unique life goals.

As a society, we are only slowly moving away from this model to embrace new ideas that will help us to break through those barriers by demystifying the concepts and the process.

The Optimal Philanthropic Guide

One way I'm addressing this gap is by creating an optimal philanthropic guide for enhanced life fulfillment. This guide includes three critical components – a Visionary Mind Map, an Intention Script, and a Legacy Blueprint.

The Optimal Philanthropic Guide provides you with a clear path to enhanced life fulfillment so that you'll come to know and trust that your beliefs and values are fully realized today, tomorrow, and in the future.

I want to ignite your imagination so you can think about and discover your vision for the future, what your world could look like, a world that you can be proud of. I want to help you set your intentions based on what's important to you and why. Then you can create a framework to take action based on your lived experience and how you want to make a difference in the world.

Through this guide, we create more possibilities with a vision for the future that ultimately binds us together. We build a better world, one person at a time, one conversation at a time, and one step at a time.

The new model for philanthropy helps us break through our barriers based on the words we use, and adopt a growth mindset that will expand our understanding of what is possible in our own lives and how that can and will impact the type of world we create.

We inspire ourselves and others to examine what is holding us back from making our dreams a reality and living an enhanced fulfilled life by how we put our thoughts and vision into action. Recognizing that individually we can make a difference in our lives and the lives of others, but collectively we are capable of so much more.

Philanthropy Is Love

When we go to the greek roots of the word philanthropy we discover it's about love (phil) of humanity (anthropos). Exploring what philanthropy means to us, is a starting point to imagining the possibilities. From there, with an understanding of our intentions and the impact we want to have, we can take action knowing with confidence that this journey is one of exploration, insight, and awareness.

This knowledge brings us to a place of seeing how we are capable of so much more than we ever thought was possible. Enhanced life fulfillment through philanthropy, ultimately, is not just about our lives but it's about the world we are creating for those who will come after us.

Philanthropy can be a complicated and controversial topic because there are pervasive viewpoints on what philanthropic action should look like. But by understanding and incorporating diverse perspectives and creating a holistic clear path, we can come to see that giving back not only helps others but ourselves as well.

Enhanced life fulfillment through philanthropy is an opportunity for personal development that shouldn't be overlooked – it's available and waiting for us all.

Enhanced Life Fulfillment Through Philanthropy

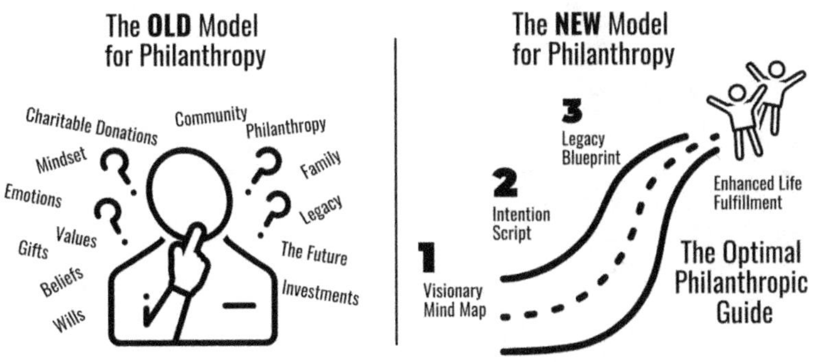

Betty-Anne Howard - The Optimal Philanthropic Guide

Betty-Anne Howard

Betty-Anne Howard, CFP, MFA-P, CLU, CHS, CEA is a Philanthropic Financial Planner, author, award-winning speaker, financial literacy advocate and charitable giving expert. For over 20 years, Betty-Anne has been guiding women, couples and families to realize their financial dreams and has shared her vision with audiences around the world. With her specialization in strategic philanthropic planning and charitable giving she has been able to direct millions of dollars to the charitable sector while dramatically reducing taxes for those individuals she has assisted. Betty-Anne lives with her life partner Maggie and their Goldendoodle, Phoenix, on beautiful Bass Lake between Kingston and Ottawa. They enjoy the great outdoors and spending time with their horses, Stella and Brooklyn.

6

The Power Within
– Brandon Fong

Anything is possible. Impossibility is a state of mind. You've probably heard a version of that a thousand times, and it's absolutely true. If you truly believe in yourself, you can do anything. The obstacles we face become our opportunities to grow. It's what we decide to do in these situations that define our outcome. We always have a choice, and the choices we make today shape our future.

Ten years ago, at the age of twenty-six, I was diagnosed with brain cancer. I was living in downtown Toronto, and I was the "corporate soldier." I was that guy; super ambitious, hustling like crazy, work-hard-party-hard lifestyle, and I was climbing the corporate ladder. I was almost there… I could see the top. But then cancer struck like lightning, and in an instant, my life changed.

When people hear the word cancer, the mind tends to go to, "Is this a death sentence?" And that's what I thought too, for a while. But cancer was not a death sentence. In fact, it was quite the opposite. Cancer was a door to freedom that I did not know was possible. During my cancer experience, I discovered many things about myself. One of the most empowering things I discovered was this; I had the *power*. Over a period of four months, I went from having four tumors in my brain to being cancer-free. And the way I did this was by focusing on *how* I was *showing up* every day. So, what exactly does this mean?

Showing up has to do with what's going on within you. If you're nervous or lacking confidence, how's that going to *show up* when you're trying to close a sale? You may be perceived as untrustworthy or lacking credibility. What's going on within you has a direct impact on your results. Let me give you a perfect example. When I was diagnosed with cancer, I was completely overwhelmed. I didn't know what to do. But I knew if I was going to survive cancer, I had to drastically change my thinking. The way I did this was by making conscious choices every day to be more grateful, loving, and appreciative. Over time, I no longer felt the doom and gloom of cancer. I became more joyful and at peace with myself. It's as if something clicked. I realized *I get to decide what type of life I want to live*. The way I started to change my life was by focusing on *how I was showing up* every day. This was a complete paradigm shift for me. I no longer felt like I was a victim of cancer. I had the POWER.

The secret to *showing up* is what I call, *The Five States of Being*. These states will help you identify where you are in your level of thinking. If you're stuck in a limiting belief, how will this affect the way you *show up* in your business, health, and relationships? If you're going to reach your goals, you have to let go of any baggage you're holding on to; the pain of the past, the old stories, or anything that might be holding you back. You have to believe in yourself. This isn't an easy process, but when you learn and master these states, anything is possible.

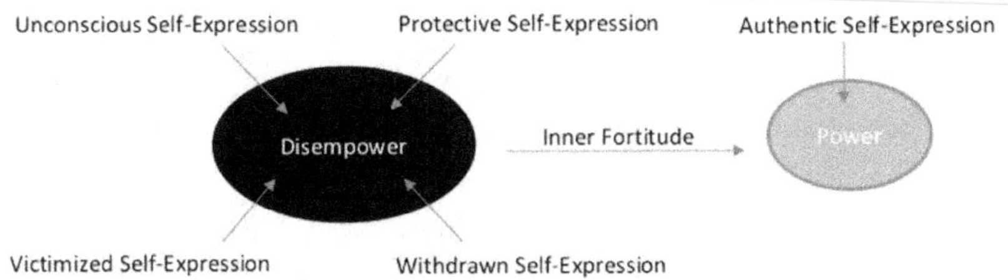

There are four disempowering states in the *Five States of Being*:

There are four disempowering states in the *Five States of Being*: Unconscious Self-Expression, Protective Self-Expression, Victimized Self-Expression, and Withdrawn Self-Expression. Each one Unconscious Self-Expression, Protective Self-Expression, Victimized of these states negatively impacts the way you *show up* and how we *show up* determines the overall quality of our lives. Inner Fortitude is what bridges the gap from these four Self-Expression, and Withdrawn Self-Expression. Each one of these states disempowering states to the fifth and final state, Authentic Self-Expression, our true place of power.

Negatively impacts the way you *show up* and how we *show up* determines the overall quality of our lives. Inner Fortitude is what bridges the gap **UNCONSCIOUS SELF EXPRESSION** from these four disempowering states to the fifth and final state, Authentic The first state is what I call, Unconscious Self-Expression. Unconscious Self-Expression is when Self-Expression, our true place of power.

You feel as though your life is passing you by. You know you're in this state when some of these things are happening: you're on autopilot, you live a life of nine-to-five, you lack a sense of purpose or meaning. You're doing things without even questioning why. You feel as though **UNCONSCIOUS SELF EXPRESSION** you're a drone just obeying commands. You find it difficult to deal with where you are, so you shut down… you disengage or numb yourself.

The first state is what I call, Unconscious Self-Expression. Unconscious

This is exactly where I was before cancer. I had this amazing job, I was making lots of money, and I was getting groomed for upper management…but I was completely miserable. I hated Self-Expression is when you feel as though your life is passing you by.

What I was doing, and I couldn't deal with what I was feeling. I didn't realize that I sacrificed my principles to get to where I was. Rather than taking a deeper look at what was going on and You know you're in this state when some of these things are happening: acknowledging my unhappiness, I numbed myself through work and drinking…, and things got you're on autopilot, you live a life of nine-to-five, you lack a sense of worse.

Purpose or meaning. You're doing things without even questioning why. **PROTECTIVE SELF EXPRESSION** You feel as though you're a drone just obeying commands. You find it The second state is what I call Protective Self-Expression. Protective Self-Expression is when you difficult to deal with where you are, so you shut down… you disengage feel trapped, and there's no way out. You know you're in this state when these things are or numb yourself.

Happening: you have become so identified by your life conditions that you can't see, nor do you want to see any other possibility, even though you know in your heart of hearts that something needs to change. Instead of changing, you resist what you're feeling, and what happens is you

This is exactly where I was before cancer. I had this amazing job, I was making lots of money, and I was getting groomed for upper management…but I was completely miserable. I hated what I was doing, and I couldn't deal with what I was feeling. I didn't realize that I sacrificed my principles to get to where I was. Rather than taking a deeper look at what was going on and acknowledging my unhappiness, I numbed myself through work and drinking…, and things got worse.

PROTECTIVE SELF EXPRESSION

The second state is what I call Protective Self-Expression. Protective Self-Expression is when you feel trapped, and there's no way out. You know you're in this state when these things are happening: you have become so identified by your life conditions that you can't see, nor do you want to see any other possibility, even though you know in your heart of hearts that something needs to change. Instead of changing, you resist what you're feeling, and what happens is you become trapped. You enter what many of us know as a state of denial. Unlike Unconscious Self-Expression, in this state, you've become aware that there is a problem.

As my health began to decline further, I had an out-of-body experience while I was sitting in my office. I saw myself looking down at my body, and I could finally see how stressed out I was, how my health was failing. It's as if I heard a voice, "You need to quit your job." But I didn't quit. I was too attached to my career and everything that came with it. My identity was wrapped up in my job, and I had no idea who I'd be without it. I had worked so hard to get where I was, and I didn't want to fail. So, I resisted. I fought. That's when I got diagnosed with brain cancer.

VICTIMIZED SELF EXPRESSION

The third state is what I call Victimized Self-Expression. Victimized Self Expression is when you're reacting and have no sense of control. You know you're in this state when some of these things are happening: you want to blame yourself or others for the problems in your life. You have thoughts of, "If things were different, I'd be different." You feel as though you've been wronged, hurt, or betrayed. This state has to do with the pain and suffering you have endured in your life, which can end up becoming a story that you relive over and over again.

When I was initially diagnosed with cancer, I felt like a victim. All I wanted to do was to blame the doctors for misdiagnosing me for three months. I was so angry. What I realized was, I was actually blaming myself. But blame wasn't going to get me anywhere, though; it just left me feeling powerless. If I was going to beat cancer, I had to start believing in myself, and that's exactly what I did.

WITHDRAWN SELF-EXPRESSION

The fourth state is what I call Withdrawn Self-Expression. Withdrawn Self-Expression is when you don't believe in YOU. You know you're in this state when some of these things are happening: You doubt yourself. You second guess your actions or decisions. You tend to think the worst about yourself. You don't feel worthy or good enough. This state is all about the relationship you have with yourself; your sense of self-worth. Many people I know, including myself, have carried this wound, and that's because, at a subconscious level, we have chosen to believe this lie, "I'm not enough."

I had no idea if I was going to survive cancer. All I could do was believe in myself. I truly felt that cancer was here for a purpose, and it became my catalyst for change. For most of my life, I used to live in the state of Victimized Self-Expression and Withdrawn Self-Expression. I used to let the experiences of my past define who I was; never believing in myself and blaming others for the problems in my life. That all changed when I discovered Inner Fortitude. Inner Fortitude is having the strength and perseverance to keep going, regardless of what happens. When I found this missing piece, I was able to let go and allow my life to unfold. I found my inner strength.

INNER FORTITUDE

Inner Fortitude is the power that comes from within, and when you have access to this *inner power*, anything is possible. When you have *inner power*, you're able to use your mind, body, and spirit as an instrument in creation. Your thoughts, words, and beliefs are what influence your results. The degree to which you exercise your *inner power* impacts how you *show up*, and how you *show up* is what determines your results.

There are three pillars to Inner Fortitude, and you absolutely need all three of them to make this work. The first is Focus, the second is Choice, and the third is Commitment. Each one of these components builds upon one another.

FOCUS

What are your goals and dreams for the future? What is it you truly want and desire? Focus is having the vision and clarity of exactly what you want and where you want to be. It's seeing it in your mind's eye and feeling it in your heart. Your thoughts, feelings, and emotions are energy. How you feel has a profound effect on your state of mind and what you think you're capable of.

My focus was my will to live, to live a healthy and fulfilling life after cancer. I spent every waking moment, and every part of my being focused on this goal. I would wake up every morning and meditate, visualize, and feel and see that life. Over time there was no doubt, just a deep, pure conviction that I was going to beat cancer. And in just four months, I was cancer-free. This is the power of a vision so strong. You become what you desire.

CHOICE

The choices you make today have a compounding effect on your life. Every decision you make either brings you closer to your vision or further away from it. So, ask yourself, "What reality am I choosing today?" Choice is about taking accountability and realizing that the only person that gets to decide is you. You have to choose to take the steps, big and small, every day that would allow you to reach your goals. It's up to you.

I had no control over the four tumors in my brain. But what I did have control over was my ability to feel. To be grateful, loving, and appreciative. This is the moment where everything changed. I empowered myself through my ability to choose. In what I thought might be the last moments of my life, I chose a life of gratitude. I would spend each day being thankful to my friends, family, and doctors. Through this simple act, I was no longer a victim; I was in control.

COMMITMENT

If you truly want to reach out and grasp your dreams, it's absolutely necessary to commit to yourself. When you have commitment, it doesn't matter if you win or lose. Commitment is unconditional. Even when you fail, you'll keep going. When you succeed, you'll keep going. When you have commitment, it leads to perseverance. Your level of commitment is what separates you from everyone else, especially during times of failure and setback. When you fully commit, you surrender and let go of the how.

There were certainly moments when I wanted to give up. Especially when I started losing my hair or when I felt like my head was going to explode after the first round of radiation. But I didn't. My commitment to myself is what got me up every day. No matter how sick I was, I kept going. I had made a personal vow to myself to do whatever it takes, no matter the challenge.

AUTHENTIC SELF-EXPRESSION

The fifth state is what I call Authentic Self-Expression. Authentic Self-Expression is when you have the freedom to legitimately express your true self at any given time. You know you're in this state when some of these things are happening: You love and accept yourself as you are. You are no longer controlled by fear. If something happens outside of your control, you're able to let go and allow it to unfold. Instead of reacting, you respond. When you're in Authentic Self-Expression, you realize that what's going on within YOU – your thoughts, your beliefs, and how you feel – are how you *show up* in every single moment. And how you *show up* determines the level of *success* in your life. When you realize this, you take full responsibility. Nothing happens *to* you. You are the one that is in control. You get to decide. This is the place of true power. Your mind, heart, and spirit are your means of creation. When you're in Authentic Self-Expression, anything is possible.

ONWARD

The Five States of Being and *Inner Fortitude* are great tools to help bring wealth and abundance into our lives. We all want to be wealthy, but what does that mean? Most people equate wealth with money. For others, wealth has to do with being part of a loving family or a tight group of friends, spending time outdoors, or being creative. The point is, wealth is subjective. It's based on the individual. No matter what wealth means to you, it can be easily attainable.

If you want to be wealthy, it requires the right attitude. It has to do with how you *show up* every day, the words you say, the thoughts you have, and what you believe. That's why mastering *The Five States of Being* is critical in creating wealth, happiness, and health. You need to program your mind in a way that works for you. You need to *become* what you desire. As Brian Tracy says, "Change your thinking, change your life."

I'm a prime example of what we're all capable of. On April 26th, 2010, when I was diagnosed with brain cancer, I had no idea that it was going to change my life for the better. It was a catalyst for deep personal growth that allowed me to find my truth, that anything is possible. By accessing the state of Authentic Self-Expression, I was able to defy all the odds. When you realize that you have the power, nothing can stop you. I truly believe that we're all here for a purpose, and I want each one of you to live your dreams.

Brandon Fong

Brandon Fong is a motivational speaker and coach. He's an expert in overcoming adversity and understanding our capabilities as humans. Through Brandon's experience as a cancer survivor, he has created a life filled with purpose and passion while finding joy in helping others to do the same.

7

Be The Unmistakable Authority – Chad Robinson

When I was first approached to be part of this book project I was unsure where to start. Of course these questions came after the gratitude and shock wore off being part of a book by Brian Tracy! I began to ask myself, "What does it mean to be the Unmistakable Authority?" "How did I become the Unmistakable Authority in the world of mortgage finance and Solution Lending?"

I define being The Unmistakable Authority as being the go to person in your field or niche. For some people it can take decades and for others it can take months or even years to achieve this. I have been a mortgage broker for over 25 years. However, it was only the last few years that I really became the Unmistakable Authority figure.

For a long time, I tried to be everything to everyone. I would say YES to clients even before I finished hearing their story or problem. Does this sound familiar to you? I say YES! Then figure it out. This approach works great when you are starting out but it definitely has its drawbacks.

This changed in late 2018. I was sitting in a conference with several business owners and multi millionaires and it struck me.

The one thing they all had in common was focus. Hyper defined, laser precise focus. You see, after the birth of my third daughter Amelia, our family spent a lot of time reviewing our career goals. My wife, Muriel, went back to school for architecture and we experimented with building homes. It was a great experience and I am glad we did it but it definitely took my attention away from our mortgage business. Of course, where attention goes, energy flows. Or in this case away from. It hit me like a bolt of lightning. Why am I messing around with all these other things?

You see, the market or universe has been telling me for years, but I was too stubborn to listen. I was the person that everyone referred all the unusual deals to. "If you need to get it done, send it to Chad and his team." Instead of leaning into this, I kept going in different directions. It is hard for a business owner to say no to business. However, resources are NOT infinite. So, when you say YES to one opportunity you are saying no to others (even if you are not aware of them). I can hear the YA BUT in your head.

Ya but, I don't have that many clients.

Ya but, I need the money.

Ya but, I have the extra time.

For every action there is an opportunity cost. You need to be aware of what those are. If you say yes to this client, or this book project or helping a friend move, it means you can't do something else. You can't prospect someone else, you skip out on going to the gym or doing the things we all know we SHOULD be doing.

For my mortgage business, the answer was to focus on Solution Lending and answering these two questions.

1. Who was my ideal customer?
2. What is the lifetime value of that customer?

Answering these two questions changed my business forever. We had to answer these questions for both our customers (aka Borrowers) and our suppliers (aka Lenders).

We determined that our ideal customers are good people that are facing a financial challenge. They could be a first time home buyer and need coaching. A client suffering from a credit challenge after a life event. A real estate investor building a property, buying a rental property etc. Generally speaking, a client that the mainstream lenders do not want because they are too much work or they don't fit into a nice little box.

The lifetime value of a client was another major surprise. We didn't include the client referral, just direct revenue. It was shocking to realize the lifetime value of a client was close to $20,000. When you start thinking about that, it completely changes the marketing conversation.

What is the lifetime value of your clients?

Do your clients have clearly defined goals?

As an aside, I was surprised to realize that we had already deployed this strategy successfully in our real estate portfolio. When Muriel and I had our rental properties, we had a very narrow tenant profile. We selected properties that appealed to young professionals in their early twenties in a very defined geographic area. These tenants all had high disposable income, and wanted a nice place to live. They wanted a fancy apartment to impress their new boyfriends/girlfriends. By focusing on this niche, it lets us easily attract the right tenants and maximise our return.

For our Private Lenders, the ideal client is what I like to call Wealthy Delegators. Generally they are successful professionals and business owners. Busy smart people with money! Our focus is to build trust by listing their individual needs and creating an investment plan that meets it.

They are generally looking for safe, consistent and stable returns. Many feel that the financial services industry is too complex and impersonal. Investing in mortgages is simple and tangible. An investor can see the security. The Life Time value of an investor is a bit more difficult to calculate but generally more than $10,000.

So I ask you, what do you need to do to become the unmistakable authority in your business or field?

Who are your ideal clients?

What is the Lifetime Value of your clients?

Here are a few steps that I took in identifying who my ideal clients are:

1. Who are your current clients?

    I know this sounds obvious, but look at key demographics of your current clients. What are their ages, demographics etc. Why did they choose you? Where did they come from? You will see a pattern. At the end of the day, people normally buy from those who they know, like and trust.

2. What problem are you solving for them?

    What goals are they trying to achieve? What problem are you trying to solve? This will help define your audience quickly. If you are selling cars, you have a very different customer base if one group is looking for the largest towing capacity vs the most fuel efficient.

3. Are they facing any fears?

    If you know the problem you are trying to solve, there is often a fear attached to it. As much as we all like to think we are logical human beings, we often buy on emotion. Helping reduce or eliminate your clients fears can be a big motivator. Using the car example, Volvo sells on safety and Porsche sells on speed.

4. Who do you like to work with?

    This is often overlooked, but key to the success of your client's experience. If you connect with your client on multiple levels, the entire experience will be easy and natural. If your business sells natural products to vegetarians, you most likely don't want to market at Rib Festivals.

Once I defined all the above, I broke it down even further.

Funnily enough, this strategy came from a friend who was struggling in his dating life. He was all over the place and never seemed to be able to find that right person. Eventually, we broke it down in the following ways:

- Must haves aka deal breakers
- Nice to have
- Ideal to have

The Must haves are the show stoppers or deal breakers.

For my dating friend, this was a person who was well read and intelligent. An academic type. (He was a professor, after all.) In my mortgage business, this is a client with a problem to solve. If someone is just coming to us to "Rate Shop" and we are not providing value beyond that they are not our client.

The Nice to Haves

This is your second filter. For my dating friend, this was an age bracket. He wanted someone roughly 5 years older or younger than him. For my mortgage business, it is a deal size. We typically want larger files $100,000 and up. It takes the same amount of time for a $100,000 mortgage or a $1,000,000. Funnily enough, the larger ones tend to take even less time.

The Ideal to Have

This is more about the feeling and the experience you have with your clients. What kind of people are they? Do you connect with entrepreneurs, engineers, etc. For my buddy, this was someone who likes to travel. For my mortgage business it was all about gratitude. If the clients are not nice people I don't want to work with them. Someone with a big ego or who "demands" things we don't have time for. I have fired many clients over the years. It is just not worth the aggravation.

Once we did all those things, I went to figure out the lifetime value of my client. There have been entire books written about this topic, but here is a brief formula.

Average Revenue x Average # of purchases in a year x Average client life (in years).

For my business it was a bit different. The formula looks like this:

(Average Revenue) x (# of mortgages in the next 10 years)

This is a great way to view referral sources or marketing channels as well.

Join our community at IQLend on Facebook or email us the answers at book@iqlend.ca

If you need a financial solution or want more information about mortgage lending, please visit us at www.iqlend.ca or email at book@iqlend.ca

Chad Robinson

Chad Robinson is a highly respected real estate professional with 25 years of valued experience in the Mortgage and Real Estate industry. Chad holds a Bachelor of Economics with a specialization in International Business from Carleton University and is both a fully licensed mortgage and real estate broker. Growing up in a real estate family, Chad began selling real estate when he turned 18 and has not looked back since. Forever the entrepreneur, Chad has worked to grow several mortgage brokerage operations and is currently the president and owner/broker of award-winning 360 Best Interest Mortgages Inc serving the Eastern Ontario area. While balancing multiple development projects, Chad also finds time to serve as a consultant to other private lenders and developers offering his sound advice and professional expertise.

Chad excels with first-time investors and investment real estate and even manages to carve out additional time to serve as a motivational speaker and contributing writer to several real estate periodicals. A valued source, Chad has become a regular on several media outlets. Chad has particular expertise working in the area of commercial development construction with several prominent construction projects under his belt and more ongoing, including partnering in several infill construction projects in the Ottawa area.

Chad has built a solid reputation serving as an attentive one-on-one expert with each of his valued clients which has allowed Chad to develop substantial client loyalty and respect.

His enthusiasm for the real estate industry and desire to address each mortgage request by looking at all possible angles enables Chad to stand out from other mortgage professionals. This client-centered approach has earned Chad respect among his colleagues and clients alike.

As well as his many professional pursuits and achievements, Chad contributes to volunteer organizations and charities and is dedicated to his growing family.

8

Understanding the Legacy Procrastination Effect – Christine Brunsden & Chris Delaney

Over the past thirty years of estate & succession planning and administration experiences, we have discovered that most people associate estate planning with end-of-life discussions, difficult processes, expensive & complicated solutions and negative outcomes. In fact, nearly 50 percent of adult Canadians do not have a will and of those with wills, a further 16 percent admit that their wills are out of date and would not achieve their current wishes. A recent online survey by Angus Reid Forum found that 45 percent of Canadians believe that end-of-life planning does not apply to them, with another 22 percent of the same group saying it makes them uncomfortable and they do not know where to start. Yet, somewhat paradoxically, most people self report a desire to do well by their loved ones and favored causes.

In trying to understand and manage this profound gap between objectives and reality, we concluded this failure to connect our present and future selves exists because of what we term the *Legacy Procrastination Effect*. The problem with this gap is that it translates into future decision-makers being inadequately prepared to perform their role with any reasonable degree of success and future heirs not being prepared to confidently manage the family wealth once it transitions to their stewardship. This gap can be bridged with the assistance of our *Purposeful Legacy Awareness Navigator*.

What was the genesis for creating a *Purposeful Legacy Awareness Navigator?*

Our clients are drawn from several, interconnected pools of interest including:

1. Clients – end users who are doing their own family wealth planning

2. Advisors – lawyers, accountants, wealth & insurance advisors, business transition specialists, coaches, planned giving specialists and elder and disability planning advisors

3. Corporate service providers – corporate entities offering comprehensive employee assistance programs

4. Channel information aggregators – groups that channel specific best practices planning information including disability networks, elder planning networks, estate planning councils

These various groups share a common area of interest where the myriad opportunities from planning and education overlap. This intersectional region offers leverage for real results by educating the connected parties on shared concepts that will allow them to move ahead together.

Legacy You was created to be a *Purposeful Legacy Awareness Navigator* to bring a multi-level approach to the family wealth succession model that is education-based and built around the simple maxim that estate planning is a process and not an event. It is a daily process of life that establishes a continuum of planning across all stages of life to create legacy. In using this approach, our design is to evolve estate planning from a sterile, asset based, event-driven step in financial wealth transfer towards an abundant, values-driven process of lifelong legacy creation, stewardship and transmission.

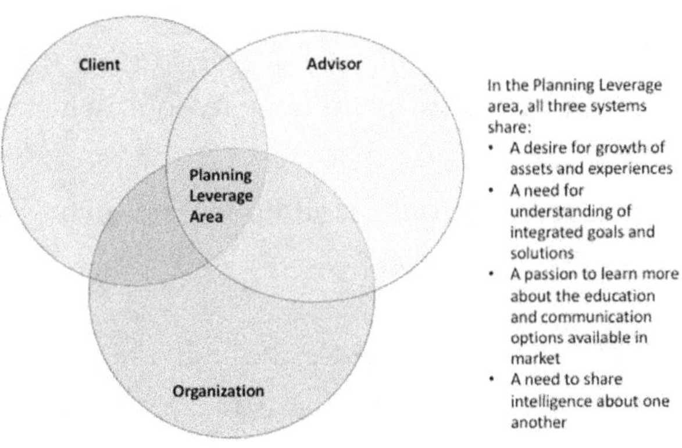

Legacy You connects the various client spheres into their areas of shared interest to maximize the leverage of educational outcomes. The central principle is that advisors, organizations and individuals share these common goals with another and have an interest in doing it together. In systems theory, there is a concept called "schismogenesis." In essence, systems (clients and their advisors, families etc.) fail to communicate and create self-reinforcing loops of increasingly poor data that ultimately collapse in a massive, entropic failure. The irony is that progressive disorder expands in a system designed, at least nominally, to provide order through planning. The core failure is in poor communications and sharing which is exacerbated by incomplete or faulty education. *Legacy You* attempts to remediate those failures and change the process from an entropic outcome to sustainable intergenerational wealth for the long term.

What is *The Legacy Procrastination Effect?*

The concept of the *Legacy Procrastination Effect* was derived from the notion that estate planning consumers typically respond to stimuli (a seminar, education event, case example, news story) in at least one of three ways:

1. They set priorities in life and respond when a challenge arises (delay)
2. They personally conduct additional research (defer)
3. They take some action (react)

Each of these "actions" provides the individual with a sense of contentment that an outcome has been achieved. The problem with contentment is that they stop planning and fall back into a generally passive and reactive planning mode. They are simply bandaging the wound rather than creating a process of positive, purpose-driven changes to their planning mindset and achieving Legacy Planning Abundance.

For example, consider Billy. He is married and has two adult children. His daughter is married with two children. She announces one weekend that her marriage is over and she will be divorcing. Billy panics that his will must be reviewed and updated to address this tsunami of change in his family dynamics. Billy has delayed a prioritized response (desire to protect family assets from risk) and is now reacting to the information stimulus. In the interim, opportunities and risk have changed in his situation and a strategically superior outcome may be compromised. By thinking of his legacy as a terminal outcome, Billy has missed chances to build a more resilient wealth transfer plan. Billy is a victim of the *Legacy Procrastination Effect*.

The Four *Legacy Procrastination Effect* Phases

Individuals and advisors generally find themselves in one of four phases within the *Legacy Procrastination Effect* paradigm. Throughout one's lifetime, they will likely progress from the first phase to the third phase and will often find themselves caught futilely looping back and forth between the second and third phases.

Innocence

The first phase is "Innocence." In this phase you haven't yet begun to think about the meaning and purpose of legacy planning. Some indications you are in this phase include:

- Wealth viewed exclusively as financial wealth (investments, real estate, business assets)
- Tactical responses seem sufficient
- No specific strategy for wealth transition planning
- No transferable, personal benefit to planning can be identified
- Define estate planning as wills, powers of attorney, life insurance, trusts
- Legacy is viewed as a terminal concept (name on a park bench or building)

Acceptance

As life progresses you generally enter into the second phase called: "Acceptance." Acceptance is when you accept that you have beneficiaries and heirs that will benefit today and in the future from your planning efforts. Indications you are in this phase include:

- Awareness and sense of discomfort with your lack of existing planning

- Unease when family and heir-related challenges arise as it pertains to your wealth continuity

- A sense of "that's not how I/we do things in our family" permeates responses to especially sad and shocking media stories and anecdotes pertaining to death and estates

- Uncertainty about the capacity of associated advisors to provide the outcomes you are seeking (a form of projection)

- Curiosity about the mechanics of specific strategies and how those tactics will implicate all members of the planning ecosystem

- A vague understanding that there is more that can and must be done, but uncertainty about where to begin

Those in the phase of acceptance may get stuck due to their fear or reticence to plan because of potential real time conflict, an aversion to the cost of engaging professional assistance or the thinking that they have plenty of time before having to take action.

Furtherance

In this third phase of the paradigm, you decide to move ahead and take action. This is an important step as it can be either the beginning of a regression back to acceptance and furtherance or the impetus to enter the final phase of the planning process. People in the phase of furtherance may do any of the following:

- Update or execute a new will
- Update or execute a new set of Powers of Attorney
- Complete an advised tax structure such as an estate freeze or family trust
- Acquire a life insurance policy to achieve specific dollar valued estate objectives
- Commit to a charitable giving amount and vehicle for the giving

Advisor and product offering organizations experience this phase as a commitment by the client to their recommendations for specific problem solving after an appropriate gap analysis.

Abundance

Abundance is the fourth and final phase that is achieved through recognition that legacy planning is a dynamic, multi-layered strategic process that is best achieved when focused on purpose and long term intentionality. This phase is not typically achieved because of the impediments caused by the *Legacy Procrastination Effect*.

The Abundance Phase is characterized by planning that recognizes that:

- Family wealth is a broad concept that includes social, intellectual and human capital as well as financial capacity
- The present value of total family wealth can be increased through strategic investment in all facets of family wealth

- Legacy development, as a broad concept, is a mindset that can be learned and recreated across generations of family wealth

- Advisors play an essential role in managing the pathway for their clients to a better level of planning

- Family wealth is a qualitative, quantitative and dynamic intergenerational process that requires effort to sustain and amplify

- Estate and legacy planning is a process, not an event

Reflecting on Billy's situation, how was he the victim of the *Legacy Procrastination Effect*? His situation reveals that he was probably stuck moving between Acceptance and Furtherance because his planning is reactive and reflects no specific strategy focused on a long-term purpose for his wealth legacy. He is just reacting to events as they happen. His daughter's stark news of her separation has just forced him, probably very uncomfortably, back into the Acceptance Phase where he realizes he needs to enter the Furtherance Phase again. However, because he has not been exposed to the Abundance Phase he will likely react to the stimuli with a specific strategy and stop. He will feel he has addressed the problem because he has been assuaged to believe that the tactic is sufficient. In this example, Billy has likely missed some planning opportunities by not viewing his legacy with a broader mindset. These "losses" accumulate and translate into missed opportunities to:

- Share values and goals with integrated, intergenerational planning

- Build resilience and decision-making skills across generations as it pertains to intergenerational wealth management

- Share and model best practises for risk management and communication

The "losses" will mount for Billy and be accretive in his family by failing to integrate the Abundance Phase early on and at every level of the planning process. These reductions in the value of the family wealth are a sad measure of the *Legacy Procrastination Effect* – lost value, lost opportunities, depleted legacy potential.

Bridging the Gap:

Transitioning from an estate planning mindset to legacy planning abundance demands awareness, effort and guidance. This is a transition from event-driven to purpose-driven planning that requires expert navigation across all life stages and into the next generation. The benefits of legacy planning abundance include:

- Purposeful living through prioritization of values and goals;
- Preparation of heirs and decision-makers (fiduciaries) with ongoing education, process guidance and improved governance (communication and decision making)
- Creating a family-centred wealth mindset that enhances entrepreneurial skills, stewardship and healthy wealth consumption skills and attitudes

Family members and advisors need tools to help them bridge the gap from early phases to the abundance phase.

Legacy Awareness Navigation System:

The various phases of the *Legacy Procrastination Effect* can be experienced in a non-linear fashion. That is to say, starting off with an advisor-client-organizational mindset of abundance in estate planning can rapidly create a legacy planning process that is purposeful and generative. In reality, most people start off in the Innocence Phase and transit, if they ever do, to the Abundance Phase more or less in the order described above. The fact that 50% of adult Canadians don't have a will is testament to the stronger likelihood most consumers will remain fixed in either the Innocence Phase or the Acceptance Phase with occasional movement to the Furtherance Phase when things are really necessary to be done.

The *Legacy You* unique value proposition is education-based and focused on the premise that change can occur when options are revealed and understood in the context of personal goals and objectives. This is a daily, lifelong process of living and experiencing that necessitates planning for aging, disability and death. To successfully achieve these outcomes and educate advisors and their clients, we have developed a *Legacy Awareness Blueprint*. The *Legacy Awareness Blueprint* is the gateway to our practical *Legacy Awareness Navigator* that is comprised of the following components:

- A Practical Methodology for clients and advisors to assess their legacy awareness, build communication skills, decision-making policies, enhanced business opportunities and abundant family wealth legacy plans
- A Co-Enrichment Curriculum
- A Multi-Disciplinary Experts Matrix

The goal is to establish a client's core values and objectives for their total family wealth. This requires a process to identify and navigate their family enterprise wealth.

The *Legacy Awareness Blueprint* helps advisors and clients identify where they are and where they want to be based on their goals, objectives and present capacity. *The Legacy Awareness Navigator* offers an ongoing, learnable process to keep the planning on course and to allow for changes in direction as desired or needed.

The Benefit:

The benefit for clients and advisors/organizations is reaching the Abundance Phase in planning where intergenerational family wealth is:

- An opportunity rather than a burden
- A generative process rather than an entropic event
- Consistent with prioritized values and goals in the dynamic family system
- Designed first and foremost to prepare the heirs to receive the wealth rather than simply to prepare the efficient transition of wealth to the heirs
- Legacy is construed as a lifelong process to prepare the heirs via education, organization and communication to be better, more confident heirs and fiduciaries

Legacy You supports these outcomes by focusing on the central principle that advisors, organizations and individuals share common goals with one another and have an interest in doing it together. The *Legacy Awareness Blueprint* and *Purposeful Legacy Awareness Navigator* break down the self-reinforcing loops of increasingly poor data that ultimately fail advisors and clients in legacy planning. *Legacy You* attempts to remediate those failures and change the process from an entropic outcome to sustainable intergenerational family wealth for the very long term via education, purposeful process and attention to the symbiotic planning relationship shared by advisors/organizations and their clients.

Closing:

The *Legacy Awareness Blueprint* is the gateway to our *Purposeful Legacy Awareness Navigator* and is an integral tool used in overcoming The *Legacy Procrastination Effect*. At *Legacy You* we are dedicated to providing a practical methodology through education and other tools designed to help you operate from a purposeful and abundant mindset in order to overcome the *Legacy Procrastination Effect*. To get started…visit us at www.legacyyou.ca and let us help you Envision, Build, Communicate and Live Your Best Legacy each and every day.

Christine Brunsden. TEP, EPC, CEA, MFA-P

Christine is the Founder of Trusted Legacy (2019) and Co-Founder of Legacy You (2020). Prior to founding Trusted Legacy, Christine gained 20+ years experience acting as a fiduciary for individuals and their families through the participation in the administration of hundreds of Estates and thousands of Trusts, Powers of Attorney, Guardianships, Donor-Advised Funds and Private Corporations at several Canadian trust companies. Christine takes a holistic approach to legacy planning by helping her clients craft an individualized legacy plan that provides peace of mind in life and better outcomes on death and beyond.

Together Chris and Christine have founded Legacy You: Evolution of Estate Planning to abundantly motivate Canadian individuals and business owners to overcome The Legacy Procrastination Effect via an educational platform which guides them through the process of Envisioning, Building, Communicating and Living their Best Legacy.

Chris Delaney. B.A.. LL.B.. B.Ed.. TEP, FEA

Chris is the author of "The Naked Opus: Growing Your Family Wealth for the Long Term" (2018). He is also a Podcaster, Professional Speaker, Family Enterprise Advisor, Lawyer, Finance Professor, and Intergenerational Family Wealth Strategist. From 2004 to 2018 he worked with Canada's two largest bank-owned wealth management firms as a High Net Worth Estate Planner and Business Succession Advisor. In this role, he worked with enterprising business families and families of wealth and their advisors to help them develop goals-based, strategic intergenerational wealth continuity plans.

9

Principles in Healing
– Darlene Turriff

*Before you heal someone, ask him if he is willing
to give up the things that made him sick.*

– Hippocrates

You are the healer you seek. You have within you the power to heal everything in your life. It is the integration of ego and spirit that will let you emerge into the life you were always meant to lead.

My story begins when being bedridden had stolen everything of value from my life. Here are the principles I discovered that healed my illness and are the foundation to living my fullest life.

I was 49 years old and I remember walking into the bank for the first time by myself and speaking with the loans officer. I was there to ask for a $50,000 line of credit so that I could buy my first vacation rental property and start my first business. I was scared AND I was ready to take the leap. This was the beginning of my purpose driven healing. I needed three things to happen before I walked into that bank. I needed to trust the habits and systems I had put in place. I needed to know and challenge myself to embody the mindset of an entrepreneur. And I mostly needed to live with what I call, "applied faith." I could not logically define why I needed to be launching a vacation rental business. What I did know is I was being called to do it. My healing journey began when I started saying yes to my intuition and my bigger purpose before knowing how it would all unfold. This leap of faith, this trust, is what allowed me to overcome my *Autoimmune Identity*™ and emerge from sick to healed.

It had been 20 years that I'd been suffering from an undiagnosed, invisible, chronic, illness and when I reached the end of that illness I had been bedridden for almost 2 years. I was in constant pain; I had brain fog, I couldn't even read; I was so physically weak I needed assistance to walk. I had migraines everyday 24/7 and I was a shell of a person. So, as you can imagine, there was no aspect of my life that was free from the effects from these symptoms. I was unable to work. We had money problems. I had relationship problems. I had marriage problems. I was a lousy parent (well not the parent I wanted to be). And the list goes on. But the one thing I wasn't, was convinced that this was all my life could be. I always knew I was going to have a big life and I could not understand how I got to where I was.

So the big question is how did I get from bedridden to running two businesses? I began to apply a new series of what I now call the Versus Principles™. My life was out of alignment with my purpose. My thinking was setting me up for disease and my actions were all about validation. I evaluated my life by what I accomplished, how I was perceived by the world and whether I was right.

I was caught in what I now know was the Autoimmune Identity Cycle. I healed my disease and life by overcoming the authority gap as seen here in this model below. When I was in full blown Autoimmune Identity, my decision response was external. All my decisions were based on external factors or as I call it, external authorities. It was when I began to trust my internal authority that I was able to increase my healing decision response. This sets us up for the first of the principles.

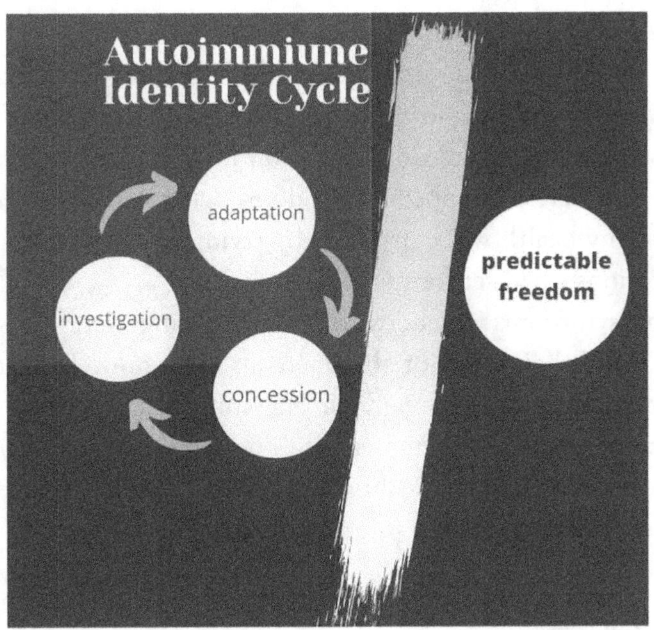

Principle #1
Personal Responsibility vs Personal Expectations

For me there were four factors in my control that needed to change. The one mindset that allowed me to identify those four factors began with shifting from my external victim mindset to my radical responsibility mindset. When I understood how much my own actions, thoughts and choices were contributing to my condition, I then understood the power I had in my own success. This is better known as being the co-creator of your own life. My results were in part due to my own thinking and doing. Just like Dorothy and her ruby red slippers in the Wizard of Oz, I always had the power. Still, there was a process to becoming well. Let me share what worked for me.

Up until this point in my life I made decisions from a defensive standpoint. My actions and habits were about placing others first. I had adopted a limiting belief that in sacrificing myself to my family and my work, I would find fulfillment. My mindset was about awaiting validation for my "good works" and I was completely wrapped up in doing what was expected. My life and my health was consumed by trying to meet unattainable expectations I had set for myself.

The symptoms my body was experiencing were a result of many things being out of alignment in my world. To bring the alignment back in, I focused on one component at a time, one element at a time and incrementally, I healed my body. I identified the four components to healing to be: diet, lifestyle, mindset, and purpose. Which brings us to principle #2.

Principle #2
Protocol vs Diet

I took personal responsibility for my physical healing by understanding that diet, stress, mindset and lifestyle choices were all common contributing factors to autoimmune disease. I began a full elimination diet for the sole purpose of personalizing my nutrition according to what my body was saying, rather than following someone else's version of what is healthy. I began listening to what my body needed from me.

Diet for me changed into what I now understand as nutritional healing. I follow what is known as an autoimmune protocol. It was a process of healing my gut, identifying trigger foods, and eating nutrient-dense with the purpose of supporting my body's natural healing abilities.

Principle # 3
Transformation vs Information

Lifestyle is about choices, choices, choices. I needed to set up a lifestyle that would support my body, my mind, and my spirit. What I learned was that 95% of our choices are automated (according to Harvard Professor Gerald Zaltman *How Customers Think: Essential Insights into the Mind of the Market*) I realized that for me to have a strong body, so that I could live the life of my dreams and follow my purpose, I would need to look at those beliefs. I would need to be deliberate, intentional and purposeful in my daily actions. My tiny choices were the ones controlling my future, not my disease.

Principle #4
Service vs Sacrifice

Mindset was the next obvious choice for my healing. My mission became uncovering all my limiting beliefs that were sabotaging my own desires. This was a journey of going deeper. What I discovered in this process was that my actions were out of alignment with my purpose.

Now these 3 actions of diet, lifestyle and mindset probably sound familiar. I used a combination of my doctors, alternative medicine and diet and exercise to reverse my autoimmune disease.

I identify this as the average approach. This only got me so far. The obvious and average action were a good part of the solution but not enough to heal me. I was still in the autoimmune identity. To heal the body, I would need a combination of external authorities AND my internal integrity. Where most people fail, where I failed initially, was only following the three most common approaches. Traditional medicine, alternative medicine, diet & exercise are the prescription of our common culture. What I now understand, is the decision response here is still external. We are making our decisions based on someone else's limiting beliefs. If I was to heal, I needed to forge my own path. After almost 20 years of living a limited life, I wanted more.

Personal responsibility means moving all my decisions to a new standard. It was not enough to follow a diet prescribed by experts. I followed a protocol dictated by my body's responses. It was not enough to meditate and do yoga to reduce stress. I started from scratch and scheduled my life for healing by no longer including stress inducing activities. My lifestyle choices were my own. It was simple enough to prioritize my healing first before anyone and anything. My mindset needed the most healing.

Principle #5
Purpose vs Plan

Choosing to ask myself WHY I was doing what I was doing versus evaluating the WHAT I was doing, became very important. We can still have a plan (the what), but it must be aligned with our soul's purpose.

The factor that got me out of the autoimmune identity cycle and into my healing was what I call the *Healing Decision Response*. Empowerment in our health is based on our choices. Our choices are based on our priorities and our priorities are based on our values. Step 1 in healing is getting crystal clear on your WHY! I now had a new filter for which to base all my decisions. I got ruthless and you should too. If any part of your daily life is not supporting your purpose, then you have the power to change it.

Our happiness, our health and our success are actually found in our mindless daily decisions. We mistakenly believe a big goal will bring us everything we want, when in fact it is the tiny decisions dictating our success and our healing. If you want to heal your life you will need a new filter to rethink all your decisions, especially your subconscious ones.

Healing happened for me in 4 steps. Step 1 was when I first identified a problem that I didn't know I had. This was the problem of an external decision response which held me in my autoimmune identity.

I was stuck in a cycle that was susceptible to outside interference, I was living in an external focus. I have identified 4 states to this cycle:

1. *Concession* – suddenly you can no longer ignore your health;
2. *Investigation* – everything you do is in pursuit of an explanation or solution;
3. *Adaptation* – you compromise your dreams to fit your capabilities;
4. *Predictable Freedom* – you are healthy and living your abundant effortless life from your passion and purpose.

My experience in the cycle was that even when I would find improvement, I was always susceptible to outside forces. When circumstances changed my reality my state would change too. I was stuck on the wrong side of the authority gap. I did not know how to cross that gap, even though I had the desire to do so. Worse, I could not figure out what I was doing wrong?

The distance from being stuck in the cycle and moving into a permanent state of *predictable freedom* is what I call the *Intuitive Integrity Formula*. Step 2 through 4 in healing, is the Intuitive Integrity Formula and can be broken down into 3 simple strategies.

Strategy #1 was to prioritize my routines by taking control of my daily habits. I am co-creating my experience and I needed to learn to control and take ownership of my own thoughts and actions. I got really honest about the results. When my body was not healthy, I did not have a system for my freedom. My health is my greatest asset, even greater than my wealth.

Having a clear goal that eliminates all other possibilities is critical. The mistake most people make is adding a goal without making room for that goal. Be ruthless. Be honest. Be decisive. Which brings me to a critical part in my story.

Setting boundaries was fundamental to reclaiming my life and making room for healing. Let me just say that when done right, setting boundaries can help everyone involved and thankfully, that is how it worked for me. But before it became something I could be grateful for, it was the most difficult thing I ever did in my life. Prioritizing for me, is having a lifestyle that is flexible and includes room for healing to occur. We cannot heal what we do not acknowledge.

The second strategy I needed was a perception shift or, as most people know it, a mindset shift. Work on mindset is needed because 95% of our decisions are made from the subconscious, and the subconscious is run on our beliefs. Shifting from limiting beliefs into abundant beliefs rocked my world.

Once I had this awareness, I developed what I call the *versus principles decision method*™. *The Versus Principles*™ are a series of principles based on the laws of the universe. Everything can be broken down into an ego decision (fear or protection) or a spirit decision (love or abundance).

I learned my results were only limited by what I believed could happen. So my emerging story does not have an ending. This leads me to the last and final strategy that you need to create your own healed life.

The third strategy that I use is what I call *purpose identity*. One key component of *purpose identity* is having applied faith. You may know this term from Napoleon Hill's *Think and Grow Rich*. But what is applied faith? Up to now everything I've shared is something you would find in most self-help or personal development books. I am a theologian and a student of *A Course in Miracles*. My understanding of our relationship with spirit is key and takes healing into another realm in this concept of applied faith. I believe the factor that moved me from my cycle of pain and chronic illness and into my life of predictable freedom is an active spiritual connection to my true self and my life purpose. I take my guidance from my inner connected self. I call this guidance, my intuition. It is not enough, in my opinion, to have a meditative life or a spiritual life unless we are taking action from that life. Applied faith is taking the courage; trusting in a bigger dream for ourselves that we have yet to understand. At the beginning of this chapter, I shared about following a path of entrepreneurship. To act on this faith I needed to trust my own intuition.

Success is not defined by the idea but by action on the idea. What I did not know is that the lessons of starting a vacation rental would lead me to being a thought leader in wellness coaching and now writing a book series called *The Versus Principles*™. As I emerge in my field as the voice on how to overcome Autoimmune

Identity, I celebrate each woman who reclaims their lives using the principles and strategies I have developed.

It is eight years and counting that I have reversed my own autoimmune disease. I wake up every day ready to trust and act with applied faith. What we believe changes nothing. What we are willing to do and be, based on those beliefs, is how we can change the world. I became the healer I sought, one incremental change at a time. I stopped looking for the magic bullet by recognizing I held the power all along.

Darlene Turriff

People who know her NOW, would never guess that Darlene suffered for over 20 years with chronic fatigue, fibromyalgia, and brain fog which left her unemployable & bedridden. NOW, her high energy and enthusiasm is the first thing people notice. Darlene and her husband of almost 25 years live in Gatineau QC and summer in Metis Beach with their chocolate lab Eugene. She is a bio mom of one and a heart mom of one. She calls her brand of living "denim woo-woo," she is deeply guided by the laws of abundance BUT her "redneck" side makes her a straight-shooter. Favorite expression is "YOU GOT THIS!"

https://www.darleneturriff.com/
https://www.facebook.com/Darlene-M-Turriff-Author-Coach-2150316975185957
https://www.facebook.com/The-Versus-Principles-1086391588218357

10

Holisticity: The Secret to Thriving in a World of Change – Denitsa Andonova

"It is our choices, Harry, that show what we truly are, far more than our abilities."

— J.K. Rowling, Harry Potter and the Chamber of Secrets

I have always wondered, is there a skill, an effective tool, which helps us to adapt easily, to transform, to shift and achieve more with lightness, love and joy? In my over 14 years of practice consulting people and companies all over the world about positive mindset, healthy habits, nutrition on cell level, energy and emotional balance, well-being and corporate wellness, through the lens of a holistic approach, I have had the blessing of meeting thousands of people who were able to achieve a goal, to fulfil a dream, to shift to a new level. How did they do it and still do it?

Why do some people enjoy extraordinary lives, why do others experience so many struggles, pain and devastation? How do some people thrive, no matter the circumstances, and why do they feel like they are the creators of their dream life? Is there a secret behind that? How can we keep our positive focus to rewire our brains and rewrite our lives? This became my passion and mission in my life and business. My dream vision is, "Thriving people, thriving business, thriving world." Especially because I am a mother of two amazing little girls and I dream for them to have a thriving life.

But sometimes the reality is very different. So many people struggle to achieve the life they desire. In fact, so many people never even try and pursue the life of their dreams because they don't even believe that it is possible (for them). That's why there is this big gap between what people believe is possible and what is actually possible. What holds people back is, what I call, their level of *Holisticity*. Holisticity is the level at which you accept your own responsibility to implement the tools at your disposal to create the life you desire. Everybody has tools available to them, especially nowadays. But so many people either don't know (and/or don't care) about them or they know about those tools, but they don't accept the responsibility to implement them in their lives. When someone doesn't have or doesn't accept the responsibility to implement those tools, this is a low level of Holisticity. But when somebody accepts full responsibility for implementing all the tools at their disposal and takes action, that's a high level of Holisticity. There are 4 different states of Holisticity that I have noticed.

The first state is called Counteractive Implementation. According to the Holisticity model this is the worst case scenario. This means that you are implementing the tools that you have at your disposal in a way that is actually making you go backwards. You get the reverse effects, not the desired outcomes. You do

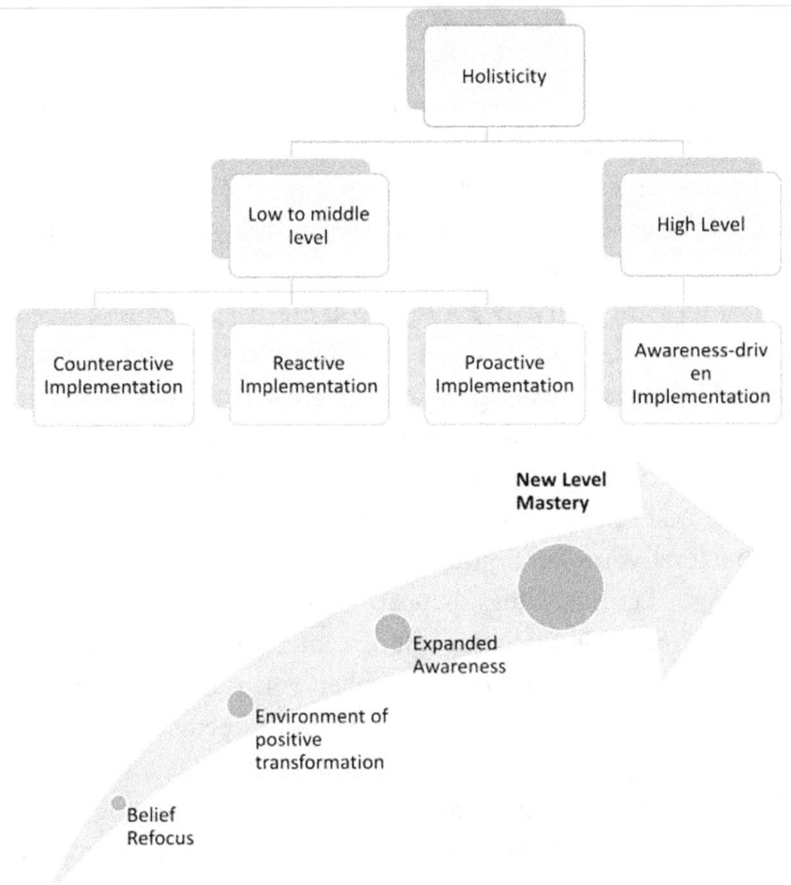

Figure 1: Holisticity Model by Deni Andonova

things in life that lead you to what you don't want, not to what you actually want. This is pulling you away from the life you desire. You know that you are in this state when you see these signs or combinations of them: bad habits, out of shape, poor health, many psychical and mental health symptoms, pain and nausea, depression, apathy, low energy, relationship problems and conflicts, business issues – low income or profit, lack of clients and growth. There is never any/enough money in your bank account. Low levels of motivation, productivity and creativity. Negative mindset, criticism and judging tendencies. Life happens to you and many times you find yourself struggling to cope, to survive. You don't "believe" in energy, you don't know about these ideas and you are not open to holistic concepts, methods, techniques, you don't want to try. Every time you create something it seems to be destroyed, every time you move forward you seem to end up going backwards, nothing is sustainable, you are always creating things over and over again and you just can't seem to move forward, because everything you do seems to get undone.

The next state of Holisticity is called Reactive Implementation. In this level you basically don't create anything as much as react to things. Letting things happen, not consciously influencing anything. Sometimes life is good, sometimes it is bad. When something happens to you, that's when you react. You don't lose weight, until you get overweight. You don't eat better, until you get unhealthy. You don't care about and improve your relationships, until you need to resolve a conflict. You don't optimize or develop your business/career, until you get stuck/fired or lose money. You never save money, until you need money in the bank. Bills are paid late and you are always reacting to things. Something bad happens and you end up fixing it. You are always fixing things as they come up. This process makes you feel tired, pessimistic, and disappointed.

Then there is a state that I call Proactive Implementation. This means that you are using brute force and will power to move forward into life. At this state you may be successful. You could have a bunch of successes in life, but they were not achieved with lightness and joy. Everything is work and every success requires hard work, effort, willpower, pressure, demand, control. You are going through life, forcing the world to create what you desire. And you find yourself exhausted all the time. You are always creating and the things that you create if you don't keep the pressure on them seem to go away. You experience a high level of distress, bad quality sleep, tension and panic attacks. You are at a higher risk for burnout syndrome, emotional eating and binge eating, heart and vascular disease symptoms. You don't have the skill to rest and to enjoy your time with loved ones and friends. You do not have time for hobbies, or daily routines for self-development. Every activity should be goal-oriented. Long working days and extra working hours. Bad work-life balance. Using Force in all aspects of life. Everything is work. You have to work, to plan, to fight for everything. You are forcing everything to happen. If something goes wrong, you are fixing it and forcing it again, going forward. Always going forward. You are always pushing, fixing and solving problems, baby step after baby step. At the end of the day you feel exhausted "What a long day that was! I have to run this hamster wheel again tomorrow. The harder I work, the bigger success I will have. I have to work and make sacrifices for it. Get things done. I push and pull things. I make them happen through Force."

But then there's this other state of Holisticity, which is called Awareness-driven Implementation. This is implementation through power, not force. Inner, authentic power, driven by your openness and awareness. You are using all the creative tools at your disposal. You have accepted your responsibility for the creation of the life of your dreams. You have the power to create life before you end up stepping into it. You know that you are there when you seem to manifest what you want with ease. You have a desire for something and it creates itself all the time. You find yourself in a situation, saying "This is exactly what I had planned. I am very aware that I have to maintain my emotional, energetic, physical, mental and spiritual balance, and I have accepted responsibility for my Holisiticity in all of these areas. I accept full responsibility for the conditions in my life. I understand that my beliefs, my mindset, my vision for my life, my energy, my emotions, my balance matter. I will use my inner power, my holistic tools for my dream life creation. Every shift in my awareness level is a shift in a desired direction – personal, professional growth, more balance and harmony in relationships, all levels of well-being and wellness. I use my energy, my emotional, my spiritual energy to use all the different holistic tools that I have in order to create the life that I step into." Desired things happen effortlessly, with ease, joy and lightness. The people who have high levels of Holisticity, experience a high quality of life, enjoy amazing loving relationships, savor quality time and an abundance of magical moments with their loved ones, friends and have time for self-development. They have perfect time management and energy management skills. Great work-life integration and well-being. They seem to have amazing stress coping strategies and find themselves in a flow state very often. They have a positive mindset and express everyday gratitude, love and support to themselves and others. They are confident, smiling and have a high level of self-esteem and clarity about what they want in life. Because of their healthy habits and wellness-oriented daily routines, they are in perfect shape, have high energy, vitality and health. They have time for hobbies, vacations and fun. Their businesses and careers are mission-driven, impactful and inspiring, they deliver massive value. The level of income and profit is high, they do a lot of charity and philanthropy. They have a high level of satisfaction, positive emotions and optimism, motivation, productivity and happiness. In this state people are far from survival mode – they are thriving and helping others to thrive.

Most people don't find themselves in the Awareness-driven Implementation state, because they don't have a high level of Holisticity. They don't accept their responsibility for the implementation of all the holistic tools that could help them to create their dream life. Every one of us has the power of choice, free will, to be in the Awareness-driven Implementation state.

In order to get to that kind of implementation, in order to score the high level of Holisticity, to implement through powerful awareness, there are 3 things that need to happen:

1. You need to have a Belief Refocus. That means to challenge the beliefs that you have, that you think are serving you. Is it possible they may not be serving you? And you must change your disempowering, limiting beliefs so you will have a belief system that is actually bringing you to the awareness and decision for the creation of your dream life. And of course to start practicing them, to put them into habits which will bring you from where you don't want to be to where you desire to be.

2. The second thing that has to happen is what I call an environment of positive transformation. We have to create this environment, this new field for the changes to happen. There are key elements that have to be in place in order to create this very special environment that allows you to transform. Sometimes it is the system that needs to be put in place, a strategy that needs to be built, the surrounding environment (people, places, the space around you and even the system of your physical body) needs to be optimized and/or the level of self-awareness needs to be shifted. Focus on where you want to go, not on where you don't want to be. There are tools that are

available to create this new field for the environment you need for transformation in your life. In this case the positive transformation is not only accepted, but welcomed, intended and expected, even influenced by the way you live, think, feel and dream.

3. And the third outcome that needs to happen is what I call Expanded Awareness. You need to have this process of expanding your level of awareness of all the creative tools that are at your disposal so that once you understand and have the openness to use and explore these creative tools, now you are in this environment of transformation and you can transform, you can shift using those tools, which is all supported by a new empowering beliefs system and positive focus. Expanded awareness state is a life mastery philosophy. Every day, using your new Expanded Awareness skills, will be a journey, a transformation, another day reconnecting to self, to your mission, to the miracle of life.

When these 3 things happen, when the Belief Refocus happens, when there is an Environment for positive transformation created and the Expanded Awareness is achieved, all these things combined together form what I call a New Level Mastery. The New Level Mastery elevates your level of Holisticity, which means you are much more accepting of your responsibility to implement all the creative tools you have at your disposal. Once you have your high Holisticity achieved through your New Level Mastery, now you are in a position to implement through power, intention, awareness and create the life of your dreams. This process will happen in love, joy, abundance and mindfulness.

And now, please take the next steps towards creating the life you want. Level up your Holisticity.

1. Set an intention to connect to yourself in an authentic way through this process and to expand your awareness. Take 5 minutes to answer these questions. Be really honest to yourself. Please write the date and the answers.

2. In which of the 4 states do you find yourself in this moment – Counteractive Implementation, Reactive Implementation, Proactive implementation or Awareness-driven Implementation? In which mode are you most of the time – surviving or thriving?

   …..

   ….

   …..

3. Do you like it? Is this what you want in life?

   …..

   ….

   …..

4. How happy/fulfilled/aware do you feel right now at this stage of your life?

   …..

   ….

   …..

5. How close are you to your dream life? What do you actually want to have, to experience, to achieve, to enjoy? Do you have your dream life vision?

   …..

   ….

   …..

6. Do you want to increase your level of Holisticity? YES/NO (circle the right answer)

7. Commit to 2 actions which could level up your Holisticity. What steps could elevate you to where you want to be? And make them a daily routine. Implement your holistic tools strategy. Track your progress. Celebrate your wins!

   .....

   ....

   .....

I'm inviting you to this interesting journey through New Level Mastery. Do not only give it a try. Take full responsibility! Decide! Commit to it! Believe that this is possible for you! Set an intention, a goal, open your mind for your dreams and desires. They are there, waiting for you to expand your awareness and to allow the alignment, the lightness, the joy of success through powerful creative manifestation. Level up your Holisticity and enjoy your creative power to achieve and savor your dream life, being the best version of yourself, supported by your new empowering belief system, your new level of environment for positive transformation and your full responsibility to use your awareness-driven creative power.

Be clear on what you want!

Know that you deserve it!

Allow yourself to live it!

Love, joy, awareness,
Deni Andonova

Denitsa Andonova

Deni Andonova is an organizational and positive psychologist, speaker, trainer, certified corporate wellness specialist, certified K-Power® instructor, HR specialist, kinesiologist, Bush flower essences therapist, specialist and certified Instructor Neurographica® – art therapy and aesthetic coaching, certified Neuro-Agility® practitioner. She has 3 master degrees in Psychology and Human Resource Management and has a PhD in Corporate wellness. Book Author: Nutrition on Cell level: Holistic guide for self-care and love; New Level: Holistic Guide for transformation and positive change. Founder of How thrive®, Thriving Bulgaria Foundation for mental health and The Holistic Academy by Deni Andonova. Deni helps people to do their desired shift – from surviving to thriving mode and to reconnect to their true selves, rewire their brains and re-write their lives. Her concept about the level of Holisticity creates new horizons for open-minded people who want to live amazing dream lives and to enjoy more love, gratitude, success, balance, lightness and joy.

LinkedIn: https://www.linkedin.com/in/deni-andonova/
Facebook: https://www.facebook.com/DeniHolistic
Websites: www.howthrive.com, www.deniandonova.com
BONUS Join here for Neurographica® practice: https://en.deniandonova.com/

Photos by Mariana Gugalova, Atelier Guge

11

Think Like a CEO
– Diana Lidstone

How to scale your business, explode your profits
& enjoy your life

Introduction

Two years ago, Cynthia and I were sitting at my kitchen table having coffee. She was at her wits end. After ten years of trying to build her legal practice, she was ready to give it up to go to work for someone else.

I realized I had seen this too many times before.
Cynthia was exhausted with dark circles under her eyes.
Her business wasn't profitable.
She worked long hard hours with little to show for it.

I've been in business for more than 35 years and, sadly, I've met too many business owners just like Cynthia! They started their business because they had a passion to help others. Yet, as the business grew, it became a time-eating, profit-less monster.

It doesn't have to be that way. I wrote this chapter so that more ambitious and growth-minded entrepreneurs like Cynthia would be able to see the possibilities that their business could bring them: joy, freedom, and profit.

In the next few pages, I'll share highlights on how business owners can accelerate their growth, explode their profits, gloriously step into their role of CEO, and truly enjoy their lives.

5 Core Entrepreneurial Tasks

The biggest problem for most business leaders is that they feel overwhelmed. They spend too much time working on the wrong activities in their business.

Here's what I mean.

When I started my retail business in 1995, I admit I knew nothing about operating a retail business. Like Cynthia, I had a passion for the business, but lacked the skills to create something profitable that still left me time to enjoy life. In those first few years, I got really familiar with business overwhelm and the hustle hamster wheel. And I didn't enjoy it.

But I figured it out. In order to get out of overwhelm and have more time away from my business, I had to think more like a CEO.

It came down to knowing which of the 5 Core Entrepreneurial Tasks I was responsible for, and which tasks could be done by someone else.

Here's a quick explanation of each of these tasks.

1. **Administration and Operations** refers to any activity related to the operations of the business which might include bookkeeping, human relations and staffing; finance; etc.

5 Core Entrepreneurial Tasks

2. **Customer Service** is dealing with any customer related issues that might arise including keeping customers happy so they become lifelong customers.

3. **Customer Fulfillment** relates to fulfilling orders and directly working with customers on those activities. If you're a solopreneur, professional, coach or consultant, this would be doing the actual coaching or consulting.

4. **Marketing and Sales** are activities that take prospects along the journey until they become clients such as blogging, networking, speaking, or holding sales conversations.

5. **Business Growth and Development** are activities related to the development of the CEO or the growth of the company. These might include improving skills; and planning or strategy days.

When I started my retail store, I was the Chief EVERYTHING Officer. I did everything: ordering inventory, hiring staff, and making sales. I was the marketing officer, strategic planner, and …. toilet cleaner. However, I soon learned I needed to stop spending so much time on administrative and customer service activities.

I also learned to ask myself a different question. Instead of asking what needed to be done, I asked WHO could do those tasks.

Take a minute and ask yourself: Where do you spend the majority of your time?

Put a number from 1-5 next to each of the core activities (#1 beside the one you spend most of your time doing). There are no right or wrong answers – just answers that you can learn from.

1. Administration and Operations   _____
2. Customer Service   _____
3. Customer Fulfillment   _____
4. Marketing and Sales   _____
5. Business Growth and Development   _____

Is it time for you to reallocate your time?

Remember Cynthia? When Cynthia and I originally met, Cynthia was acting and thinking more like an employee than the CEO of her business. She was spending the majority of her time doing administrative tasks and customer fulfillment. She worked long hours on everything from hiring, training, and sales conversations to doing the actual 'lawyering.' Because her law practice was seen as 'just another law practice,' she was unable to attract high-value clients.

However, Cynthia started thinking differently about her business as we worked to re-focus her efforts on positioning her business (marketing) and business growth and development. Then she started building a strong ecosystem to support her as the CEO.

Today, Cynthia's business generates more profit than she could ever have imagined. She has more free time. Although she sometimes works weekends, she takes time off during the week for self-care. Strategically, she has hired more team members and has built a strong ecosystem to support her business growth. She is also well known as the go-to-expert in her field of specialization which brings her tremendous joy!

Thinking differently about your business, like a CEO, and spending your time working in the right areas of your business will allow you to accelerate growth, explode profits, and live the life you truly desire.

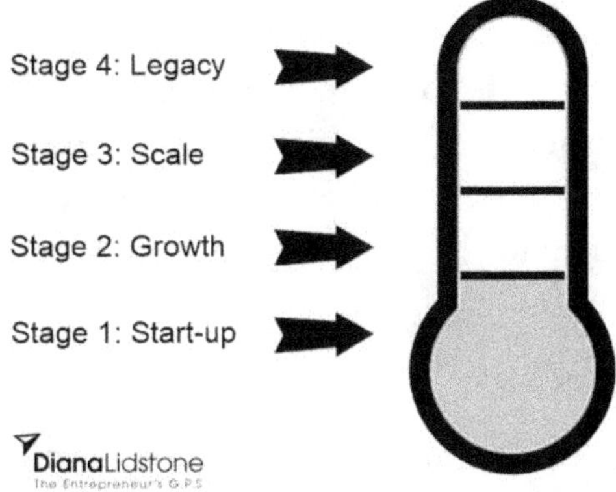

GPS Business Grow-Meter*: 4 Stages of Business Growth

We all grow. We come into this world as newborns, then transform into toddlers, teenagers, adults, and seniors.

Generally speaking, every business goes through four stages of business growth: start-up, growth, scale, and legacy. I like depicting these four stages as a thermometer (see diagram). And just like newborns, a start-up has much different characteristics than a legacy business.

Just a reminder: a business doesn't go to sleep one night in start-up phase and wake up the next morning in growth phase

– it's a transition and transformation that happens over time, just like the temperature rising in a thermometer.

If we examine the 5 Core Entrepreneurial Tasks (discussed earlier) and look at these through the stages of growth, you'll understand why successful entrepreneurs are able to shift from crazy, overwhelm to sane profitability.

START-UP

The name of the game at this stage is survival (unless you've had the Good Money Fairy hand you a wad of free start-up cash). In other words, entrepreneurs in this stage are working long hours, with very little money, struggling to cover expenses.

With respect to the 5 Core Entrepreneurial Tasks, start-ups spend the majority of their time doing Administrative and Operations tasks. However, when a business stays focused on these tasks throughout the growth cycle, they find that it is not sustainable and it's not profitable.

GROWTH PHASE

As a business starts getting more and more clients, they enter the Growth Phase. Growth can be exciting and overwhelming as revenue soars - but so do expenses. In this phase, often there is little profit and little freedom.

The growth phase is where many entrepreneurs get stuck and stay stuck.

Again, if we look at the 5 Core Entrepreneurial Tasks, business owners in the Growth phase are often overwhelmed with a massive to-do list which includes administration and customer fulfillment as well as marketing and sales.

Also in the Growth phase, entrepreneurs often feel trapped by their business! They find that their business is the driving force in everything in both life and business. They have no freedom or joy. Profits are low.

Shifting to the next phase of business growth requires thinking about your business differently or what I call, Thinking Like a CEO.

SCALE PHASE

Scaling is different from growth! Growth is the increase of both revenue and expenses. Scaling means that there is growth in revenue with little or no increase in expenses. You could call this the profit phase! (This is where Cynthia is now.)

Here, the business owner truly steps into the role of the CEO leading an aligned business (and not just another hard working, underpaid employee).

In the Scale phase, the CEO focuses:

1. foremost on marketing and sales to drive sales and growth,

2. then business growth and development,

3. and lastly on administrative & operations type tasks.

In this phase, the CEO learns how to:

- **A**lign business growth with their vision of success, and with their clients' needs.

- **B**uild an ecosystem to support the growth, the vision and their customers so that the owner can reclaim their life.

- **C**reated a rinse & repeat marketing roadmap to drive momentum and profit that is aligned with the vision.

LEGACY PHASE

It's a rare breed of entrepreneurs who want to build an empire, but that's not the only way to create a legacy. In this phase, the entrepreneur may diversify and create other companies and/or even start a charity. By the time a business owner reaches this phase of growth, they have built their ecosystem and profit model.

Consider the four phases of business growth.

What's your current stage of business growth?   ________

Where do you want to be?   ________

Are you where you want to be?   ________

3 Proven Secrets to Accelerate Business Growth & Enjoy your life

Carl Richards is the creator of Podcast Launch Made Simple and The Podcast Authority Builder. He enjoys time spent camping with his spouse and confessed to me recently that he has never been as profitable as he is now.

But it wasn't always that way. When I first met Carl, he was a full-time radio broadcaster and a part-time speaking coach. His coaching business limped along for several years and then …. The pandemic hit and he found himself out of a JOB!! He came to me ready to grow and scale his business to create full time income.

Like the majority of coaches, Carl was just one of many in a crowded industry. He knew he had to differentiate himself from his competition.

Let me tell you how Carl rapidly went through the three phases of business growth.

In the early stages of re-starting his business, Carl:

- Shifted from a general speaking coach to podcast launching, repositioning his business to a narrow audience.
- Created his own visual framework called "The Podcast Authority Builder."

- Struggled to meet expenses (survival mode).
- Wore all the hats in the business (bookkeeping, marketing, production, etc.).
- Worked long hard hours just to cover expenses.

In Phase II, the Growth Phase, Carl found that he:

- Stood out from his competition by using his visual framework.
- Built a rinse & repeat marketing system that attracted a consistent flow of qualified clients from around the globe.
- Outsourced activities (team) so he could focus on marketing.
- Grew his revenue and expenses (growth phase).

As he moved into Phase III, Carl found he was truly stepping into the role of CEO and scaling his business. He is now:

- Working only in his zone of genius and having fun in his business.
- Leveraging his team and systems to optimize revenue and profits.
- Scaling his time down because he has built a proficient ecosystem around him to allow profits to increase.

In order to achieve predictable and sustainable profits like Carl and Cynthia, here's what absolutely has to happen. You need what I call the **Aligned Profit Engine**.

The **Aligned Profit Engine** contains three specific tools that, when combined, will transform you from a stressed out, overworked business owner into a happy, profitable CEO.

These three keys are Strategic Growth, Authority Positioning and Sales & Marketing Roadmap.

1. Strategic Growth helps you stay aligned to your vision and build an ecosystem to carry out that vision. Of course - Stephen Covey said it first – begin with the end in mind! Once you clarify your destination and what you want your business to look like, this vision helps you guide your business growth, set well-defined goals, pinpoint the metrics to measure your progress, and define the ways you want your business to support your lifestyle.

In Carl's instance, he knew specifically what type of business he wanted to build. Carl and his significant other love camping and boating – his business need to leave time for those joyful experiences. So, with his clear vision in mind, he started to build the foundation for his predictably profitable business.

2. Authority Positioning is the 2nd key to Predictable Profits. Are you perceived as obscure (best-kept secret) or are you considered the go-to-expert in your industry or field?

Creating your own unique visual framework, like Carl's Podcast Authority Builder or my GPS Business Grow-meter, is one way I help my clients demonstrate their difference so that they easily stand out from their competition and attract high-paying clients.

3. Sales & Marketing Implementation Roadmap is a comprehensive <u>rinse & repeat strategy</u> that is aligned with YOU at your stage of business growth! When your marketing is done right, you are no longer are the best kept secret and sales conversions become so much easier. (Who doesn't want that?!)

Carl's sales and marketing roadmap was based on his gift – a combination of his past experience as a radio broadcaster and his amazing voice. Podcasting, live videos on social media, speaking and videos were all a natural fit for him and were included in his overall marketing strategy. But these might not be a perfect fit for you!

You can do this!

Like Carl and Cynthia, you will need all three of these keys to work in alignment so you can accelerate your growth and reclaim your life!

Conclusion

It is possible to love your business and make darn good money!

It is possible to build a business that gives you joy, income, impact, and influence.

But it doesn't happen without doing business differently.

It doesn't happen without some guidance and support.

Do you know someone that's built a time-eating, profit-less monster but who is truly brilliant at what they do? Then let's help them discover a better way of living and doing business.

Your business should fit into your life. It should bring you joy and income to live the life you always dreamed of having.

YOU CAN DO THIS!

I'd love to be your guide along your entrepreneurial journey.

Diana

Diana Lidstone

The Entrepreneur's G.P.S.

After 35+ years in business and working globally with coaches, consultants, and experts, Diana Lidstone has gathered rock-solid wisdom and advice that has helped thousands of entrepreneurs and professionals double or even triple their profits while freeing up more time for the things they love.

As the creator of the GPS Growmeter, The Marketing Proficiency Effect, ᵀand as best-selling author of* Shift into Rich: Navigate the 9 Roadblocks to Small Business Success, *Diana's signature Profitable Marketing Engine teaches entrepreneurs how to get noticed, get clients and get profitable.*

Diana and her husband love boating in the Thousand Islands, Canada. She is often found walking her dog and drinking champagne (not at the same time)!

Schedule your complimentary Growth Strategy Session on my website; www.dianalidstone.com

Connect with me at:
diana@lidstone.com
www.dianalidstone.com
Facebook – https://www.facebook.com/TheEntrepreneursGPS
LinkedIn - https://www.linkedin.com/in/hiredianalidstone/

* GPS Business Grow-meter was described in Diana's book, Shift into Rich, page 33; she has slightly modified the names of the stages since that time.

** Successville – page 21, *Shift into Rich: Navigate the 9 Roadblocks to Small Business Success* by Diana Lidstone

12

From Confused to Happy Using the Self-Empowerment Blueprint – Dr. Yasmilde Rodriguez Gonzalez

It's April 2014 late afternoon and I am in the living room of my apartment, standing frozen while looking at my phone, reading an email my godmother had just sent me from Cuba. Something she had written had felt like a hammer to my head! I can still remember hearing the background noises of my husband moving around in the kitchen and of the traffic outside. Inside of me though, everything had gone cold and quiet, as if the world just stopped turning. In a split of a second, the details of the life I had been living for the previous 20 years started running through my head as if watching a movie acted by someone else: the stresses, the sacrifices and losses, the depression, the chronic illnesses, the unhappiness, the rushing, the betrayals and the many issues in my 3rd marriage. It rapidly dawned on me that I had been slipping down a rabbit whole for a long while; that I had been ignoring my body, my mind and my intuition for years. Suddenly, I realized that I wanted badly to feel happiness, for my smile to be honest and not forced. I wanted to be done with struggling through life, having to solve one problem after the other and making everyone else a priority.

Right then and there, something shifted. I decided that day that I was DONE with suffering and illness and that **I would seek guidance to DO whatever it would take to become healthy and happy for myself**. THAT right there, became the biggest step forward I had taken so far in my life (never mind the four scientific degrees and other achievements!). That step led me into a journey of healing and self-discovery that I never saw coming.

During the next two years, I discovered energy work and learned how to heal my body; I became malleable to coaching and guidance and learned to shift and heal my mind; I started meditating and discovered the infinite nature of my spirituality and the powers hidden within me. And in all that process, I fell deeply in love with myself. I stumbled into my life purpose as a Healer and realized that I had always been one without knowing it. And, eventually, I decided to leave my 30 year long career in science behind to start serving humanity the way I was meant to from the beginning.

Finally embracing my new path, I realized that I had always been in tune to other people's moods and actions, capable of 'reading between lines' and detecting what was really going on with them, totally unaware of what I was doing. Once I founded EQUALLIBRIUM as a medium to fulfill my life purpose, every interaction with clients became a personal lesson and an opportunity to hone that gift.

So, looking back into the hundreds of people I have had the opportunity to help find health, relaxation and happiness within themselves, I noticed that at the time they came to me they were suffering (like I did for so many years) from low levels of something I decided to call the **APPARENT INNER CERTAINTY**™ (AIC).

I define the AIC as the mix of sentiments about identity, self-worth, self-lovability and self-confidence you may have at any given moment. Our AIC reflects the mix of everything that has contributed to the subconscious opinions and beliefs we have ABOUT OURSELVES. I have been able to identify 4 possible states we may be at, based on our level of APPARENT INNER CERTAINTY.

The first state is what I call the **PUNITIVE** state. Here, the lowest possible level of AIC keeps us in constant self-attacking mode. The hallmark of this state is a permanent negative outlook. You know you live here if you suffer from insomnia, often feeling exhausted, lethargic and even depressed, under the impression that you live under constant pressure. If you are here, you might be unable to perform tasks or even work since it is hard to start or stick to anything. You might be unwilling to make decisions, based on having lost interest in almost everything and not being able to see how anything could actually change. In the PUNITIVE state, you might see life as miserable, evil, hopeless and tragic, experiencing emotions such as guilt, despair and regret.

The second state I have identified is the **PERPLEXING** state. At this point, your AIC keeps you in constant confusion. The hallmark of this state is the presence of one or several chronic conditions that probably require constant medication and visits to a medical doctor for check-ups. You know you are here if you are unsure about what you want out of life, or your career, or even your relationships. You might be pretty good at what you do and have a steady job, but chances are you don't particularly like it or know how to make it better. If you are here, you are probably not able to take compliments gracefully, either denying you deserve it or becoming seriously embarrassed by them. In this state there is also emotional unbalance that shows up in extremes; you either have intense emotional episodes (breakdowns and crying bouts) or are emotionally stuck (and experience anxiety or even panic attacks). If that is the case for you, chances are that the fear of not being able to prevent or control such episodes significantly adds to the anxiety. When living in PERPLEXING AIC, life might 'feel' frightening and disappointing, while experiencing anxiety and craving.

The third state is what I call the **ASSERTIVE** state. This happens when your AIC keeps you seeking constant control over everything. The hallmark here is a strong sense of independence, usually accompanied by a very successful career. You know you are here if you are an excellent executive type (or a control freak, depending on who you ask), even outside of your professional life. You get things done! As high as your standards for things and other people can be, they are even higher for yourself, and you probably value personal growth. Here, you are always busy and in a rush, often experiencing frustration and anger. The one very challenging aspect in your life is relationships! Unsuccessful at many of them, you might have felt confused or irritated by the behaviors of others towards you, experiencing many flavors of betrayal. Chances are you have developed trust issues, making it hard to be vulnerable with others. Then, depending on what aspect of your life you are facing, in this state you bounce from seeing life as antagonistic and demanding or as feasible and satisfactory. Because of that, you experience flips from resentment and scorn to affirmation and confidence.

You might find that you are either purely in one of these three states, or at a combination of them. Regardless of the case, everybody I've ever known wants to be in the fourth. I call that one the **IN FLOW** state. Here, you have the highest level of APPARENT INNER CERTAINTY possible, in perfect alignment with your TRUE SELF. The hallmark of this state is that you have mastered unconditional love for yourself, for everyone else and life in general! You know you are IN FLOW if your passion has become your profession and you have a sense of purpose that goes beyond yourself. You embrace challenges as opportunities for personal growth and step towards discovering everything you can become. IN FLOW, you live in health, joy, playfulness and happiness. You have embraced your spirituality and see yourself as the creator of your own human experience, feeling empowered to do so. You are IN FLOW, when you see life as harmonious, meaningful, and complete; experiencing understanding, serenity, and bliss. Here, living is an adventure!

And you have probably perceived, like I did, that there is a BIG jump between the first three and the last state. At some point it became clear to me that the driving force to personal and spiritual development is fueled by awareness. So, the first hurdle to conquer to start moving towards living IN FLOW is a Self-Awareness Threshold, just like the one I jumped over while reading my godmothers' email.

But what brings us all the way there? How can you navigate your human experience from any of the first three states to the amazing fullness of living IN FLOW? I discovered over the years that we all need to implement what I call the **SELF EMPOWERMENT BLUEPRINT™ (SEB)**. And that is what I do, provide it and facilitate your healing and growth through it. But what is it?

The SEB is a unique approach to transformation that is based on two main principles. The first one is that healing only truly happens when three steps are completed: Awareness, Clearing and Replacing. Most of the approaches I have encountered out there, only include one or two of them and barely ever the replacing part. The second principle is that for transformation to fully occur, we need to target all three facets of us: the emotional, the mental and the energetic one. Again, most healing modalities address only one or two out of the three. Infused by both principles, the SEB provides the tools and experiences needed for us to be able to reproduce the results on our own, for every loop of growth and expansion we are willing to experience in our lifetime. And it does that through the power of FOUR components.

The first component is the DEFICIENCY AWARENESS. This one is all about creating a constant state of curiosity regarding ourselves. It is about learning to connect and interpret the INTERNAL cues that our body constantly gives us, developing our intuition and our capacity to follow it. The best compass we can ever use to guide us through life is already inside of us. The goal is that we are able to answer questions such as 'Do I resonate with _____?', 'How does ____ make me feel?', 'What am I feeling right now?', 'What is my body doing?', 'What inside me is creating ____?', 'What is the lesson?', 'What is ____ trying to tell me about myself?'

The second component is the ENERGY INTERACTION CODE. The code is about recognizing and applying daily the fact that we are energy. It is about adopting practices that allow us to interact with it, exercising our power to tune our own ENERGY FIELD. Our field is the blueprint for physical and circumstantial experiences, and because of that, energetic awareness is required for health and transformation. Simple tools and practices can have profound effects in our levels of Mental, Emotional and Physical Health. Self-awareness then, also includes our energy states: 'Is my field expanded and fluid? Connected? Defined?', 'Is my energy vibration in alignment with my intentions? My purpose? My vision?'

The third component is the INTERNAL LOCUS OF CONTROL. This one is all about taking responsibility for our MIND, which is the driving force of our human experience and doorway to our spirituality. It is about learning how to access our subconscious mind to clear fears, doubts, beliefs, stories that hold us back and replace them with ideas, beliefs and behaviors that support our growth and transformation. And do all of it with intention! Like Danielle Delgado says, "Intentional everything to overcome occasional anything." So, checking in with ourselves also includes our mental processes: 'What am I afraid of?', 'Why am I afraid?', 'What are my values/beliefs regarding _____?', 'Are those beliefs really mine?', 'What do I believe in?', 'Is what I believe supporting what I want/need?'

The fourth and last component is the HEALING AND GROWTH ECOSYSTEM. The ecosystem is all about connectivity and community; about learning to balance Giving and Receiving through practices that support both. Believing and acting as if we are individual entities is profoundly damaging to our health and integrity. We not only need to acknowledge that CONNECTION but learn how to use it as it's meant to. COLLABORATION is the key to our unlimited capacities. So, checking in with ourselves also includes our community: 'Am I open to receive?', 'What should I become to be able to help?', 'How do I recognize when I need help?', 'What can we become, TOGETHER?'…

It has been my personal and professional experience that, for us to be able to live IN FLOW, we need ALL four components and all of them AT THE SAME TIME. I have been privileged enough to be part of and witness amazing transformations through the Self-Empowerment Blueprint approach, while my clients' journeys have enriched my own to beautiful levels.

So, remember that late afternoon back in 2014? Fast-forward 5 years and I am in my home office/ treatment room, just out of a meditation session and it hits me: I AM happy AND healthy. That

I had left behind for good a life of enduring, existing and struggling and replaced it with inspired and motivated THRIVING. All of that happened, because one day **I decided to stop hiding from myself and start taking action towards my own wellbeing.**

Would you be willing to do the same? To show up for yourself and take action? I recognize that not everyone would be ready to answer 'Yes.' And I respect it and suggest you honor it. I still remember how reluctant I was once upon a time, allowing the image of myself to blind me to my own vulnerabilities, until I felt embarrassed to admit that I was not perfect in my personal approaches and experiences. This is a good opportunity to acknowledge that staying where you are now would mean to keep reproducing the series of unfortunate little decisions that brought you to the patterns you are experiencing today. And when we are stuck (paralyzed, depressed, overwhelmed, doubtful, or just plain trapped), nothing changes. The question to really answer would be: How many years of living in health and happiness is it costing you to stay where you are?

But what if you answer 'YES'? There is nothing more powerful than falling in LOVE with ourselves. When that happens, EVERYTHING CHANGES. And you show up in the world paving the road for a better future for you and everyone you care about, convinced that the real you is the finest piece of art that has ever been created.

Then, my challenge for you is to give yourself one hug a day, every day for a week, and then self assess: "What good would freeing the real me bring me?" And the moment you feel that you are willing to experience what FLOW would mean to you, contact me to have a chat and evaluate how we can make it happen. I'll be looking forward to it!

Dr. Yasmilde Rodriguez Gonzalez

Dr. Yasmilde is an Intuitive Healer that combines science, coaching, energy work, mindfulness and meditation in her approach. Since she was 13 years old and decided to help humanity by becoming a scientist, she has defended four science degrees, the last one a PhD in Neuroscience. She had already dedicated over 25 years to science research, when her own personal healing and growth journey led her to discover that she had always been a healer. Her mission is to guide as many people as possible into developing their own power to increase their Inner Certainty to levels high enough to create a life of intense happiness and flow. She founded EQUALLIBRIUM in 2017 and has since touched the lives of hundreds of people.

As part of her signature program, she provides her clients with what she calls the SELF-EMPOWERMENT BLUEPRINT, an experience that guides them through a journey of healing and growth that brings them AHA moments, provides them with tools to create new habits, shifts their current mindset and introduces them into a community that keeps them accountable and supported. All of that, so that they discover and connect with their REAL SELF. She can be contacted at info@equallibrium.ca or at any of her Instagram (@equallibrium.ca) or Facebook (@YasmildeBalance) profiles.

13

Find Your Spark During Divorce – Fauzia Khan

On a harsh day in November, my life crashed when my husband said he needed space to figure out his life. I hoped it was a brief midlife crisis. I was shocked to learn he met someone else. I was embarrassed and disappointed. I felt alone and paralyzed with shame that I couldn't share with anyone. This rejection led to depression and anxiety. After three months, I finally told my immediate family about my marriage failing.

At the age of 45, I left a successful career in the financial industry to start a new life with my husband. Our marriage expanded as business opportunities developed. As a spouse and business partner, I led four different companies ranging from property management to transportation logistics. My marriage became my priority which left little time for hobbies, friends, or even my family. All of my dreams came true with this financial success. I lived in my dream home, drove my dream car, traveled frequently, and could work from anywhere in the world.

Divorce is a Significant Change

Divorce felt like death to the dream life I built. I invested everything into my marriage. My income, my social life, my identity were anchored in the partnership with my husband. I felt lost and unsure. I didn't realize it at the time, but I was not alone. Fifteen percent of adult women in the United States are divorced compared to less than one percent in 1920. Almost 50 percent of all marriages in the U.S. end in separation or divorce - with a divorce occurring every 13 seconds. While divorce is declining for younger couples (ages 25 - 39), it is climbing for older folks. Studies from the Pew Research Center indicate the divorce rate for adults ages 50 and older doubled since the 1990s (2017). The rate increases for people like me who are married for less than 10 years (21 people per 1,000 married persons in 2015) and for those like my husband who were in their second or higher marriage (60%).

Though our marriage failed, I hoped for an amicable divorce since our relationship was entangled in several businesses. Financial insecurity after divorce is a real and reasonable fear. Like many women experiencing divorce at midlife, I no longer had a job to go to. We expected to continue working together as we jointly owned three companies and my income was dependent on a company he created prior to our marriage. Operations ran smoothly as I managed responsibilities for our companies while he was in Thailand with his new girlfriend. He suggested separating on our own without involving lawyers to save money. I agreed. Then disagreements spurred heated confrontations which threatened my personal safety.

Naïve about the divorce process, I was blindsided by the level of scrutiny I'd face. The emotional turmoil was a constant storm I couldn't escape. I didn't know the toll it was going to take on me mentally and physically. Divorce impacts women as they struggle to redefine themselves while grieving the end of a relationship. The process elicits emotions ranging from sadness, pain, grief, and uncertainty.

Taking responsibility of your financial situation is part of taking control of the next chapter of your life

The financial untangling of the relationship adds to the loss. Simultaneously we discussed dividing our financial assets (home and several businesses) while paying our household bills and business expenses. Since my dream car was under the business name, it was taken away and I had no transportation. Disagreements about listings and ownership put the sale of our home in limbo. He canceled the cable, phone, and internet. He blocked me from our companies which I helped build. I was jobless and alone. I had no idea what I was entitled to or how heavy the financial burden would be for me.

I panicked and charged day-to-day expenses like food and utility bills to my credit card as a short-term solution. Joy felt elusive as depression, anxiety, and sleepless nights weighed heavily on me. My health deteriorated and I was prescribed antidepressants, anti-anxiety medications, and sleeping pills in order to function. Months passed, I charged my medical and dental expenses and legal fees to my credit card. Desperate for money, I opened a new credit card to hold me over. I assumed once the house sold, I could pay everything off and start my new life. I was wrong. When we sold our matrimonial home, I expected my share of the proceeds - only to find out that the funds were to be held in trust until the divorce was settled. Later, I realized what I thought was rock bottom was truly a blessing. Accepting that one's financial life will be different is the first - and sometimes hardest - step to take.

Managing finances is part of the healing process

Reaching back to my years in finance, I strategized how to manage my money as best as possible. First, *I assessed my current financial situation*. I *created a budget* based on my limited income that included groceries, utilities, home insurance, entertainment (dinner with a friend), personal care (hair cut), etc. I developed a spreadsheet to *track my spending habits* and adjusted my budget accordingly. I *ordered my credit report* to confirm there was no suspicious activity and realized the negative impact of paying only the minimum monthly amount due. Knowing my credit score determined whether I could buy or lease a car, rent or buy a new home, etc. Immediate action was needed to improve my credit score.

Next, I *cut back on spending*. I cancelled my gym membership and found cheaper workouts online. I stopped buying clothes, going out for coffee, and traveling. Without a steady income, I rented a place as it was less expensive. I swallowed my pride and applied for social assistance which challenged my ego. I borrowed money to clear up my debt and further tightened my finances. It was hard. There were times I wanted to give up. I couldn't believe this was happening to me. I'm an educated, successful woman... how did I get myself into this mess?

With my life feeling out of control, I focused on what I could control. I went for early morning walks and long drives to clear my head. I cleaned my backyard and sat outside to enjoy the weather. I found peace in my own backyard - hearing the sound of the leaves rustle in the wind., the birds chirping and children playing nearby. I reminded myself this was temporary and redirected my attention towards gratitude. I said, *"I am so grateful for the house and food I have available to me. I am grateful for my health."* As I spoke out loud about what I was grateful for, I felt stronger.

I felt more confident about myself as I took control of my finances. My credit score rating increased. Though I had significantly less than when I did when I was married, I felt grateful for what I had. Realizing other women faced worse struggles, I donated extra items as well as 10% of the money I received to a women's shelter, food banks, and other community organizations. My spirit brightened as I balanced giving and receiving. Helping others allowed me to appreciate the healing and growing I experienced.

Avoiding costly mistakes before marriage and during divorce

Before and during my marriage, I took my finances for granted because I had the funds to do anything I wanted. I should have **documented all of my investments, properties, loans, credit cards, bank accounts, car, and other valuables** the day before I got married.

When I was married, I should have **kept my accounts separate with a joint spending account for common bills** like utilities, food, rent/mortgage, and entertainment. I should have **kept one vehicle and my credit cards in my name** as the primary cardholder to prevent negative impacts on my credit history. I should have kept **my own emergency fund with at least six months of savings** to pay day-to-day expenses such as food, utilities, insurance, rent/mortgage, etc.

A major mistake I made was trusting family and friends for legal advice. One of my closest friends drafted a separation agreement to save me money. I was lost and didn't know the right thing to do so I allowed them to make the decisions for me. When I met with a lawyer, they discovered areas that I could claim that my friend wasn't aware of. It cost me more to undo and revise what my friend drafted than if I met with the lawyer originally.

Another mistake cost me thousands of dollars. I mistakenly took a gift of money from my mother and applied it to our joint line of credit. Later I learned that gifts I received during the marriage would have been best to keep under my name as it exempts them from the overall assets that need to be divided. These were costly lessons to learn. Now I help other women rebuild themselves when they face divorce.

DO	DON'T
Document investments, properties, loans, credit cards, bank accounts, cars, and other valuables -preferably the day before getting married	Follow advice from friends and family regarding legal or financial matters
Maintain bank accounts separate with one joint account for common bills	Apply gifts of money to you (as an individual) to joint debts (ex. Loans, credit cards, etc.)
Have at least one vehicle and credit card in your name as the primary owner	Assume your financial situation will return exactly to what it was before you married
Create an emergency fund with at least six months savings	Cut ties completely or close/ freeze joint credit cards
Keep a budget (projected spending), financial journal (actual spending) and divorce calendar (court dates, money paid/received, etc.)	Increase your debt
Determine how common monthly bills will be paid	Forget assets

Strategies for strengthening your financial health before and during divorce

LESSON 1. Assemble a financial support team (Ex. Divorce/Family law attorney, estate attorney, CPA/accountant). They can advise you on what happens regarding joint accounts & bills from the moment of separation until the divorce is final (ex. Can you freeze accounts? How long are you covered by insurance?)

LESSON 2. Define shared assets (if possible whether to divide or sell them). Figure out who will be responsible for each asset. Make a complete list and include any homes, joint properties, vehicles, and securities. Assets can be sold with the proceeds divided between the spouses. Alternatively, one half of a joint asset (ex. house) can be awarded to a spouse as long as the other party is paid either in cash or other assets in the divorce proceedings. This is best handled by a lawyer.

LESSON 3. Keep track of YOUR investments, accounts, credit cards, etc. before and during marriage. You need to declare them at the time of separation and this becomes difficult if you've been married for more than five years.

LESSON 4. Advocate for yourself - and your dependent family members. Do not assume your spouse or even your lawyer will take care of you.

LESSON 5. Make changes to fit your new life. Set small goals. Don't be afraid to downsize. Explore creative financing - like using points for a quick getaway.

Self-care is critical

Divorce is a highly emotional time which can lead to feeling alone, abandoned, isolated, overwhelmed, scared. You are not alone. Many communities provide support both in-person and online to help women through this transition. Engaging in these groups brings fresh ideas and approaches to managing the challenges during the divorce journey. We frequently avoid or delay self-care as we're distracted by other perceived crises. **You are the only person who can make yourself a priority.** This involves seeing yourself as capable to do whatever you want - which is empowering and overwhelming at the same time. Self-care includes:

- *Emotional health* - Reconnecting with friends, engaging in supportive communities, etc.

- *Physical health* - Sleep, exercise, healthy eating, awareness of alcohol/caffeine

- *Spiritual health* - Practicing gratitude, re-examining beliefs, self-awareness

Working with a therapist put my life in perspective and opened the door to my emotional healing. I became accountable with my emotions and actions. As challenges arose, counseling allowed me to come to terms with my divorce and how my life was changing. Instead of wallowing in sadness or behaving irrationally, I felt empowered to act in my best interests.

If you are not making self-care a priority, you hold yourself back. Self-care is a stress reliever. Lack of self-care prevents you from being your best self which makes the divorce process heavier and more difficult. If you feel guilty about self-care, imagine giving your best friend advice. Treat yourself to the compassion and care you give to someone you care about. **You are your best advocate.**

CONCLUSION

Divorce is an ongoing journey involving continuous adjustments even after the proceedings are completed. **Hope comes from empowering yourself during this emotional transition.** You may feel uncomfortable, vulnerable, or ashamed when approaching your financial situation. However, **developing a system to manage your money brings you control.** Creating a financial plan is like using a map when traveling to a new place. These tools outline where you are going and can develop alternate ways to reach your destination. Embracing autonomy and **self-care develops confidence** and makes the divorce journey manageable. **Remember, you are not alone and you can become stronger during this process.**

RESOURCES:

- *Led by Baby Boomers, Divorce Rates Climb for America's 50+ Population* (Pew Center of Research) - https://www.pewresearch.org/fact-tank/2017/03/09/led-by-baby-boomers-divorce-rates-climb-for-americas-50-population/

- *The Four Step Divorce Recovery Guide* (Second Saturday) - https://www.secondsaturday.com/the-four-step-divorce-financial-recovery-guide/

- *5 Tips to Recover Financially From a Divorce* (SmartAsset) - https://smartasset.com/personal-finance/5-tips-recover-financially-divorce

- *How Will Divorce Affect Me Financially?* (YourDivorceQuestions.org) - http://yourdivorcequestions.org/how-will-divorce-affect-me-financially/

Fauzia Khan

Fauzia developed a career in the finance and software industries. With more than 25 years in the profession, she earned accolades for leading her team and was on the fast-track as a rising executive. However, the path she thought would lead to happiness caused her to lose herself in a toxic marriage and difficult divorce.

While the divorce ended her marriage, it was the catalyst to the path of redefining and rediscovering herself. She immersed herself in learning and reclaimed her self-identity. She found hope and built a practice based upon inner strength and outer support. She discovered the key to moving through adversity is to recognize you are not alone.

Today Fauzia is an entrepreneur with experience in retail and ecommerce sales and supply chain management. She is a coach and consultant who supports clients on their journey. Her services are based on struggles rebuilding her life from divorce both personally and professionally. Fauzia helps clients explore their emotions, overcome shame, reclaim their power, and become better than before.

Website: www.findyoursparkduringdivorce.com

14

Anxiety Deactivation
for High Performers
– Faythe Buchanan

Do you dream of being a prodigiously successful executive or entrepreneur without wasting energy on anxiety and feeling drained at the end of the day?

Do you want to get rid of frustration when people are difficult or things do not go according to plan?

Do you want to have cosmic calm when there are problems or things go wrong?

Do you want to eliminate the moments of panic - that maybe only you know are there - or the endless anxious buzzing at the back of your mind?

What others are not telling you...

Unlike what others are telling you, there is a way to have all of this. You can go beyond relaxation techniques and meditation, you can have real answers instead of "common sense advice" (that doesn't work). You can resolve and deactivate anxiety rather than just managing this ancient impulse that gets in the way of modern-day success.

There are simple, proven frameworks that, when applied to your life, will give you the ability to live virtually anxiety-free. You learn to use your mind in a totally different way that deactivates anxiety whenever it shows up and teaches your brain not to worry.

So let's back up the bus and see *how I know what I'm telling you is true.*

The cost of anxiety

It's noon on a summer day in rural Nova Scotia. My family is walking into a small cafe. I am 5 years old, my sister is 2. My father towers over us at 6'2, in contrast to my mother who measures in at 5'1", but in spite of my father's height, our little group is almost invisible as we enter the restaurant, because we are all so thin.

My father goes over and looks at the menu, while the 3 of us wait. I will never forget the inside of that cafe, it looked so beautiful to me. There's fake black and white cowhide on the booths, the walls are a pale green and the cafe is immaculately clean. The light smell of food makes me so hungry. After a moment, my father straightens, turns and walks out the door. We follow, out into the sun, back into the car.

I don't know if I knew then, or learned years later that there was absolutely nothing on that menu we could afford, nothing within our means that would give us a simple lunch.

Fast forward 13 years. I am 19 and weigh 95 lbs., not because I am anorexic, but because our family is still what I call "empty refrigerator poor."

Anxiety = No Solutions

You see whenever there was a problem in our family, and that was often, my mother would get incredibly anxious and my father would go into a panicky rage. So nothing ever got solved! Our family struggled with conflict and poverty the whole time I lived at home.

From these experiences I realized that I did not want to live like that, nor did I want others to have to live with unsolved problems and unlived dreams!

The Quest

So I set out on a quest for solutions, though not consciously at first. I became an occupational therapist, a psychotherapist and then a coach. I worked in hospitals, mental health and crisis units, for Victim Services, and then in my own practice for several decades.

Through the thousands of hours of working with people, "sitting at the door to people's souls" listening to their stories of pain and struggle, I discovered that it wasn't just my parents who were thwarted by anxiety: it stops **everyone** from solving their problems.

I learned that even high achievers:

- run out of energy at the end of the day
- lose focus when things are uncertain
- get anxious when people or circumstances are difficult
- experience immobilizing frustration when things do not go according to plan
- miss opportunities because they are afraid of risk
- procrastinate when they are anxious or don't know what to do next

Without anxiety, people are amazing, creative and happy, and their productivity is unstoppable.

So through all this listening and working with people and their challenges, figuring out what works and what doesn't, I began to put together frameworks and strategies that deactivate anxiety.

What doesn't work to get rid of anxiety.

In my journey I also discovered **what does not work** to get rid of anxiety.

1. Common sense advice is useless, because the survival brain where anxiety is created has very little language, and no logic.

2. Meditation and relaxation techniques - while very good things - tend to manage rather than get rid of anxiety. They also don't work for everyone and are time-consuming.

3. Exercise, again a really good activity, burns off the stress chemicals, but does not eliminate anxiety. It comes back with the next difficult circumstance.

If what the self-help gurus were selling worked, there would be no anxiety left!

The stress management gurus have been selling the same strategies for decades now, and they are rather affluent as a result. But if what they are peddling worked, by now there would be no anxiety left. Instead, we have an epidemic of stress-related misery.

In my experience, *everyone has some kind of relationship with anxiety* which can be quantified in a model I call the **Anxometer**. This framework measures what I describe as the "Anxiety Disruption Factor." In other words, just how much anxiety is interfering with someone's life.

The Anxometer: Measuring the Anxiety Disruption Factor

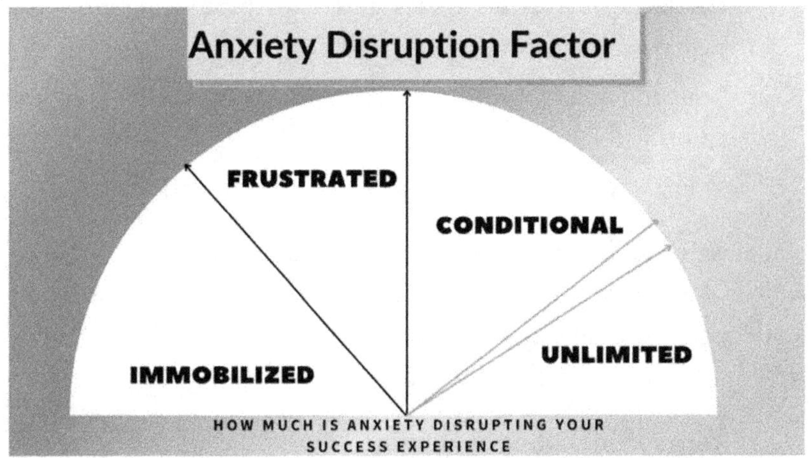

Measuring the Anxiety Disruption Effect

In this model, the worst-case scenario is what I call **Immobilised**.

This is where entrepreneurs and executives are in real trouble because anxiety stops them from doing almost anything.

You know you are here when:

1. You don't try anything new. You feel there is no point: you will just be trapped by fear.

2. You have frequent panic attacks, or constant background anxiety/stress.

3. You believe this is how your life is and there is nothing you can do to change it, these are just the cards you have been dealt.

4. You rely heavily on medication and maybe even become hospitalized. You have very few relationships, and the ones you do have are there for support or to fill in where you can't move forward.

5. You can barely work or be productive.

6. You have health problems such as fatigue, joint pain, headaches, digestive issues and high blood pressure. You never really feel well.

7. Your life is very limited and repetitive because that is all you can stand.

8. Every day is a struggle just to get through and survive.

The next worst scenario is what I call **Frustrated**.

This is where you are frantically looking for solutions to the anxiety that is dragging you down.

You know you are here when:

1. You spend hours meditating, repeating affirmations and reading self-help books.

2. You think you have found ways to be calm, then when there is a new challenge, another wave of anxiety takes over.

3. You see opportunities but can't take them because fear won't let you move forward.

4. You build all kinds of support into your life - people and resources to call on when you feel you can't cope.

5. People tiptoe around in case you get upset.

6. You can perform with lots of support and sick days, but each day is exhausting as it is so much work to manage anxiety.

7. It is hard to maintain your health with the effects of the stress chemicals in your body.

8. You keep trying new medications in case that helps.

The third and most common state I call **Conditional**.

This is where your energy, mood and productivity are all related to outside circumstances.

You know you are here when:

1. If life is going well, you have no anxiety.

2. When there are problems (things are difficult, unpleasant or unknown) you get anxious, worried and stressed.

3. You believe everyone has to get anxious if they don't like what is happening and you feel your relationship with anxiety is normal.

4. You look for support when you are anxious and rely on people around you when you feel stressed.

5. Your productivity is related to how you see your circumstances. When you see difficulties and become anxious, your productivity drops, which creates inconsistencies. But you feel that is natural.

6. You miss opportunities because that 'sliver of fear' that is almost unconscious prevents you from taking action.

7. You have good relationships unless circumstances are really difficult. Then you lean on those around you, or distance and close off.

8. You may be really good at hiding this, especially at work. But personal relationships suffer from your ups and downs even when you try to keep the anxiety a secret.

9. Your health is generally good, but you are vulnerable to increased blood pressure, digestive discomfort or headaches when life presents you with problems.

Then something happens.

Between state three and four there is a shift. In the first three states people respond to difficulties by getting anxious. In state four, they do not. In that gap they have learned what I call **Anxiety Deactivation Secrets**. They no longer approach difficulties, problems, unpleasantness and the unknown, by getting anxious. There has been a mindset shift and they have acquired the tools and frameworks to get rid of anxiety whenever it shows up and train their brain not to worry. This is what I do, and this is what I teach.

State four is what I call **Unlimited**. This is where you have learned to LAF -- Live Anxiety Free.

You know you are here when:

1. *You see anxiety as a signpost that something needs your attention*, rather than an abyss of pain that is overwhelming.

2. You don't use anxiety as a way of responding to difficulties: you have other ways to respond.

3. You have tools to resolve anxiety if it shows up and your brain has learned not to worry.

4. You have laser focus for solving problems and creating the life you want.

5. You have energy left at the end of the day.

6. You take action when there are opportunities, and accept circumstances that are out of your control.

7. People love being around you. You are a go to person when things are tough as it is known you provide leadership in the face of difficult issues.

8. You are capable of deep, consistent love as you are at peace with yourself.

9. Your health and energy are excellent. You grow stronger and more resilient as you move energetically through your life.

May I ask you two questions?

1. Which of the above states are you in?

2. Are you in the state you want to be in?

Why are so many people stuck in anxiety if there are solutions?

At this point you could be asking, if there are solutions, why are so many people struggling with anxiety and worry?

There are three reasons that make it easy to stay stuck in anxiety.

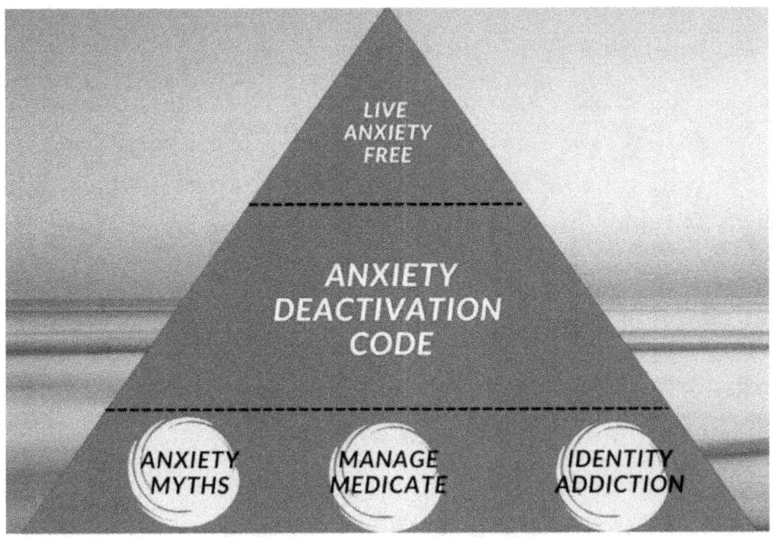

The three Reasons people stay stuck in anxiety.

1. Anxiety Myths:

We believe the many *cultural anxiety myths*, such as

- Everyone has anxiety, so why should I be different?
- People will think I don't care if I'm not anxious
- If you don't like something you need to get upset
- People won't do what I need them to do if I am not anxious
- Anxiety is a normal response to difficulties .....
  . . . and many other false beliefs

2. You can only manage or medicate:

We have been taught that *you can only manage or medicate anxiety*, you can't resolve it or teach your brain not to worry.

3. Addiction and Identity

We become *addicted to the stress chemicals* produced by anxiety, and when we have experienced anxiety for many years it *seems like part of our identity*, a part of who we are. We don't like the thought of getting rid of what we have come to feel is a part of ourselves.

To step out of anxiety we need the three components to Anxiety Deactivation Secrets.

Secret 1: Changing Your Anxiety Mindset

The first part of this shift is education to understand anxiety and change our anxiety mindset. When I created training programs for Peer Support Counselors for Survivors of Sexual Abuse, I watched the students heal just by getting the information about how trauma works, what to expect and how to resolve it. I realized the principles of education could also be applied to deactivating anxiety.

Einstein said something to the effect that *if we understand a problem and where it comes from we are 80% of the way to solving it.*

This is why I have divided anxiety into 9 types according to where it comes from.

These anxiety types are not diagnoses, but a way to understand where different kinds of anxiety come from.

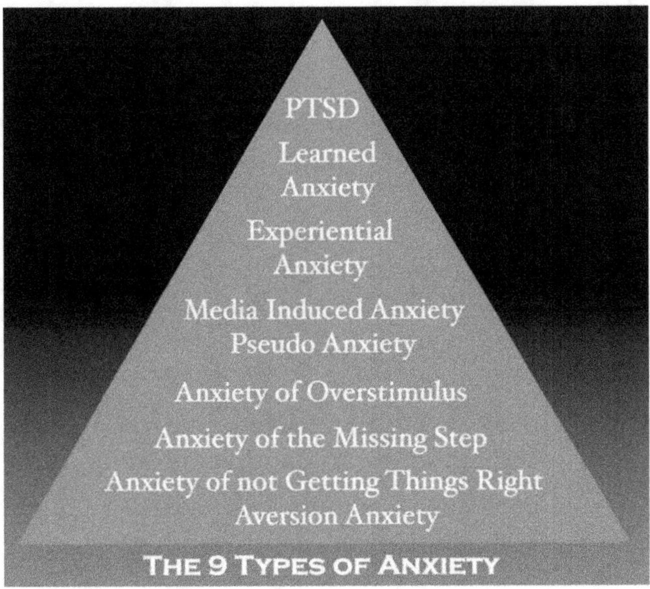

Summary of Anxiety Types:

Aversion Anxiety: this is where the brain activates anxiety because you don't like something.

Anxiety of not getting things right: this is when life or circumstances will not let you meet your own standards.

Anxiety of the "Missing Step" : this is when anxiety is activated because there is missing information or you don't know what to do next.

Anxiety of over stimulus: this comes from overwork, or just having too much on your plate.

Pseudo-Anxiety: this is where you unconsciously use anxiety to get others to do what you want.

Media-Induced Anxiety: this is when you are afraid because of the background presence of bad news, or feel invaded by social media events.

Experiential Anxiety: this is when you have had actual experiences of physical danger growing up and have learned to code the world through the lens of fear.

Learned Anxiety: this is where you have had a parent or significant caregiver in your early life who was anxious and you learned from them that there must be danger.

Post-Traumatic Stress: this is where anxiety is constantly off-gassing from traumatic experiences that are stored in a part of the brain that has no sense of time, so does not know the event is over.

Secret 2: The next Secret is the Frameworks and Strategies to deactivate anxiety.

For each anxiety type I have developed simple, proven frameworks to resolve that type of anxiety. This gives step-by-step, proven strategies to resolve that type of anxiety and move towards living anxiety free.

Secret 3: The third Secret is Implementation.

This is where we take the frameworks and apply them to each major area of life. This declutters the subconscious and gets rid of the 'fuel' that supports anxiety. These strategies prevent anxiety from occurring and train your brain not to bother with worry.

The Good News

Discovering how to spend your time on high value work without dealing with anxiety or feeling drained is possible through the Secrets of Anxiety Deactivation.

The results are :

- Cosmic calm when there are problems and unknowns,
- Elimination of procrastination and risk aversion,
- Access to your own amazing energy and creative productivity.

If you are ready to experience the power of Anxiety Deactivation Secrets to elevate your success and supercharge your productivity while experiencing peace of mind, reach out and let's have a conversation.

Faythe Buchanan

Faythe is an expert in helping highly successful, driven entrepreneurs spend time on high value work without dealing with anxiety or feeling drained.

If you really need to feel less stressed, have cosmic calm when things go wrong, and have laser focus when things are uncertain then she can definitely help you.

Although many do not realize that Anxiety comes in the guise of 'Limiting Beliefs,' 'Lack of Confidence,' 'Fear of Success,' 'Fear of Failure.' Faythe has uncovered that all of that is just Anxiety under different labels. Faythe leads the field in removing mindset roadblocks through Anxiety Deactivation and her accomplishments include:

Education:

- Honours Degree in Occupational Therapy
- Certification in Neuroscience of Conversation
- Certified Coaching Professional
- Language and Behaviour Profile Trainer

Work History:

- Health Professional in Hospital Units, Crises Units, for Victim's Services
- Psychotherapist, Coach and Consultant in Private Practice
- 40, 000 hrs. of client interviews

Awards, Titles, and Designations:

- Past President CAPS Atlantic
- Author: Learn to LAF - Live Anxiety Free
- Anxiety Deactivation Expert
- Deep Thought Strategist
- BSc.O.T.

Other Info:

- 40,000 hrs. sitting at the door of people's souls, listening to what hurts, what works and what doesn't to solve problems and create the life they want.
- Single parent of three small children, worked full time and went to University half time for four years. Learned about the value of time and energy.
- Earned Intermediate white water canoeing certificate even though I can't swim and am afraid of water.
- Have moved 34 times.
- Met my husband online 11 years ago. He moved across the Continent from Washington State to marry me and we are living happily in Nova Scotia.

When you want to spend time on high value work without dealing with anxiety or feeling drained, most of what you need is help, instruction, and encouragement from someone who has "been there and done that!" with success in business.

The Secrets of Anxiety Deactivation include the frameworks, strategies and mindset transformation to help you feel less stressed, have cosmic calm when things go wrong, and have laser focus when things are uncertain! I look forward to empowering you to perform at your highest level by learning to eliminate anxiety as a disruption to your productivity and an obstacle to your success.

Faythe Buchanan, Anxiety Deactivation Expert
BSc.O.T., HT, CCP, Cert. Neuroscience of Conversation, LAB Profile Trainer, Deep Thought Strategist, Professional Speaker, Past President CAPS Atlantic
faythe.buchanan@gmail.com
livanxietyfree.com

15

The Leadership of Transforming Crisis – John Robertson

Do you want to be the leader people want to follow through storms? The ***traditional crisis response*** requires a leadership style that's inverted from one that many utilize. The person who encourages, inspires, through real values is the one who enables others to thrive through crisis. The followable kind which people trust, respect, when things are changing and uncertain. I call them shepherds as they walk in front, walk the talk, and are not behind driving people [ranchers].

- ***Believe you are a* leader? *Look behind, is anyone following?***

If no one is following, beyond what they can buy/get from you, you are just taking a walk.

I know you can be this type of leader, in fact people are counting on you to lead, but it's not about title, degree, or position. When you hear 'leadership,' change the word to influence. Influence is something all have, the choice is whether its good or bad, which is leadership.

Most leadership care <u>about</u> their people yet few have ever been shown <u>how</u> to do this. Responsibility to support mental health and well-being is another leadership expectation. Leaders are to be genuine, authentic, transparent and keep productivity and profitability up. It's not one more thing on your overcrowded plate. It's not as complicated as some make it out to be.

Crisis can be the catalyst, to lead in a way that others want to follow, be more than just resilient but thrive. Maybe you're at the pinnacle of a career, yet what takes years to build, a crisis can undo in minutes.

Workplace leaders tell me they feel like they are simultaneously juggling running chainsaws. Chainsaws like engagement, performance, grievances/complaints, culture, stress/sick leave, turnover, results, and their own well-being. Sometimes feeling like people are waiting to pounce when something goes wrong, whether it's supporting people the right way [*whatever that means!*], not providing the right training, or promoting the wrong people. When the workplace is unhealthy, who gets blamed!

Three things I've learned in 30+ years of crisis intervention work and leadership coaching, two of which I have shared many times before. First, ***the event is never the real crisis***. Secondly, ***that crisis can be an opportunity***. The third is the ***shepherd's values***, a followable leader, ***which emerge*** during a crisis.

- **What's inside, always leaks out**

How organizations and leadership handle a crisis determines engagement, mental health, and well-being of all personnel.

Whether it's a pandemic, death of a special colleague, retirement of some key person, downsizing, a significant shift in customer expectations, these moments create a series of quakes, or shock waves. These quakes can result in a tsunami affecting trust, and credibility of leadership. These shock waves affect people's wellbeing, culture, engagement, productivity and can set things back years.

What a leader, organization, is made of leaks out in hot water [like a tea bag] when they are in hot water – even if no one says anything openly.

Last fall I got a call from a senior leader, Tom.

He informed me that one of his employees was having some significant crisis reactions impacting his work. Brian has a wife and two young children and was also a volunteer firefighter in a small town. But what makes it even more challenging is he is a manager for several dozen people in a 24/7 operation.

Tom added, *there's some serious performance concerns, and feedback is not helping, in fact things have become worse. I asked for you to work with him, but HR have told me that they want him to speak with EAP. What should I do?*

I asked - *what's going on that you're asking for me?*

He informed me *a couple leaders remembered what you told us would happen after our last crisis if it was not handled properly. It has happened exactly that way even including the negative impact on morale and culture, some people use leaves to be off & on since then. We can't afford these results again. Right now, there's a struggle between those of us doing business and those checking boxes.*

I responded to him, *Tom first there needs to be an outline of costs and spell them out for the nay-sayers including your lost time and productivity. No threats or fortune telling but simple walk through, in writing, why you cannot afford the same thing to happen this time. If they do not support your approach, then you will be putting a note in your budget for these costs that were not supported.*

He said, '*John, they do not allow us to do that.*'

I said '*that's fine, then Tom I will have to say No to being involved. They have no skin in the game and you are eating all their costs.*'

Ten minutes later, I received a phone call from the HR manager. She and I talked about whether it was better to do the counselling with an EAP. I asked whether she and the leadership wanted to change this **traditional crisis response**, starting with leadership then personnel?

She informed me that they just needed someone to support Brian and his work. I wished her the best of luck. I would help if they wanted to do things differently.

Then I got a call from Tom venting, *that they have just wasted 4 months, things have become worse in their workplace, including Brian. Would I be willing to assist the leaders? Would I be willing to let Brian connect with me immediately?*

We started into this approach.

The **Traditional crisis response** trips up wellbeing, trust, leadership, and culture [engagement]. It is the leadership that makes it work. The visual is a *Teeter Totter*.

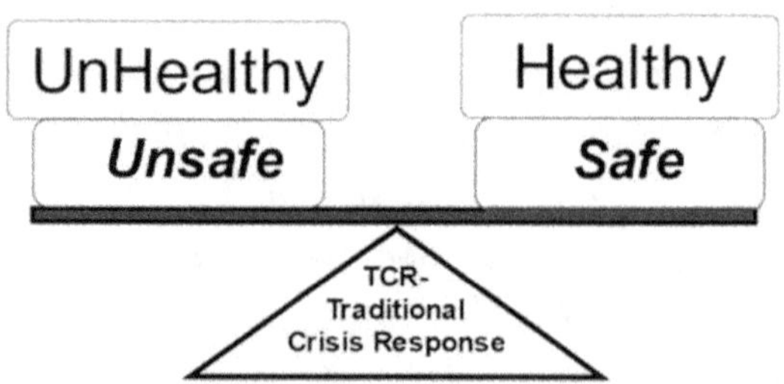

- 2 workplaces - healthy and unhealthy
- 2 leadership models

- 2 patterns of progression, same phases
- 2 <u>very</u> different results

2 workplaces - healthy and unhealthy

Unhealthy is the workplace where crisis is not addressed, and well-being is not actively being promoted. **Healthy workplace** is defined as the safe workplace and culture where crisis response support and well-being are being promoted.

In an abbreviated format, this results in 4 types of workplaces balanced by this traditional crisis response fulcrum. There are two phases in an unhealthy workplace. The unhealthiest I call **<u>Toxic</u>**, but safer I call **<u>Tense</u>**. There's little trust, cynicism and gossip abound, while absenteeism, turnover, leaves are increasing. Productivity usually drops after events, maybe never rebounds. As a leader you can start to doubt your own competencies and capabilities, so feeling safe at work is not an option.

The **<u>Tense</u>** phase is less Toxic, but like a classic airplane flight of moments of smooth flying then things get bumpy. It feels like walking on eggshells as you're not sure what the reaction will be, or who will be blamed. Feeling 'safe' is rare but it's happened. There's a job to do, so it is getting done. You care but no one is sure how you should respond.

On the healthy side of the fulcrum, there are also two phases called **<u>Treated</u>** and **<u>Thriving</u>**. Perhaps you show you care so personnel are less hesitant to ask for support, but consistency is not across the company itself. It is happening, and people are becoming more aware.

There's a chasm between these two phases because symptoms are **<u>Treated</u>**, not causes, so things drift back into old ways. Lineups form to join the departments with the right leadership.

The healthiest workplace is the one I call **Thriving**. The safe, supportive, workplace where leaders, and personnel, are aligned even when there are differences, disagreements. People are supported for as long as required. There is an intervention plan beyond reacting. Relationships and culture are constantly being strengthened through TLC [trust, leadership, communication].

Crisis Response is the fulcrum which tilts things towards healthy or unhealthy, towards thriving or towards surviving. The chasm between **Treated** and **Thriving** is because it requires values not just accountability. There can be an unhealthy leadership providing **Treated** solutions, however enough reactions using the **Treated** phase moves it to the unhealthy side of the fulcrum. The perception is all talk, no walk.

2 leadership models

There are two Leadership Styles resulting from the choice you make between reaction or responding, doing the same things over and over or choosing the different path.

On the unhealthy side is the leadership culture of accountability. It is easiest to describe as the workplace of the P's. There is a lot of talk about Policies, Procedures, Protocols, Paperwork, Performance, Productivity. These are the ranchers as they are driving things forward, personnel included, which results in Pushback during the crisis.

On the other side is the values-anchored culture leadership style – VERI© -**V**alues are known, **E**ncouraged, **R**esponsibility grows as people take the **I**nitiative. These are the shepherds who walk the talk, reinforce, and recognize, so people are strengthened and safe.

2 patterns of progression but same phases

When a critical incident or a significant event/change in an Unhealthy Workplace or healthy workplace, the phases are the same, however the leadership causes dramatically different effects.

Starting in an **<u>Unhealthy Workplace</u>** culture an **Event** is the stimulus. It may be nothing for some, but personnel's engagement is negatively impacted, and things are out of alignment. You know you need to do something as a leader. You want to support people, but you are not sure what the best approach is. You also have a job that needs to get done and want to get back to it ASAP. You might even catch yourself blaming or thinking *life happens, and life goes on?* Maybe you're unable to focus on your work with your own stress reactions.

Next is the **Intervention**. It's the mad flurry for immediate on-scene support to do something. The EAP does its thing but shortly after the complaints follow. Maybe you're thinking you're not a parent or babysitter, *come on, let's just get back to work!* Pressure from the 'experts in the stands' tell you that stress leaves and sick time are your responsibilities. You start to feel isolated and misunderstood.

Transfer of Information follows with a never-ending amount of resilience and wellbeing, education consisting of training, courses, workshops, keynote speakers, and even certifications. The treadmill has started with a proliferation of options. It seems to be a never-ending series of programs ending with questions like ***Now what?*** Or ***What about the change? What about the difference?*** There's a constant financial drain of new training or new programs without a real sense of a measurable ROI. People may be talking but transformation is not.

Often people hear the comments that the leadership and the organization is just checking a box not actually being supportive?

You want the best for your people but who do you trust? What to do? Who to listen to without getting sold on something else?

Dissension is the phase where things boil over as raised expectations do not match workplace practices, basically *all talk and no walk.* Now there's grievances, complaints, cynicism, or blaming different generations, cultures, values, personalities. The leaders get whispered about. Trust, wellbeing, and mental health have eroded to affect your family, or your health.

You're tired of feeling beaten up, the personal attacks sting. There's got to be a better way or maybe you've started looking elsewhere. The healthy leaders have a lineup of people applying to work in their section/department. You are too exhausted and have less time or interest to build relationships at work, resulting in distancing yourself from people. Nothing is good enough.

The ***TCR*** [*Traditional Crisis Response*] is the pivot point between the two workplaces. An ***unhealthy workplace*** is always in react mode, so the New Norm gets Defined for them, it's about survival. In a ***healthy workplace***, the ***TCR*** is to respond to enable thriving. Defining a Refinable New Norm, which is called growth. Growth is never just a program.

Leaders struggle because their ***TCR*** is fundamentally flawed in four areas.

- No crisis intervention plan beyond react
- Right People not in the right places
- Motivation & Focus is about accountability – legal, policy, sick-care costs
- Cultural leadership style of the organization

When an **unhealthy workplace** reaches that *react-response chasm* in **Dissension**, it results in a phase I call the **Institutionalized** phase.

This is frequently called the *death spiral*. Except for a governmental model, a couple crises at this point of an organization will maim it or kill it. The commitment to engagement, personnel's well being, is writing new policies, procedures, or rules.

Things are managed by committee, decisions are made by rumors and gossip, while leaders held in high regard are leaving. People are more focused on what caused the problem and fixing what caused it then to learn from it. People judge something based on information they currently have but you did not. There's a sense of complacency and accommodations for all sorts of issues. Wrong behaviors seem to get rewarded. People talk more about retirement than growth.

2 <u>very</u> different results

It takes real leadership to transform the **TCR** towards the thriving **Healthy Workplace**. That safe workplace, culture, where well-being is promoted through support. Where leaders, values, and personnel are purposefully aligned despite their differences, disagreements, or crises.

When leaders focus on the VERI approach, walking the talk, supporting themselves, and their personnel the result through these phases -***Event, Intervention, Transfer of Information, Dissension*** - it works like a springboard in raising the bar.

<u>**Business works when people thrive**</u> and that needs real leadership.

The result is the **new Norm is being Defined and Refined!**

A couple of weeks ago, I received an email from Tom.

John, I really want to thank you for supporting me and my leadership, including our personnel. Our engagement is back to what it was before the first crisis.

Brian is back at work full time; he has reorganized his priorities including his family [which I completely endorse].

You have helped us get through this hurdle. I know we have not done our work with you, but I wanted to let you know how beneficial this has been. I am so pleased for Brian as well. We look forward to our next steps… We are very grateful…

To **Define the Refinable New Norm** means transforming the **traditional crisis response** in four ways

- The crisis intervention plan where people, and crisis reactions, are cared for because it is the right thing to do which ironically results in people engaged and caring for the workplace, therefore lowered costs
- The right people are in the right places - *for the right reasons*
- The motivation and focus is about trust, leadership and culture, increasing engagement, lowering costs.
- Strengthened VERI approach through leaders that people want to follow

The key to adjust your TCR starts with you leading. The process I call SHIFTRAP which describes a series of chess pieces that absolutely must be in place to make the state of thriving sustainable.

To do this I work with leaders to strengthen the VERI leaders who are needed. To start leading in the way people need you, allow me to ask the questions we would start with. Your responses are vital if you want to thrive and people to follow your leadership.

We follow people we trust, even when at times we may not like them, start with self.

- ***How do you want people to describe you in a non-physical way?***
  - These will be your values shown by your day-timer and bank statement. Where we spend our time and our money are our real values, not what you tell people.

- ***How do people describe you?***
  - If you have the courage, ask honest people [teenagers are great for this].
  - <u>Special note</u> - if you do not like their answer, please do not get angry with them.

- If we were to meet in two or three years from this day, for you to know the sense of achievement and contentment in your growth, what needs to have happened during that time?

- What are the biggest opportunities that you have that you would need to focus on and capture to achieve those things?

- What are the biggest rapids or falls (barriers, hurdles, or fears) you'll have to address to achieve that progress?

- What strengths will you need to reinforce and maximize, and what skills and resources will you need to secure so that you will overcome and seize those opportunities?

To support you in transforming the **TCR** and thrive, let's discuss these questions together?

Let's explore how your leadership can be the VERI difference between survive and thrive.

In a world of Presents, People need Presence.

Let's make your Presence Thrive

John Robertson

John Robertson, founder, and President of FORTLOG Services Inc., an established and trusted company focused on workforce wellness and culture alignment. With over 30 years in crisis intervention in a variety of contexts, John helps forward-thinking leadership transform organizational crises, in a values-anchored approach, into the opportunity to develop a thriving workplace with fully-engaged people, where leaders can lead.

John's education and certifications include Certified Coach, MHCC's The Working Mind, Advisor in National Standard for Psychological H&S in the Workplace, Grief Resolution Specialist, Trauma Treatment Specialist, numerous psychometric tools & assessments, and a Bachelor and Masters Degrees from Queen's University.

16

Longer Content Meets Human Craving for Stories – Katherine Burrows

No one knows exactly when humans started telling stories. But we do know that stories were told orally long before the invention of the written word. Thousands of years later, we still live our lives in stories. Stories help us connect with others, learn about ourselves, and search for meaning.

The Power of Storytelling

According to research by evolutionary psychologist Robin Dunbar, 65% of all human conversations take the form of storytelling. We tell each other about our day. We talk about how a meeting went at work. We give play-by-play accounts of sporting events. We share stories about our children and with our children involving family activities and history. We relate world events and celebrate cultural milestones. We tell each other stories.

Stories provide us with a way to make sense of our world and even to feel like we have some control over what happens to us.

- Stories connect us with others past and present (heritage, traditions, family, culture)
- Stories give us space to explore our values (ideas, goals)
- Stories create meaning and patterns (in our circumstances and relationships)
- Stories allow us to feel hope and inspiration amid discouraging situations
- Stories help us come to know ourselves better

Psychologist Pamela Rutledge says stories "connect us to a larger self and universal truths." She also notes, "When you listen to stories and understand them, you experience the exact same brain pattern as the person telling the story… Through imagination, we tap into creativity that is the foundation of innovation, self-discovery and change."

In psychology, this complete immersion in the world of a particular story is known as "narrative transport." Action-oriented, suspenseful stories cause cortisol release, which creates a more intense reaction in the reader, viewer, or listener. Stories with strong, well-developed characters cause the release of oxytocin, a hormone that helps people to bond and feel empathy. They can identify with the characters in the story.

Some of the greatest lessons and progress in human history have come about through stories and parables.

The Longevity of Storytelling: Facts vs Stories

Jennifer Aaker, a professor of marketing at the Stanford Graduate School of Business, says that people remember information when it is weaved into narratives "up to 22 times more than facts alone."

Paul J. Zak, author of *Trust Factor: The Science of Creating High-Performance Companies,* notes that his findings on the neurobiology of storytelling are relevant to business settings. He says, "For example, my experiments show that character-driven stories with emotional content result in a better understanding of the key points a speaker wishes to make and enable better recall of these points weeks later."

Do an experiment. Compare this...

List of facts:

- *Ted, 65, is an avid golfer, now retired from his accounting firm, which he sold last year.*
- *Ted's son, Jack, 38, is an entrepreneur whose company builds fitness apps.*
- *Mountain climbing trip celebrating Ted's five years in remission from cancer.*

...with this:

It was a warm August evening in the Rockies. Jack took a moment to admire the setting sun, then crouched down, extending his right hand to his father and helping him over the last outcropping. They had reached the plateau where they would make camp for the night.

It hadn't been easy for Jack to get time off work. But building fitness apps for other people would have no meaning for him if he couldn't take a long weekend to celebrate the health of his own father. It had now been five years since Ted was declared in remission, and Jack was grateful for that fact every single day.

You can see how weaving the facts into the context of a story is much more impactful and memorable.

The Impact of Storytelling

In this day and age of the internet with short memes at a glance and social media character limits, our society still craves stories. And not just five-minute bedtime stories, but the deep, epic sagas that span generations and often take place in entirely different worlds.

Think about *Star Wars, Game of Thrones,* or the Marvel Universe. These rich, involved tales take place in detailed settings with well-developed characters that have comprehensive backstories. The tales are played out in plots that are full of action and intrigue. Part of it is escapism for sure, but we are drawn to stories we identify with and that show us versions of ourselves that are greater than the ones we think we are in our regular lives. Stories inspire us to dream, help us find the courage to act, and serve as a medium to celebrate and immortalize our achievements.

The pull to identify with stories is a powerful tool that business owners can use to connect with their ideal clients. A successful brand story will elicit a positive response from the ideal client who can see themselves in the story in some way. They may identify with the company values expressed, place great importance on the benefits achieved by the product or service offered, or desire the status perceived to be associated with the brand itself.

This isn't about forcing people to buy something they don't want or need. It's about a dynamic and organic way to connect with those customers that are the best fit for the product or service offered by your business. Stories encourage the many prospective clients who will come across your content to self-select their participation with your brand. Those who aren't a great fit will naturally move on, and the people who are more likely to make a purchase from you will gravitate toward your offering.

Your offering must provide genuine value and come from a place of heart-centred customer service. Your authenticity will shine through in your brand story to resonate with your client. When that happens, your product or service sells itself.

Stories Help Fill Our Communities with Strong, Independent Businesses

I love stories. Words have been my passion since I was a young child. I have always felt called to use my words to help people.

Beginning with short stories in elementary school, I've been writing all my life, experimenting with poetry, prose, playwriting, fiction, travel writing, memoir, and business content. As so often happens, my life path was filled with a few twists and turns that, for a time, led me away from my goal of writing as a career. But I never lost the feeling of being strongly called back to writing.

In 2009, I began writing professionally for a large organization. In 2016, I left this typical office environment to start my own business, something that would give me more flexibility to meet family obligations as both a mother and a daughter. As I looked into what type of business would be the best fit, I found myself returning to my original passion of words and writing. I began copywriting blog posts, newsletters, press releases, and even social media.

I met other business owners and entrepreneurs and formed relationships with them as we worked to support each other on the journey. These connections inspired me to combine my love of writing with my desire to be of service by helping entrepreneurs find the right words — the right stories — to describe their business that would resonate with their ideal clients.

I want to see our communities filled with strong, independent businesses. When I help businesses tell their stories, I know that I am part of growing those communities.

Show Don't Tell!

In the writing world, there is a saying: "Show, don't tell." I still remember the first time I heard this storytelling wisdom. I was 15 years old, and I was taking a fiction workshop with author Diane Schoemperlen, who had recently won the Governor General's Award. Thirty years later, I still hear her voice saying those words. And I can look back over the intervening years and see just how true this teaching is. Writers around the world know it. Business owners can also apply it.

Think about my Jack and Ted story. Showing you how they interact is much more engaging than just giving you facts about them. And I could have continued on, telling you about the relationship between Jack and Ted, the previous trips they'd taken together, and so on.

My **Creativity Intensification Strategy** helps entrepreneurs do just that: find the right words to "show" their business in a way that resonates with their ideal clients rather than merely "telling" facts that have no impact.

Let me show you how it works!

Step 1: Measuring Your Level of Authentic Connectivity™

As a lifelong writer and a professional copywriter since 2009, I've noticed that so many coaches, speakers, and entrepreneurs really struggle to get the response and the impact they expect when they publish their business content. They encounter an Audience Engagement Ceiling™, and their messaging has limited impact.

What I call the Level of Authentic Connectivity of your business content can be categorized into one of four states: Full Disconnection, Disingenuousness, Isolation, or Symbiosis. Most coaches, speakers, and entrepreneurs fall into one of the first three states.

State #1: Full Disconnection

(Which I define as "without authenticity and without connectivity")

In the State of Full Disconnection, you:

- Are not creating content because you have no idea what to create and may fear making mistakes.

- Are losing touch with clients, not getting repeat clients or referrals, and not connecting with new prospects.

- Feel as if you have nothing of value to say and regularly discount prices to close sales.

- Completely lack a brand story for your business.

- Find that prospects have never heard of you.

State #2: Disingenuousness

(Which I define as "inauthentic and having minimal connection")

In the State of Disingenuousness, you:

- Create and post content inconsistently. Since you're unsure of what will work best, you try a lot of different voices and personas.

- Get some casual inquiries, but ultimately most prospects are not interested in making a purchase. Connections within your network are tentative.

- Feel you frequently have to explain why you and your company are the best choice.

- Operate your business with a weak or disconnected brand story.

- Are still hearing "I didn't know you were here" after several years in business.

State #3: Isolation

(Which I define as "creating from an authentic place but failing to achieve connection")

In the State of Isolation, you:

- Create lots of authentic content, but it doesn't connect well because you have no plan.
- Get only minimal interaction because your content is not accessible or relatable. It is difficult to create relationships when prospects and clients don't feel understood or valued.
- Think you have some idea of what to say but still feel that people don't really get who you are or what you do.
- Have a fairly detailed brand story that makes sense, but you are not using it well.
- Realize that although people have heard of your company, they don't know the specifics.

The fourth state is where most coaches, speakers, and entrepreneurs would like their business content to be.

State #4: Symbiosis

(Which I define as "reflecting the authentic character of the entrepreneur and connecting strongly with the audience")

In the State of Symbiosis, you:

- Are confident about the specific message and purpose of your content. You create and post consistently with engaging, on-brand content.

- Achieve deep connections with new prospects who regularly become clients. You develop long-term, mutually beneficial partnerships and collaborations with colleagues who are happy to provide referrals.

- Feel extremely confident about exactly what to say and how to say it. You may give people discounts but only by choice (such as scholarships).

- Produce and curate a strong, connected, complete brand story.

- Know that prospects recognize your company and know the value of your brand. Your products or services sell themselves.

Storytelling Increases Your Level of Authentic Connectivity

From the perspective of my personal alchemy of literary storytelling, human psychology, business marketing, and unwavering passion — as well as my unique insight into brand stories — I've developed two unique and powerful tools. The Business Character Analysis™ and Creativity Intensification Strategy™ (steps 2 and 3 below) are specifically for entrepreneurs, speakers, and coaches who are fed up with failing to produce content that connects them with their ideal clients in the way they need to grow their business.

Let me challenge you to think of yourself and your business in a way you never have before!

Step 2: Business Character Analysis™

Through in-depth, interview-style questions and your **Business Character Analysis**, you will discover your:

- **Defining Characteristic™**: the one overarching characteristic that shows up in everything you do.

- **Supporting Characteristics**™: three additional characteristics that enhance and support the Defining Characteristic.
- **Culminating Result**™: the power and impact achieved by combining the Defining Characteristic and the Supporting Characteristics to benefit your ideal clients.

Step 3: Creativity Intensification Strategy™

Using your Business Character Analysis as the foundation, I will help you build your own **Creativity Intensification Strategy**, which includes your:

- **Unique Brand Motif**™: your distinctive, recurring brand identity and voice.
- **Relatability Drivers**™: values and situations that make your prospects want to be part of your brand story.
- **Allurement Generators**™: information, entertainment, and education that keep people coming back for more.

Step 4: Creating Content That Is Relevant, Relatable, and Real

Together, the Business Character Analysis and Creativity Intensification Strategy are woven into your brand storytelling to build authentic connections with your market through longer content that resonates with your ideal client.

When you focus on putting this longer content in blogs, articles, and books, you can build your credibility and authority in a way that shorter content doesn't – to demonstrate shared values, what it's like to work with you, and results you have achieved for real people just like your prospects.

That's what I do!

Let's showcase your authentic business character in your content to break through the Audience Engagement Ceiling and create that deep connection with your audience in a state of Symbiosis – a deep, reciprocal, collegial relationship with high value for both parties, resulting in exceptional customer delight and tremendous customer lifetime value.

When your brand story has resonance, you will challenge their brain, win their heart, inspire their soul, and earn their business.

Katherine Burrows

Founder, CEO, and Creative Content Strategist at Katherine Burrows Creative

Business Character Analysis™ Creator

Creativity Intensification Strategy™ Creator

The Write Connection Podcast Host

Katherine Burrows is passionate about helping entrepreneurs find the right words to describe their business that resonate with their ideal clients. Through the power of storytelling, she wants to strengthen small business foundations and create communities filled with strong, independent businesses. She is known internationally for her perceptive observations, her ability to write accurate descriptions, and her intuitive understanding and unique insight.

Connect with Katherine at https://katherineburrowscreative.com/

17

Empowering Patient and Family Participation in Medical Care – Kathy Pendleton

The sunrise is beautiful on this warm morning in late December as I arrive at my sister Carole's hospital room in Fort Lauderdale, Florida, following the knee replacement surgery that ended late the previous afternoon. She's clutching the barf basin and praising the machinery that supplies painkillers with the mere push of a button.

Carole tells the nurse about her high level of nausea. The nurse assures her that it's caused by the anesthesia and will be gone within 24 hours. When the breakfast tray of cereal, milk, and yogurt arrives, Carole tells them she's allergic to milk products, but the tray stays.

The doctor arrives and begins looking at Carole's leg. He moves between the bed and his bag as he presses the button to lower the head of the bed. Carole props herself upright with her free arm, cradling the barf basin with the other. I finally ask why she's holding herself up and she replies that if she lies flat, she'll vomit. The doctor finally looks at her and takes in the situation, raising the head of the bed. "We'll leave it up then," he says.

Minutes tick by as he performs the exam, with Carole still clutching the barf basin. Eventually I ask the doctor if they can give her anything for the nausea. "Yes, of course," is the answer, and it's done. The nausea abates.

The nurse asks about the untouched breakfast tray. Carole replies that she can't eat milk products. The nurse offers her a consultation with the dietician, but no additional breakfast items appear. The dietician hasn't heard of the milk additive that Carole's allergic to and suggests that she order a grilled cheese sandwich for lunch.

The nausea returns in less than an hour. Carole mentions to the nurse that she's never had this reaction to anesthesia before but is assured again that it will go away on its own within a day. In the afternoon, I suggest that Carole ask if there's an alternative to the painkiller she's currently taking. The change is made, and the nausea is gone for good within the hour.

Instead of taking the expected 24-hour trip just to check in on Carole, I spend three days in south Florida, making repeated trips to Whole Foods to bring in food that Carole knows she can safely eat.

What's going on? Are these bad doctors and nurses? No, certainly not. The knee replacement was a success and healed well. The focus of these doctors, nurses, and nutritionists was on providing medical care, rather than patient care. I inserted myself with the doctors and nurses to aid Carole in receiving patient care.

Families Can Be Empowered to Participate in Health Care

These experiences and more during my 20 years of teaching families to navigate the medical system have shown me that for families to experience

- peace of mind and
- confidence that they're doing the right things

...participation is essential. When a family member requires medical care, both patient and family have to be involved in caregiving and decision-making. I call this process of patient and family participation Healthcare Participation Empowerment.

At its most basic, Healthcare Participation Empowerment means that we are in charge of our own healthcare decisions. Sometimes that means questioning out loud what's going on at the time. Sometimes it's the gentle determination of the patient and family to be involved in the evaluation and choice of care plans during an illness. It even means being involved in the extreme decision of refusing care. Families and patients can recognize those situations where that's not as extreme a decision as it appears at first.

Healthcare Participation Empowerment

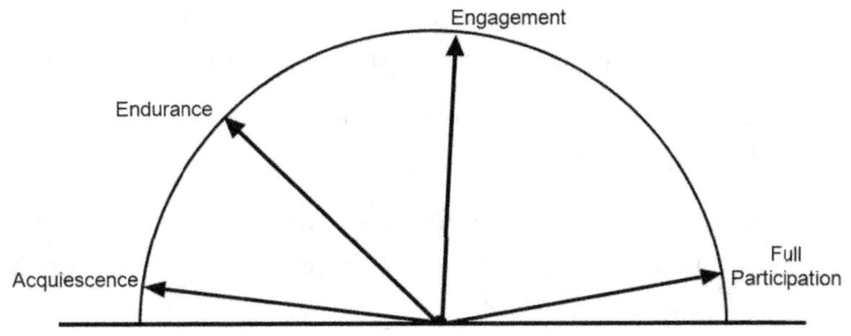

Patients and Families Can Be Involved With the Healthcare Team

As a Board Certified Patient Advocate, I've observed four levels of patient and family involvement with the healthcare team in Healthcare Participation Empowerment.

I call the first level **Acquiescence**. In this level, you're healthy and take it for granted. You're mostly detached from the process of occasionally consulting a doctor. You know you're in this level when:

1. You avoid going to the doctor when you feel bad until you can't stand it anymore. Your condition may have become more serious than it originally was.

2. The doctor has to pull information out of you about your condition, and you often can't give a detailed description of what you've been feeling.

3. You remember the basics of a plan for your recovery and don't pay attention to the details.

The second level I call **Endurance**. In this level, you recognize that you have a responsibility to provide information to the doctor. You know you're in the Endurance level if:

1. You go to the doctor when you recognize a problem, and you describe your major symptoms to get the exam started.

2. You ask a couple of questions about what you don't understand in the recovery plan.

3. You don't ask questions about allergies or interactions with other medications. This can leave you open to adverse interactions that could have been avoided.

The third level I call **Engagement**. In this level, you recognize the positive effects of your involvement in the process of health care. You know you're in the Engagement level when:

1. Before going to the doctor or the ER, you review in your mind all the symptoms you're experiencing and how long they've been going on.

2. You ask questions about everything the doctor tells you.

3. You take notes on what the doctor tells you to do.

4. There's no need for you to do research on your own, because you believe you'll get better.

Can you see yourself in any of these three levels? I've seen myself in all three at various times, every one of them.

The fourth level I call **Full Participation**. In this level, you recognize the importance of your involvement and insist on understanding your illness and treatment, and you make the choices and decisions about your care. You know you're in the Full Participation level when:

1. You've thought about your own healthcare goals and discussed them with your spouse, partner, or close family, and you've designated a Healthcare Proxy by completing the paperwork.

2. You learn about your diagnosis and any prescribed medications.

3. You ask for additional treatment options and evaluate them based on your own health goals.

4. You or a family member are taking notes during all care discussions with the care team and ask questions when you think of something more.

You can see that there's a big gap between the first three stages and Full Participation. Why do we want to bridge that gap?

Think about this for just a second:
Health is the ultimate personal asset!

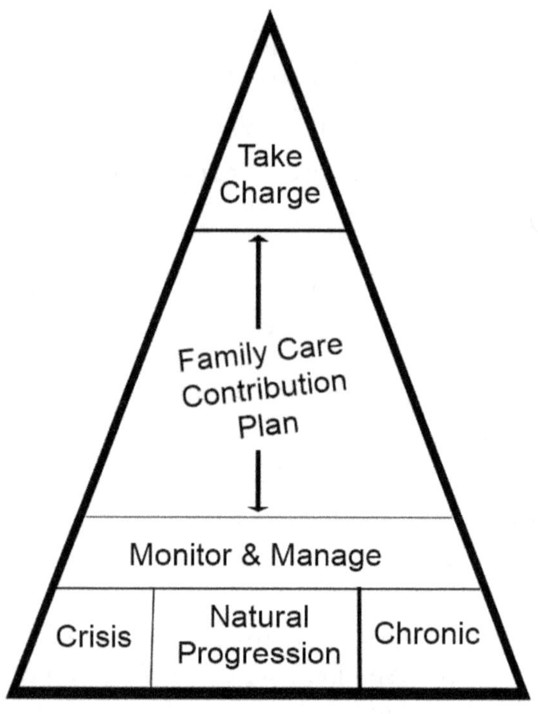

Why Patients and Families Participate in Health Care

What is it that motivates individuals and families to take more interest and be more involved in their own health care—to move themselves from Acquiescence through Endurance and Engagement to the Full Participation stage?

Keep in mind that we can, and often do, move between each of these participation levels in communicating with our care teams. Our participation depends on several things:

1. How tired we are as family members
2. How sick or injured we are as patients
3. How likely recovery is

Occasionally we simply need some time to absorb the information we've received from the doctors. Sometimes we're able to grapple with the situation and sometimes not, so we rely on the expertise of our medical team completely. In these circumstances, we often don't say much, don't ask questions, and don't inform ourselves.

But what happens when an illness is serious or complicated and recovery is lengthy? I was completely unprepared for the possibility of any serious health issue with Carole's knee replacement; maybe you were taken by surprise too, and maybe you still feel unprepared.

Doctors and nurses provide procedures, treatment plans, or medications based on their assessments. As patients and family members, we want to find out what to expect and hear details about how to recover in language that we can understand.

This is exactly when we (you and me) tend to get more involved in our health care.

In my experience, the kinds of health events that motivate us fall into three different categories.

The first is CRISIS. Suddenly something occurs that's serious and unexpected. It requires a doctor's immediate attention. It could be something like a reaction to medication or pneumonia. Decisions must be made quickly, and you depend on the expertise and experience of the doctors. Following this crisis, the family dynamic might change to avoid a similar situation in the future.

The second category is CHRONIC. You or a family member receive a diagnosis that's going to be around for a long time—maybe the rest of your life. Something like diabetes or arthritis. You must manage the treatment plan and your family members may participate in ongoing caregiving.

The third situation is NATURAL PROGRESSION. As we age, health often advances to the forefront of our minds. We receive regular checkups to detect cancer or heart disease, which are more common in the elderly. Perhaps we develop conditions that could progress into serious health issues.

Contributing to Patient and Family Health Care

Throughout these health events, we want to better communicate with our doctors and nurses and to be more attentive to the care provided to our sick family members. I call this the **Family Care Contribution Plan** and there are three parts.

The first part is **Comfort Care**. It makes the patient feel homey and comfy. It includes the knowledge we have as family or close friends because we're familiar with the person who's sick, such as:

- Information that keeps our loved one safe. We know because we've lived with them, i.e., allergies or medication reactions. We don't have to consult a chart for this information; it's top of mind for us.

- What our loved one likes, i.e., cold drinks (with or without ice) or snuggling under a special blanket. And we know what they don't like.

This is how I helped my sister end the nausea. I trusted her assurance that she had never experienced nausea after anesthesia and looked for a different possible cause.

Families also provide **Environmental Care**. This includes making the environment safe and convenient. We move items that could cause a fall and keep needed items like a cell phone or ice chips close by. It can also include patient safety issues, like:

- Handwashing for visitors as well as medical and healthcare professionals.

- Keeping a record of treatment and medication changes, especially during discharge planning, so that everybody is ready when it's time to move from the current environment.

Once we couldn't find hospital foods that my sister was comfortable eating, I brought in food for her that she had confidence in.

The last of these essential care tools I call **Mom's Care**. So much of what Mom does makes us feel loved and valued, and it helps recovery to go smoothly. Mom figures out how to get it all done and adopts a mindset that it will get done. These things include:

- Keeping a list of questions to ask the doctor or nurse.
- Taking notes on answers to questions.
- Preparing needed consent forms, Powers of Attorney, and Advanced Directives before they're actually needed.

Even though my sister's doctor was made aware of her suffering from nausea, it required my suggestion to get her something to control that awful feeling.

Mom's Care, Environmental Care, and Comfort Care together build the Family Care Contribution Plan. All three parts are essential for us to know that we've done the best we can for our parents, our children, and other family members. We can expect to use these essential care tools alongside the care we receive from the doctors and nurses who make up the medical team.

Success With Patient and Family Care

We become more involved in our sick care very naturally, and yet we often continue to allow doctors to make most of the decisions for us!

And THAT'S the problem!

The goal of feeling well and being able to do the things we love to do is way up there! In between the illness that requires medical care and the goal of feeling well resides Mom's Care, Comfort Care, and Environmental Care. And that's what I do!

I teach individuals and families to ask questions, evaluate choices, and speak up. We can reduce the suffering of ourselves and our loved ones—suffering from fear, worry, and discomfort—simply by voicing the suggestions that we think of automatically.

If you've experienced frustration or concern about how you can help with the health care you and your family receive, you can reach me through my website www.GetTheCareYouDeserve.com

I'd love to talk with you!

Kathy Pendleton

After more than 25 years as a technical trainer with various computer software companies, Kathy has directed her analytical fervor toward healthcare solutions through patient advocacy.

Kathy's frustrations and observations during the extended hospitalizations and recoveries of her own family members have convinced her that errors occur regularly, although not maliciously. In her business, she teaches people what to do to effectively manage their own health care and the health care of their families.

She is especially passionate about including our preferences in our health care and avoiding treatment and medication mistakes. Her fifteen years of experience in watching, helping, and asking endless questions during her family's health care has strengthened her belief that:

- No one cares more about your own health or your family's health than you do.

- To help ensure that we avoid medical treatment and medication errors for those we help, it's necessary to pay close attention and ask all questions, both big and small.

- While doctors have years of experience and medical knowledge, we have even more years of experience and knowledge of the bodies of our family members.

Kathy is a best-selling author and educator. She enjoys traveling, cooking, and spending time with her family and friends in Florida.

18

Power Up Your Profitability!
– Linda P. Cousineau

Consider this true scenario.

Meet Mark. Mark worked as a senior employee in the IT department of a large company for fifteen years. He loved his job and excelled at it. He was a great asset to his team and he enjoyed sharing his knowledge. Mark was praised regularly for the quality of his research, his expertise, and his ability to think long-term. He never did anything halfway, everything had to be logical, accurate and precise. He was eager to learn and had been identified as a future potential leader. Being forward-thinking, the company had gone from being small to large rapidly. Mark knew he was going to be there for a long time… So he thought!

After fifteen years, the company went through a restructuring and Mark's department was replaced by a third party. Because he was so great at his job, Mark was moved to the Sales Department and was given a sales target. Despite his best efforts, he failed miserably. Wanting to help, the company transferred him to another department. Again, Mark failed. Mark left the organization a year later, feeling "broken" and unable to figure out why he failed not once but twice. Failure was not something he had ever experienced. He went into a three-year depression. Last fall, Mark decided to attend an *Empower Growth*'s conference. During the training workshop, Mark learned about environmental values and realized he "was not broken." The company he worked for did not know about environmental values and moved him in two roles that were not aligned or congruent with his environmental values. Mark's ability to succeed was compromised!

Sounds familiar? Mark's personal story is not unusual. Both Mark and the organization paid a high cost for their lack of awareness and understanding of environmental values.

At Empower-Growth Inc., we empower Leaders and employees of an organization to connect, collaborate and perform better at all levels by discovering their own environmental values as well as those of their colleagues. Our *HBCT Operation Model*™ systematically connects the operation, the leadership and the personnel components of an organization through the practical application of environmental values in a proven step-by-step process. Whether your organization is a "mom and pop" company or a large organization, environmental values impact **performance, productivity and profitability (3Ps).**

Imagine having the ability to consistently increase the performance, productivity, and profitability (3Ps) of your company, organization, or team...

WHAT ARE ENVIRONMENTAL VALUES?

Environmental values are personal preferences which, when respected, allow an individual to be most productive and successful. People can be divided into four groups, each one operating differently within their environment, making it easy or difficult to work together, communicate and collaborate.

The four groups consist of the acronym **FISH**:

- **F**lexible
- **I**nformed
- **S**tructured
- **H**armonious

Everyone's code is a combination of the four groups (FISH) but not necessarily in that order. People typically see, experience, and respond to their environment based on their first two letters. Their ability to be creative, productive, make decisions, take risks, be proactive, envision short versus long term goals, inspire or be inspired, be organized, and so much more are all related to their environmental values. Most people are not aware of their environmental values and how they affect their personal and professional lives. Yet, their environmental values are the foundation of who they are, and how they like to operate within their environment.

Below is a brief description of each group (FISH).

The Flexible people

Flexible people like to operate in a stimulating, and flexible environment. They look at the world as a place full of opportunities, and possibilities. They like to take action, try new things and be spontaneous. They want the freedom and flexibility to do things their way. Flexible people are creative and have a winning spirit. They thrive on being successful. They make decisions on the spur-of-the-moment and are comfortable taking risks. Flexible people are action driven.

The Informed people

Informed people like to operate in an information driven environment. Knowledge is key. They have a thirst for learning and need to research various sources of information! They love a challenge and like to look at what is possible. Informed people are curious and question everything. They are guided by logic, expertise, and accuracy. They like and need to understand what is and what could be. Informed people tend to have difficulty making decisions as they feel there is always more information to gather. Informed people are information driven.

The Structured people

Structured people like to operate in a structured environment. They need to be able to plan and predict everything. They like to follow a well-established routine and are much more comfortable when their life is organized according to systems and processes. The Structured people make decisions based on the past, they do not like to deviate from the "tried and true." Predictability and familiarity are key. They are not comfortable with change, disruption, chaos or the unknown. Structured people are task driven.

The Harmonious people

Harmonious people like to operate in a friendly-people oriented environment where all are treated fairly, welcome and made to feel part of the whole. They want everyone to be happy, interact and collaborate. It is important that all team members and teams get along. They build strong relationships, are personable, and compassionate. Harmonious people inspire, encourage, motivate, and support others. Emotions prevail over logic. Togetherness and connectedness are key. They make decisions based on trust. Harmonious people are people driven.

The company Mark worked for did not have knowledge of the environmental values. Mark was placed in two different roles and forced to operate in an environment that was not congruent with his environmental values. This situation prevented him from performing as well as he had in the past and impaired him from being as productive as he could be which negatively impacted the bottom line of the organization (the 3Ps).

Change and risk are inevitable in an organization. When change is imminent, Leaders who use their knowledge and understanding of environmental values (FISH) can execute the four leadership functions of the *HBCT Operation Model*™ (which follows) more effectively.

Empower-Growth's HBCT OPERATION MODEL™

The **HBCT** *Operation Model*™ consists of three layers: the Operational layer, the Leadership layer, and the Personnel layer working conjointly.

The Operational Layer

The success of an organization rests heavily on the four critical leadership functions of the Operational layer:

1. **H: Hiring** the right people for the right role (or placing them in the right role when change occurs),

2. **B:** Inspiring long-term **buy-in**,

3. **C:** Training, coaching and empowering to increase **competencies**, and

4. **T:** Building cohesive **teams** for growth, expansion, and potential.

The Operational layer is under constant external and internal pressure. The external pressure comes from the Leadership Layer because the skills and abilities of the Leaders determine their ability to execute and sustain four strong HBCT functions. The internal pressure comes from the Personnel Layer because employees have personal aspirations, issues and concerns about their family, finances, and health. These aspirations, issues and concerns affect the employees' behaviors which consequently put pressure on the four HBCT functions.

The Leadership Layer

Leaders must be able to execute and sustain four strong HBCT functions.

1. **Hiring**

    When those hired are interested, excited, dedicated, and enjoying their work, they perform well and expectations are met. When an employee is moved around due to layoff, acquisitions, rapid growth, or restructuring (as was the case with Mark), it is equally important to ensure the employee is moved to a role that is congruent with his environmental values in order to be productive, and successful. When the wrong person is in the wrong role, expectations are not met, other employees start resisting, conflicts arise, and productivity goes down.

    When a hiring manager uses environmental values, it is a simple process to match the environmental values of the prospective employee with the required competencies of the role. When an applicant matches the competencies required for the role, now the right person can be put in the right role.

2. Buy-in

When people buy-in, retention is high, employees are involved, absenteeism is low, there is a sense of belonging and people are willing to go the extra mile. When buy-in is low, employees lose interest or belief in the organization's vision and mission, attrition increases, tension and stress are felt, people are not participating or sharing, and there is a sense of apathy or nonchalance.

Leaders lead, coach, inspire, train, communicate, behave and interact with their employees according to their natural environmental values. Only once aware of their own environmental values, can they adjust and customize their approach and communication. As a Leader, "one approach does not fit all!"

Consider the quote by Kenneth Blanchard, *"The key to successful leadership today is influence not authority."*

The risk of not knowing how to inspire buy-in from employees, comes at a high cost to a company. By understanding employees' environmental values and personal aspirations, Leaders are better equipped to influence and inspire buy-in.

3. Competencies

It is never easy for an organization to go through change. Change always feels risky. Yet, change and risk in an organization are inevitable. Leaders must consistently train, coach and empower their team members to further develop their skills as the company evolves. When that does not happen, mistakes and quality issues increase, deadlines are missed, team members start to blame each other, conflicts increase and so on.

When Leaders provide the tools and support required for team members to grow their skills and abilities and use their understanding of environmental values to train, coach and empower, employees are better equipped to perform at an optimal capacity.

4. Teams

An organization's profitability is influenced by the performance and productivity of its personnel. Environmental values allow team members and teams to work to their strengths. Conflicts, misunderstanding, miscommunication diminish while performance, productivity, and profitability (the 3Ps) increase. Leaders no longer have to spend much of their precious time dealing with team issues. The "us versus them" mentality disappears and the sense of jealousy or envy amongst team members diminishes as well.

When the right people are on the right team, this creates a synergistic effect wherein the performance of the team is greater than the individual performance of each of its team members. Consequently, when environmental values are used to put teams together, the teams' productivity outperforms the capacity of each individual on the team. This has the potential to accelerate the profitability of the organization.

Once aware of their environmental values, Leaders can execute the four functions (HBCT) of the Operational layer effectively. The Leaders become more flexible and learn to customize their approach and communication with their employees (Personnel layer).

Without these four critical leadership functions being executed effectively by the Leaders, an organization is at risk for poor performance, lack of productivity and decreased profitability. So how does a Leader execute the four critical HBCT functions? By understanding the environmental values and providing the necessary conditions for team members to be most productive and successful.

The Personnel Layer

Employees of an organization have personal aspirations which drive them and affect their behaviors. They also have concerns and issues about the well-being of their family, their health and their finances. All these factors have an impact on the employees' behaviors at work. Cultural diversity is also becoming an important factor as employees now work with people whose beliefs, traditions, and needs vary substantially.

The greater the number of employees, the greater the risk for conflicts, misunderstanding, miscommunication, and so on. Conflicts can arise for different reasons and they are not always easy to resolve. When trained on environmental values, employees gain an awareness of themselves and their colleagues' strengths, likes and needs and can now collaborate, communicate, and interact better. There is a greater sense of respect and understanding amongst team members or teams.

One simple strategy to improve **performance, productivity, and profitability (3Ps)** is to identify, understand, and apply the concept of environmental values. By executing the HBCT functions flawlessly and applying the environmental values, Leaders empower their team members to be productive and successful.

Now let's look at Mark and the four critical leadership functions of the Operational Layer:

H: Mark was hired fifteen years ago. When it was time to restructure, Mark was moved into two new roles that were not aligned or congruent with his environmental values. He failed.

B: After being part of the company for 15 years, Mark became demotivated, anxious and depressed. Feeling helpless, he lost respect, trust, and belief in the company and left.

C: Mark was a praised employee, eager to learn. Had the company been aware of Mark's environmental values, and placed him in a "suitable" role, Mark would have embraced the opportunity to learn new skills. He probably would still be there, maximizing his potential.

T: Placed in the wrong roles, Mark's ability to be successful was minimized. He was unable to perform as a valued team member. Team members started resenting him. The impact on Mark and both teams was devastating.

The potential risks for an organization when "incidents" like Mark occur are huge and the cost is also great. All of Mark's fifteen years of expertise, experience, knowledge and training were lost to the company he worked for.

Knowing that environmental values allow an individual to be most productive and successful, what are the risks for an organization not to consider environmental values in their daily operational activities?

Angelina Farrell, workplace conflict resolution practitioner, and writer for YFS Magazine wrote an article in 2014 which was updated in 2019, regarding the 5 workplace conflicts every small business will encounter. They are:

- Leadership conflict
- Inter dependency-based conflict
- Work style differences
- Cultural-based dissension
- Personality clashes

Consider your company. Which of these conflicts are prevalent? Based on the short description of environmental values, what aspects of the above conflicts could be mitigated at the Operational, Leadership, and Personnel layers. Imagine how the implementation of environmental values could positively impact the 3Ps—performance, productivity, and profitability.

Conversely, consider the cost of conflict within the organization because environmental values are not intentionally used organization wide. Companies are at risk for decreased performance, productivity, and profitability when environmental values are ignored or not recognized.

All of these can be minimized by introducing environmental values to an organization. Leaders become better equipped to execute the four critical leadership functions (HBCT) and what follows is increased performance, productivity, and profitability (3Ps).

How many Mark examples do you have in your organization? What is the perceived cost?

If you want to better equip your company's Leaders to execute the four critical leadership functions (HBCT) flawlessly, please schedule a call with us at www.empower-growth.com.

If you want to learn more about environmental values, request your free environmental values' assessment at www.empower-growth.com and book a call with us.

A more complete free e-book version of this chapter is also available at www.empower-growth.com.

Linda P. Cousineau

Linda P. Cousineau, Founder, and CEO of *Empower-Growth Inc.,* is a global bilingual Entrepreneur, Award-winning Speaker, energetic Trainer, Certified Coach, Negotiation Strategist, Certified Jack Canfield Trainer, Facilitator for the University of Ottawa and SAIT (Southern Alberta Institute of Technology) and Best-Selling international Co-Author.

For more than 20 years, Linda has empowered business owners, leaders, and teams of small and medium-sized businesses to increase the 3Ps—Performance, Productivity, and Profitability. *Empower-Growth*'s proprietary *HBCT Operation Model*™ systematically connects the operation, the leadership, and the personnel components of an organization through the practical application of environmental values—those personal preferences which dictate how people succeed or fail within their environment.

Email: linda@empower-growth.com
Website: www.empower-growth.com
Facebook: Empower-Growth
LinkedIn: lindapcousineau
Instagram: empowergrowthforbusiness
YouTube: https://www.youtube.com/channel/UCXM6pOD6G
w8WGz4JI-MT_-A

19

Riding the Waves of Change to Freedom
– Lisa Cavender

My passion is to empower people with the business tools and inner resources they need to be happy, healthy and wealthy, however they define it. I dream of a day where individuals, families, companies and schools are equipped with these important skills so that life becomes more calm, joyful and abundant for all.

If you have had a lot of stress and overwhelm in life or business, and you're not sure how to overcome it, if fears and doubts have been sabotaging your success, then rest assured that you can easily learn the strategies to immediately improve your results, maintain your health and grow your wealth in the process.

I know that this sounds easier said than done. Like many of you, I've had a bumpy ride during this COVID-19 pandemic. Even though I rolled into the beginning of 2020 on the positive momentum of having shared the stage with Jack Canfield and Kevin Harrington in November 2019 and then co-authoring a book and sharing the stage at Emerge Virtual 2020 with Brian Tracy, I was definitely put to the test this year!

It all started in March 2020 when I got separated from my kids for 4 months when the borders closed down, my dad who lives in long term care caught COVID in April, my sister was hospitalized with a life- threatening illness in May, my mom passed away in July and my sister was back in the hospital in September and we almost lost her. I lost a close friend to cancer in November and my uncle after that. So, I speak from experience when I say that I know that it can be a huge challenge to keep your health, wealth and happiness stable when unexpected change and stressful obstacles get put in your path.

I know many of you have had similar chaos with juggling home schooling of children, caring for elderly parents, pivoting into new lines of work and business all while running your teams remotely as if it was "business as usual."

So, before I sat down to write this for you, I went for a walk along the beach near my house in the beautiful Turks and Caicos Islands and asked myself, "what are the key elements necessary to emerge on the other side of this time of immense change and upheaval with our health and wealth intact?"

I discovered that **the gap between surviving and thriving** during periods of immense change is best managed when you do the following:

- Calm your mind and body
- Accept what is
- Focus on what you can control
- Get clear on the priorities
- Simplify your daily schedule

- Dedicate yourself to a self-care routine
- Search for positive meanings and lessons learned from life's events
- Celebrate the small wins
- Be grateful for what you have
- Reassure yourself that the situation is temporary
- Remind yourself that you have what it takes to weather the storm
- Tune into your inner guidance for insight and creative solutions
- Surround yourself with calm, positive-minded and experienced people to mentor and assist you
- Take action with confidence and conviction
- Accept responsibility for your results and course correct as needed

The reality is that **the only three things we can control** are the thoughts we think, the pictures in our mind (i.e. our imagination) and the actions we take. Our thoughts and pictures in the mind generate emotions and feelings, which we feel in the body. If certain patterns and habits of thought and strong emotion are repeated and reinforced enough over time, they become beliefs.

Our beliefs then dictate the type of actions we are likely to take. Since the brain likes what is "familiar" and does its best to keep us in our comfort zone and away from danger, we will find it extremely difficult to take any action that is inconsistent with our beliefs about ourselves or the world around us.

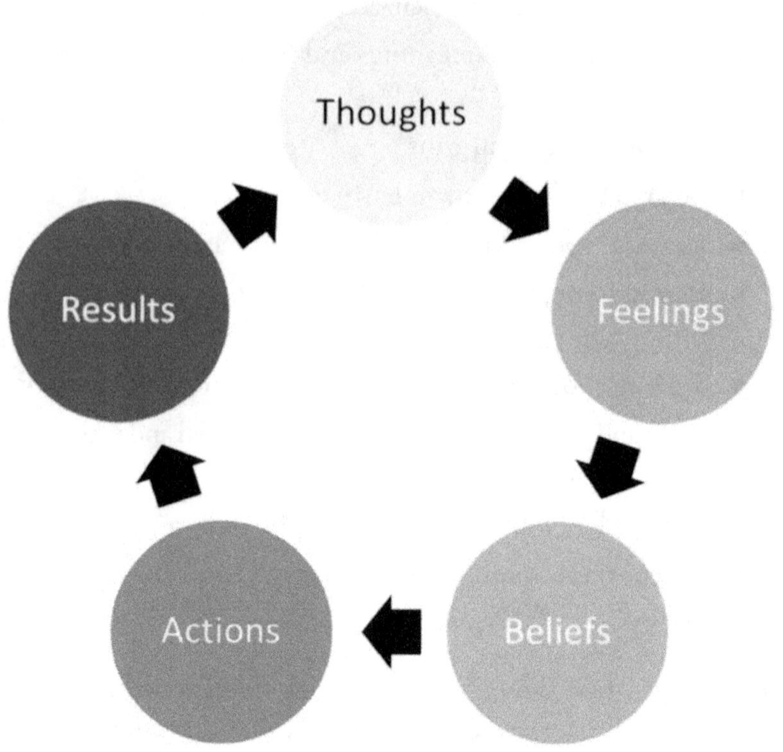

Our actions or inactions then dictate the results we get in any area of our life. If we take actions towards our goals and the results match or exceed our expectations, it leads to positive thoughts, which lead to good feelings, which lead to improved beliefs about our capabilities, which lead to more positive actions and more positive results and the spiral continues upwards in its momentum.

"We cannot outperform our self-image" – Lisa Cavender

However, the opposite is also true. If we take actions that sabotage our success, or take no actions at all, it negatively affects our results. This leads to "I told you so" thinking, feeling terrible and reinforcing the negative beliefs. Instead, I encourage you to learn the tools and techniques to master your responses to those events. That is your point of power, and the only thing you truly have control over – yourself.

When we are stressed about something happening in our life or business, it can be easy to blame others, the government, the climate, the job market, our co-workers, spouses, kids, friends, etc. for our undesirable results. When we take 100% responsibility (response-ability) for ourselves and our responses, we learn to master our ability to respond to life instead of reacting.

Improvements to your mindset and perspective will free you from excessive amounts of stress, worry, fear and self-doubt so that you take the needed actions to keep moving forward.

"If you can't fly, then run. If you can't run, then walk. If you can't walk, then crawl. But whatever you do, you have to keep moving forward"

- Martin Luther King Jr.

I would love to tell you that I have a silver bullet or a magic pill, but I can't. I CAN tell you that resilience, wellness and success are created from the inside out.

I am so grateful to have learned and developed this comprehensive set of tools that can easily be learned by anyone and is the thing that will allow you to master your responses so that you go from surviving to thriving!

I've called it the **Personal Freedom Code™**.

The Personal Freedom Code™ is the culmination of my 30 years of experience in business and personal development studying the latest tools on stress reduction, energy work and mindset techniques and high-performance habits.

> **The Personal Freedom Code™ will empower you to jump that gap from surviving to thriving, and keep you calm in the chaos.**

My friend and teacher Jack Canfield tells his students that "success is like knowing the combination to a lock. You have to know the right numbers in the right sequence to open the lock. If you have the right numbers but use them in the wrong order, the lock won't open."

The Personal Freedom Code™ works just like that. It is the secret combination of simple yet powerful tools to open you up to health, wealth and happiness.

The Personal Freedom Code™ is made up of 5 core elements:

1- Calm

The power of the mind over the body has been widely researched and documented. We now know that the body does not know the difference between something "real" and something imagined. Case in point, when you wake from a bad dream only to notice that your heart is racing, you are sweating and your breathing is rapid and shallow. So thoughts in your mind create feelings in your body. Are you mindful or Mind Full? Start by noticing how you are feeling. Are you stressed? Is your body tight or relaxed? Do you feel tension anywhere?

Breathing is the easiest and most effective tool for rapidly changing your state. When we breathe deeply our body sends a signal to the brain to let it know that "things are calm, all is well." Your brain will stop the flood of stress chemicals and bring blood flow back to the prefrontal cortex so that you have more access to creative thinking, problem solving abilities and executive decision-making functions.

Start and finish each major segment of your day with some deep breathing. In through your nose for a count of 4 and out through your mouth for a count of 4 is a great starting point, but there are many different styles of breathing exercises. Pick the one that works best for you and commit to do it every day for the next 30 days. You will definitely feel a major reduction in your stress level.

Until it becomes second nature, set a chime on your phone as a reminder to stop, pay attention to how your body is feeling, release any tension and breathe deeply for 2 to 3 minutes. After breathing, drink some water, stretch and get back to your day refreshed and with access to more of your inner resources so you get back into inspired action.

2 – Clarity

If you haven't yet learned how to meditate, I strongly encourage you to do so! Meditation is simply a vehicle to calm the mind in order to tap into the higher mind - the Inner CEO™ as I call it. The part of you that sees the big picture, that has access to the birds-eye-view of your life and knows where you are headed.

Anything can be a meditation. Running, doing art, playing music, walking in nature, cooking can all be tools to focus the mind on a singular task to the exclusion of the background chatter. Have you noticed that you will often get your most inspired thoughts when you are not making an effort, such as doing something simple like driving or showering, etc.? That is because the mind is focused and alert but disengaged from the chatter, so a clear path opens up for the ideas to flow easily.

My favorite way to teach meditation for beginners is through walking meditation. Imagine how much more wealth you could generate if you had regular and easy access to such creativity, inspiration and higher knowledge?

Another aspect of Clarity is knowing what makes you truly happy and what you would like to accomplish in your life. As a result of the pandemic, many of us are reevaluating our priorities and future plans to be more in alignment with our values. In my masterclass called "Passion, Purpose and a Plan for Profit" I walk participants through *The Passion Test*™, we tap into their vision for life purpose – what Simon Sinek would call your "Why" and then make a 90-day plan to work towards a life of more passion, purpose and success.

3 – Courage

Once you have clarity, we will need to build up your courage muscle so that you will allow yourself to take some new actions. Small and consistent steps outside your comfort zone build positive momentum, minimize fear and resistance and build confidence.

When fear shows up, embrace it and listen to what it has to say. Fear can show us where we have not considered all the aspects of something or it can be the doorway to our limiting beliefs. Either way, fear is a gift. In my sessions with clients, I regularly facilitate a process which allows them to discover what the beliefs are that hold them back, what was the meaning they took on as a young child, reframing the meaning on the level of the mind, feeling where it is stuck in the body and then releasing it from the whole system.

A holistic approach to working with your beliefs is the most effective – remember beliefs are a combination of a powerful meaning/thought and a strong emotion. Thoughts are the language of the mind and emotions the language of the body, so engaging only the mind or only the emotions will fall short.

4 – Confidence

Once you have taken some new actions and start getting some new results, it will build confidence. It is so important to celebrate your "wins." As part of your end of day routine, I encourage you to journal about the things that were a success, where things flowed easily and were fun, the goals and profit targets that were met. We often gloss over what we did well and are too hard on ourselves for the things that we didn't do as well as we expected. Break that cycle and focus on your wins. For maximum results and wealth activation, remember to really feel it in your body how satisfying it was to have things flow.

5 – Conviction

Imagine how life will feel when you have developed such calm, clarity, courage and confidence that you can handle whatever life throws at you with conviction and self-trust! That power builds more positive thoughts and the spiral continues upward! You will feel better and better every day and more and more abundance will flow as a result.

Bonus Step – Avoid the Isolation Trap

In order to keep your spirits and energy up and moving towards your goals, it is so important to surround yourself with people who can inspire you, support you, mentor you and coach you through the rough spots and help you to stay calm, centered and on track. Remember that vulnerability is a strength, not a weakness. It takes courage and confidence to ask for help when you need it. Reach out!

Imagine A Less Stressful Life and Business

Whether you need to apply the Personal Freedom Code™ to just one area of your life or several, it will work its magic and bring you back into flow, ease, prosperity and happiness.

And once you have learned the Personal Freedom Code™, you will always have these invaluable tools at your disposal for life and business' inevitable future challenges and obstacles.

The Personal Freedom Code™ will give you the shock absorbers you need to absorb the bumps in the road easily and get back on track faster and easier than ever before, saving you from stress and loss of profit.

Imagine a life with more freedom, ease, flow and abundance in all areas of life! Every small increment builds momentum and makes a massive impact on your happiness and results!

If you are ready to close the gap between where you are and where you want to be, it would be my honor to guide you and/or your team in implementing the Personal Freedom Code™ in your own life or business!

> *"We must be free not because we claim freedom, but because we practice it." – William Faulkner*

Reach out by email at lisa@lisacavender.com to book a complimentary call with me, request to join my newsletter or to find out more about upcoming workshops, retreats and mastermind groups.

Lisa Cavender

Meet Your Mentor and Coach…

Lisa Cavender is the CEO of Innergy Ltd., a company located in Providenciales, Turks and Caicos Islands dedicated to empowering people to transform their personal lives and businesses from stress to success!

Lisa is an international speaker and bestselling author who has shared the stage with business development legends such as Kevin Harrington, Jack Canfield and Brian Tracy.

Lisa is one of Jack Canfield's Certified Trainers of *The Success Principles*, *How to Get From Where You Are to Where You Want to Be*™ and also one of Janet and Chris Attwood's Certified Facilitators of The *Passion Test*™, *The Effortless Path to Discovering Your Life Purpose*, for both adults and kids & teens.

Lisa is also a graduate of the Richard Ivey School of Business, a CPA, an accomplished entrepreneur and the proud mother of two daughters. She has been practicing and teaching meditation and energy work since 1994.

www.lisacavender.com

20

The Business of Intuition
– Lisa LaJoie

When you start a business, you create an entity that has vibes and a soul. It has a current of energy created from a vision deep in your heart — your entrepreneurial dream.

Grow Your Business Vibrations

All businesses have vibration because all things — including our dreams — have a desire and purpose that starts the energy itself. Like soul and human coming together as energy and matter, manifesting creative birth, this vibrational DNA gets birthed inside the foundation of the business.

The vibes of the idea grow into a business that serves clients through an interaction which satisfies a need for that client or the business in some way. Vibrations are the connector energies that come together like magnets, attracting each other. When our needs align with what our client needs, there is full satisfaction on both ends, and our business growth is happy.

The Role of Intuition in Business Success

These vibrations are always present and part of our business growth. Once people get what they need from us and trust us to deliver it, our business starts to grow wings to fly on its own.

Successful business people use intuition, often without knowing it, simply by being in tune with the soul of their business and the trend vibrations out in the world. As part of their regular business planning and operations, they can intuit what people need, and then create it, using their inner knowledge to decide on the best next steps for business development, extension, and expansion.

When we believe this higher version of our business exists already, we are able to manifest it easily. Imagine how much better our businesses will be if we intentionally call on our intuitive guidance and use it as a resource to improve the bottom line for people we serve. As business owners, we feel on fire, and we find fulfillment in serving the client ever more deeply.

Making Business Intuition Intentional

Intuition is the ability to connect us and the client, helping us to visually conceptualize both sides together, and providing the mapping to the business and its best potential to serve our clients. It also helps us understand the next right things for each client and what the client needs to feel satisfied and fulfilled in our interaction.

Intuition can tell us when we're off-track, when we're going to fail, when we need to turn left instead of right, and when our idea has to be put on hold or be started right away.

Intuition can also help us know what to do to stay on top of our overall vision, future plans, marketing, and projects. Intuition can help us know who to hire and fire, and how to get to the next level. Intuition can inspire direct methodical actions to ensure we reach our goals, and manifest the abundance, appreciation, and joy that comes from doing what we love and loving what we do.

We're the core foundation of our business. Intuition is the best way to build that foundation. It can alleviate stress, help us know what to do next, and create a sense of profound strength inside us as we start getting results from using it.

Learning How to Use Intuition to Better Serve Clients

Intuition is a guiding source of the highest kind. Have you ever "just known" that you shouldn't do something? Then, after you did it, you thought back and said to yourself, "I knew I shouldn't have done that." You might not have known how you knew, but you did. That was your intuition trying to guide you — to prevent you from creating chaos of some sort.

We can access the guidance of our intuition in any life area. It has the potential to accelerate our learning, make us incredibly adept at avoiding conflict, and successfully move us through life's obstacles. When we know how to use it, we will create a flow that speeds up our manifestations of positive results, and creates exponential growth in our inner and outer life.

To keep on top of the next steps to build our own success, we need to be in charge. Being deliberate and methodical in the intuitive practice when working with business gives us the best results when using our intuition.

Cynthia's Story

Cynthia was a franchise owner who wanted to sell her franchise. She came to me because she was having a really hard time working with the other people in the franchise itself.

Franchises are complicated and often more than one person makes decisions. Cynthia found this very difficult because she couldn't do her own thing without direct hold up from the others. It felt like she was being challenged for no reason. Intuitively she knew this was not good for her or the sales.

Having worked extremely hard to make the business profitable, it was hard on Cynthia to have someone undercut her work and integrity, treating her with arrogance instead of the appreciation she had earned.

Using my ability to tune in to all the different scenarios, I started by working with her areas of conflict in the present moment and with the company who was a potential buyer of the franchise. Cynthia had trouble because the other party was very stubborn and controlling. He wanted things the way he wanted them. I helped Cynthia to understand the energetic and vibrational triggers between herself and others and why she was being triggered when their energies came together.

Intuition Helps Us Handle Challenges

We can be challenged by others, ourselves, our beliefs, and our insecurities. It's a lot to manage. But we can learn to use our intuition to guide us in successfully navigating these challenges. Having intuition as a guiding force helped Cynthia develop faith in herself. She was able to take my guidance and implement it to get the results for herself.

Once she had the information she needed, Cynthia could manage those energies independently. As business owners, that's ultimately our goal: using our intuition to serve our highest potential for ourselves, for others, for our clients, and for our business.

Intuition as Strength

I worked with Cynthia to recognize the opportunity to learn, grow, and challenge herself to become a stronger individual. She began to heal her insecurities as a person, and the results are still showing up in her life as today she's able to manage these types of arrogant people. In life and in business, it's important to deal with and heal our triggers.

Learning that she could use her intuition has served Cynthia long term. Now she only comes to me when she's really not sure about something. Otherwise, she uses her own inner guidance to deal with situations herself. Her interactions with different people have dramatically changed from insecure to powerful.

Cynthia learned to use her intuition as part of her team. Through my work, she understood that, like me, she had an intuitive ability to get out of the way, ask three basic questions, navigate through the business goals and desires, and work with the challenges to turn them into positive conclusions.

Asking Questions of Our Intuition

Owning a business is a big challenge. The past, present, and future all influence what's happening now and where we want things to go. We exchange co-creative energy with a variety of people, which also influences our business.

Being on top of our business intuitively requires a methodical, intellectual and purposeful direction of questions. The bigger picture of a business and its success has many different variables. Our questions must be clear and concise. We must understand what questions to ask and when they're important.

I work to develop the right questions because the intuitive approach we take is key to accurately hearing what our intuition has to say. The clearer the questions the clearer the answers.

We move through our questions to attain information offered by our intuitive guidance. Then we take the answers and turn them into a strategy. Using intuition to navigate accurately requires us to be clear, courageous, confident, and committed.

Intuition gives us answers that are truth, to make sure we reach the true success potential available for us. If we become afraid of the answers we're given, we miss the point. Our intuition is a messenger for us, our clients, and our business. Our business wants to thrive because it came from our heart and soul, our deep dream, and our purpose.

It's our job to show up to that mission with conviction and deep love, ready and willing to receive the guidance that's offered, and then turn that intuitive guidance into intelligent, sensible action steps that change things in the right ways.

Intuition Is an Essential Business Asset

Called to be entrepreneurs and business owners, we have a drive to accomplish and shine in the world. It's imperative that we use our intuition as a business asset to create circumstances that produce our desired results.

Having a plan to achieve optimal results is crucial for a successful business. Keeping the business on track, it creates a current and vibration that makes people feel good. Clients grow and get what they need. They feel fuelled and fulfilled, becoming happier human beings.

A magnificent tool for business, intuition is a key part of our built-in life tools. Many of us express our life purpose through our work. Our business offers the opportunity to expand ourselves deliberately and consciously as we experience and explore our full potential.

Take Your Intuition to Work with You

Why do we feel we must leave our intuition at the door when we go to work? Often, people think intuition is only a soul or spiritual tool. It's not. Intuition is a practical, everyday part of your life, and you must choose to make it so.

As business owners, intuition offers us the attainment of creative strategy to change the course of our success dramatically. Our business gets information crucial to its success. Knowing that we can tune in to something bigger creates a sense of certainty in the unseen.

We often leave our intuition at the door in business, because it's a bit risky to talk about all that woo woo. Also, we don't realize we can use it efficiently. By asking the right questions and having methodical, practical steps, you can shift your reality from where it is to where you want it to be.

Use Your Intuition in Business Relationships

Although some are more skilled than others, every person has some level of intuitive ability. Develop your intuition and use it at work. When we comprehend challenging relationships from a different perspective, using intuition and insight, we can manifest a better workplace environment. Instead of judgement, we can use our intuition as a guiding tool for interactions, resulting in more positive relationships.

Business owners can use intuition to work more effectively with difficult people - for hiring, firing, and interactive compatibility solutions. We can choose the right people for our team that fit into our business success model. When our team is happy, they want to serve our clients and our business even more.

It's endless how many areas are improved once you've mastered the how. Remember: your partnership with your intuition in business is an ongoing relationship. Be open. Be ready and willing to help yourself with the intricate details of the business and its relationships.

How to Make Intuition Part of Your Life

We must make a conscious and active decision to embrace and explore our intuition. Allow yourself that potential of living bravely and seeking out answers and guidance about what might not be in your favour, so that you can turn it around by being willing to see it clearly.

Intuition gives us the gift of having a larger scale of control over the intricate details of our life, relationships and business success. The truth will set you free. But more importantly, the truth will kick your ass to awaken your ability to transform anything anywhere anytime to something more positive.

If you are already seriously in the intuitive flow, congratulations. Your intuition supports you already because you're in tune.

If you don't take advantage of your intuition, it's like having a secret weapon that you never use even though it has the power to help you in ways that you actually need.

If you keep making mistakes impulsively, you really need to slow down and activate this life-changing helper. Your intuition will help you understand why you keep repeating the same things over and over again and end up frustrated, conflicted, and confused. Your intuition will allow you to see things from a different perspective and navigate challenges as a deliberate solution maker instead of an impulsive runner going nowhere.

Time to Tune In

You've made the choice to work with your intuition. It's time to tune in and learn. The first step is to open up and be ready.

Get serious in your heart about getting to know, and build a relationship with, that untapped part of yourself.

Your intuition has its own language, its own way of helping you understand things. Be patient. It takes time to get intimately acquainted with this aspect of who you are. You might not understand for a while, but eventually you will.

Learn How to Ask Questions

Be simple and sincere. Open your heart to your whole self. To create good conversations between your intuition and you, you need to have good communication skills. Learning how to ask questions will develop the protocol for your journey with your intuition.

Start by asking these three questions. Grab a paper and pen and sit somewhere quiet.

On a blank page, write this: "Intuition, I need some help. Here are some questions I need answers for. I am asking for guidance from my higher consciousness through my intuition. Please help."

Then write the first question. Be sincere, open, and serious. It takes a few minutes to get warmed up. Don't judge. Be still. Sit and write even if it makes no sense at first. Don't worry, it will.

1. Intuition, what do I need to know that is important at this moment about _____________________ in my business?

2. What information can you offer to improve the situation/project/path of _____________________ in my business?

3. What within me is causing conflicts about _______________ in my business?

Continue the Intuition Journey

This is the beginning, so take it easy on yourself. No judgement. Just write and stay focused on your intuition as the part of you that you are talking to. See how it goes.

Intuition is the tool that can make the difference in your business success. Be persistent. You'll be surprised by the results you achieve.

We want our business to give people the results that we're hoping for so we feel deeply and completely fulfilled by their accomplishments. We want our business to be something that's lasting. So does the heartbeat and soul of the business — our intuition.

Lisa LaJoie

Lisa LaJoie is a high-performance mentor and intuitive business strategist for entrepreneurs and 7 figure business owners. A dynamic force with a fierce faith in the soul's human potential, Lisa empowers entrepreneurs, business owners and seekers of consciousness to unlock their innate power by learning to trust and tap into their own intuitive intelligence.

She weaves her deepened knowledge of quantum reality and intuition into a cut-to-the-chase full embodied mentoring style that helps to ignite her client's personal and professional purpose. They quickly become able to move beyond paralyzing fears, play-bigger in their lives, negotiate like a boss, develop solid business boundaries, connect to their higher calling and transform their passions into profitable businesses and life happiness.

Lisa is the creator and host of Unstoppable Consciousness, an inspirational podcast with evolutionary conscious leaders from all over the world who have taken themselves from feeling unworthy and out of place to confidently creating the life of their calling. The show highlights topics on consciousness leadership, high performance ascension, making impact in the world with powerful purpose.

Lisa is the grateful founder of Tapping into It (Inc), an Consciousness Leadership company that offers intuitive business consultations and coaching for self, life and business.

21

Awakening The Leader Within
– Lisa J. Weiss

We are all on a journey. A journey that defines how we act, what we say and who we believe ourselves to be. In this chapter I'm going to describe four states that run in the background of our thoughts and actions, as well as a process that invites you to lead and empower yourself, and others, differently.

It doesn't matter where we live, the job we have or our cultural background. Each of us learned how to be in the world through our family system and our cultural conditioning. It has also been documented that intergenerational trauma impacts our behavior. Imagine all that information residing within us that we are unaware of, driving the choices we make and who we believe we are.

In our lived experiences from our childhood, through adulthood, we develop brilliant strategies to cope with what we see, hear and perceive. We make judgments of ourselves and how we engage with others, based on internal conversations that we are often unaware of.

When we are feeling stressed and under a lot of pressure our perceptual filters are sometimes clouded, and we often engage and respond in ways that we feel we have no control over. For example, we may lash out or react in a way that appears extreme. That results in us feeling alone, misunderstood and frustrated. These reactions can lead us to ask the question "Who is that?"

Feeling misunderstood, alone and unheard are common statements I have heard from clients in my many years of working in the areas of communications, facilitation and coaching. I noticed often unbeknownst to us, deep underlying beliefs, values and attitudes were at the root of who we project outwardly when we find ourselves in conflict with our self and others.

It's taken me over 30 years interacting, observing, journeying and living to develop the models you are about to read about. I have the knowledge and the experience to guide you to awakening the leader within.

Let's begin with identifying four underlying states you might find yourself in. I call this process:

The Sensory Identification Cycle™

This model invites you to consider some of the behaviors, language and perceptions associated with four states: Disembodied, Cerebral, Aware and Aligned. I will illustrate them using moments from my life.

Disembodied

In August 1970, I stepped off an Air Canada plane and my whole life changed. From November 1968 I had been living with my grandparents in Trinidad, when my parents immigrated to Canada. During that time, my little brother was conceived and born without my knowledge. As children, we perceive our world as black and white and because I have no memory from that time, I assume I felt like an outsider, that I was just here for a visit, not really a part of the family.

Fast forward to February 1971. My grandmother was going back to Trinidad and I thought I was going back with her as well. I packed my bags and was singing "I'm leaving on a jet plane…" only to find out I wasn't going anywhere. I imagine I was devastated and felt abandoned. That's when it happened. I shut down by going silent and refusing to participate at school.

I *disembodied*. This happens not only to children. As adults, significant and painful events can cause us to separate, compartmentalize or disembody. I disembodied again as an adult when I went through two failed in-vitro processes. I was 34 years old and my then-husband and I had been trying for a few years to have kids. When it didn't work, we tried in-vitro. The first round seemed to be going well until the retrieval when the results were nothing like we expected. Only one viable egg, which didn't fertilize. I received the news just before heading off to facilitate a three-day event in Toronto. The only way to get through it was to push down my disappointment and pretend everything was ok.

What Disembodied looks like:

- In the worst-case scenario, you numb yourself to not connect to what's happening in your life and in your body.

- Feelings, other than those that are highly intense, can be very difficult to pinpoint and articulate.

- It takes extreme circumstances to get a reaction and you are often perceived as being cool or aloof.

- You sometimes fake what you're supposed to feel and how you are supposed to act in certain situations.

From a sensory perspective:

You float above your body and walk around more like an observer. What you feel is very intense and causes you to shut down. You look and act like everyone else, only you are not really present. You might find you often have no cognitive memory of events. Daydreaming, removing yourself from the current reality may also be a sign of disembodiment.

> *Trauma happens to us in many ways, takes many forms, and can be experienced mentally, physically and/or spiritually. Sometimes we remember, sometimes we don't. As an intelligent response we separate/disembody, as a way to protect our self. The one place that does remember is the body. It remembers everything the intellect can't or won't allow.*

Consider…What life event(s) caused you to be disembodied?

Cerebral

As a pre-teen and teenager, I was insecure and shy. I was neither with the 'in or out' crowd. I was a keen observer of everything and everyone. I acted in a way that was expected. No one knew what was really going on inside of me. My mind was sharp, analyzing every situation, conversation and environment I was in. I was quick at assessing any situation and always had a backup plan. My mind was my greatest friend and protector. It felt like it never took a break and I didn't comprehend the notion of people who said they had nothing on their mind.

I was efficient, a master planner. Having scenarios for every possibility. I was quick to assess and shape myself into who I needed to be. As I got older, my intellect made me really good at whatever job I had. I was always able to predict, with great accuracy, several outcomes and act accordingly. I was *cerebral.*

What Cerebral looks like:

- In this state you live in your head, creating stories, playing out conversations and tend to not communicate your thoughts.
- You have trouble expressing your feelings.
- You are good at being a chameleon, able to adapt quickly to changing environments.
- You are highly attuned to your surroundings and excellent at risk-management.
- Emotions are secondary and only rise to the surface when intense.

From a sensory perspective:

Our awareness of the sensations in our body is minimal and noticed only when things are intense. The intellect runs the show in letting us know how we should be feeling and doesn't allow us to go into any depth of feelings.

> *Being in the Cerebral state is an amazing intelligent reaction and way of engaging when we have a painful experience. Our intellect becomes our protector and defender. We don't allow our self to 'feel' because it elicits a body memory we chose to forget. Cerebral is a great skill, unfortunately it can cause us to miss out on experiencing the depth of emotions we are capable of.*

Consider… What situations cause you to immediately be in your head?

Aware

As a young adult I travelled, got a degree, met a boy, got married, got a job, and settled into life. Things were good…for a while. I thought I was happy. I was working, started a business, lived comfortably, had the house… Yet, every now and then I would feel restless and wonder if there was *more*. Life had become habituated and I noticed we were repeating the patterns of our parents' marriages. Every now and then I thought "What else is there?" *After many years of living what I thought was the 'perfect life,' I discovered I was dying on the inside and needed a shift.*

What Aware looks like:

- When you try to express your feelings sometimes your mind goes blank and you find yourself asking a lot of questions.
- Life seems comfortable with hints of restlessness thrown in.
- You may choose to sit on the fence rather than take action.
- You might read self-help books, do yoga and meditate.
- From the outside everything looks great and you're not ready or willing to rock the boat.

From a sensory perspective:

You are aware of the feelings when something's right or not right, though you may have trouble expressing what it is. You seem to have a good handle on things.

> *In the aware state, we have the ability to choose to feel certain things and at times our intellect fights us to gain control. We begin to get curious about what's going on and look for ways to shift or change how we live our life. Life is tolerable. For some this is ok…for others it can feel like a slow death.*

Consider… What life situations do you find yourself sitting on the fence or holding yourself back?

Aligned

Being **aligned** is a continuous invitation for me to trust myself fully, to know that I could withstand the intensity of what I feel and express myself in a way that creates a deeper connection with myself and the people in my life.

Alignment was my invitation to see vulnerability as a strength. It invited resiliency, flexibility and creativity to shape my world beyond what I thought. It also required courage to really see myself and discover I wasn't who I thought I was, and a willingness to surrender to something so much bigger than the limits of my intellect.

What Aligned looks like:

- In this best-case scenario, you notice what is going on from a sensory perspective in your body.
- You trust yourself and your choices implicitly, without feeling compelled to always explain yourself.
- You express your thoughts from a place of honoring yourself and others, and are genuinely curious about the people you engage with.
- You experience deep connections to the people in your personal and professional lives, and you are inspirational to others.

From a sensory perspective:

You are aware of and able to engage the depth of your emotions, such as anger, joy, frustration, jealousy, rage and happiness;

and see them as invitations to grow and discover more of who you are.

> *To BE aligned is to be willing to dive off the high diving board and go to the depths our self. In that place we find a calmness, an ease that emanates from our core. A strength we didn't know existed and a capacity to become an invitation to others just by being our self. Alignment has a positive impact on your mental, physical and emotional well-being.*

Consider… Are you ready to explore what being Aligned could look like for you?

*   *   *

I have lived in pretty much all the states of ***The Sensory Identification Cycle*** ™ throughout my life. At times occupying more than one. I just didn't know that was what was driving my behavior.

Can you self-identify where you are?

It is possible to be in multiple states at the same time.

Sensory Identification Cycle ™
© Lisa J. Weiss, 2021

As humans we develop intelligent strategies to cope when we feel under pressure and stressed. Unfortunately, after a while the strategies stop working, which is why we find ourselves in one of the three states. These states in turn impact how we lead ourselves and others.

*   *   *

The Core Guidance Realignment Process

Over the last 30 years I have worked with individuals, professionally and personally, and with groups in various sectors such as: healthcare, high tech, government and various private sectors. In that time, I noticed that many of the issues that surfaced in engaging with others resulted from individuals not recognizing the underlying causes, drivers and patterns which affected how they experienced the world and those in their world.

The process to Alignment and *BEING* the leader of your life is made up of three key foundational pillars **Cellular Identification, Engagement and Capacity Building**. This is a dynamic, experiential and powerful process, designed to take you from whichever state you are in, to Aligned.

The process is designed to teach you how to notice, identify, engage, integrate and build capacity. You learn how to move through the underlying beliefs, values and attitudes running in the background dictating how you think and feel in your response to your emotional, mental, physical and spiritual ways of being.

In this process you:

- Learn to trust yourself.

- Discover you don't need to be afraid of the sensations (feelings) that move through you.

- Become able to clearly articulate and share your thoughts and feelings, in order to communicate more effectively, and create deeper more meaningful relationships personally and professionally.

Cellular Identification: A way to notice, identify and articulate your emotions and what is happening in your body. You learn how to pay attention to your thoughts, feelings and words.

Engagement: A non-strategy outcome-based way to engage the intensity of the stressful moments and strong emotions that accompany them, in a way that invites and allows you to process and integrate the information. Creating the space for you to find more creative and innovative solutions to problems.

Capacity Building: A space is created for you to stand in the present moment to address whatever comes along, no matter what the situation is. This frees you from defaulting to old patterns, habits and strategies created from your past experiences. You become the best version of yourself!

This is the magic of **The Core Guidance Realignment Process™**

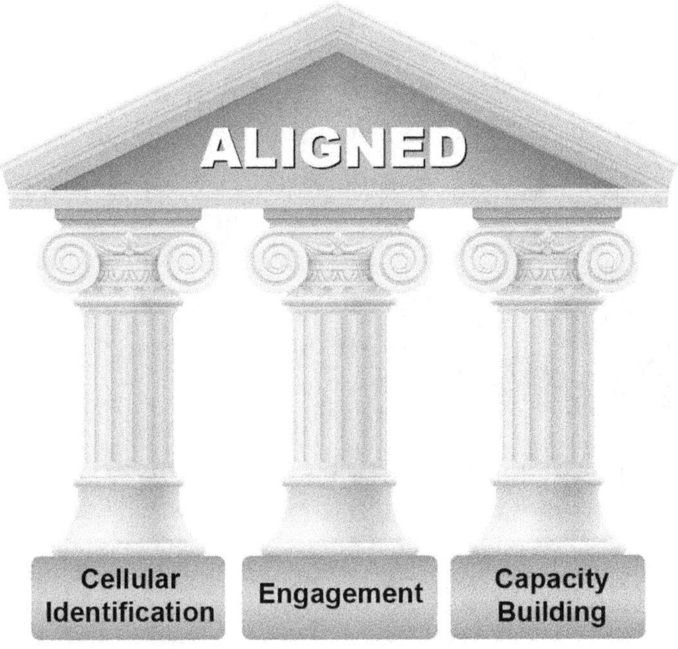

Core Guidance Realignment Process ™
© Lisa J. Weiss, 2021

Consider this process, if:

- You have reached the edge of what you think you can handle.
- You are fed up of walking around not knowing who you are.
- You are ready to connect more meaningfully with yourself, your family and colleagues in order to live from a different state of being.

Every journey begins with a first step… are you ready?

*   *   *

Lisa J. Weiss

Lisa J. Weiss, Transformation Maven, Speaker and Author is the creator of The Sensory Identification Cycle™ and the Core Guidance Realignment Process™. Combined, they invite you to know what sits under the surface of your behaviors and empowers you to make the choices which result in you becoming the leader you are meant to be, personally and professionally.

It all begins with a conversation. Reach out to explore what's possible for you, or your organization! Visit my website www.lisajweiss.com and Let's Talk!

22

Realizing Economic Gain
– Lorraine Wilson

Realizing Economic Gain is not about making the choice to start a business, it's a process! If I am being completely honest with you, starting a business is a journey that will make or break you. I hate statements like that, but what I hate even more, is not being completely transparent or sugar coating something that makes you unprepared for the tough realities of being a business owner.

I have, and continue to have, many successes in my businesses. Although my successes are not always easy, the hardest lessons are always my greatest successes.

My work over the last 25 years has brought me here to share what I have learned and cultivated into what I call Realizing Economic Gain.

As entrepreneurs we all have been chewed up and spit out many times over and for some crazy reason we all get back up, dust ourselves off and keep going. A great description of a true entrepreneur is that they have Grit and Mental Toughness.

I love how Angela Duckworth, a Psychology Professor explains Grit and being Mentally Tough.

How to Be Mentally Tough

Step 1: Define what grit or mental toughness means for you.
For you, it might be…

- going one month without missing a workout
- delivering your work ahead of schedule for two days in a row
- calling one friend to catch up every Saturday this month

Whatever it is, be clear about what you're going after.

Step 2: Build grit with small physical wins.
So often we think that grit is about how we respond to extreme situations, but what about everyday circumstances?

Mental toughness is like a muscle. It needs to be worked to grow and develop.

Choose to do the tenth rep when it would be easier to just do nine. Choose to create when it would be easier to consume. Choose to ask the extra question when it would be easier to accept. Prove to yourself — in a thousand tiny ways — that you have enough guts to get in the ring and do battle with life.

Step 3: Build strong habits and stop depending on motivation.
Grit isn't about getting an incredible dose of inspiration or courage. It's about building the daily habits that allow you to stick to a schedule and overcome challenges and distractions over and over and over again.

Mentally tough people don't have to be more courageous, more talented, or more intelligent — just more consistent.

Grit comes down to your habits. It's about doing the things you know you're supposed to do on a more consistent basis. It's about your dedication to daily practice and your ability to stick to a schedule.

If you are like me, and every other entrepreneur out there, we like fast hard data that we can skim and process to see if we want more. I won't bore you with the small stuff......yet. Let's just get right to the meat and potatoes of this conversation of why we are here.

Most entrepreneurs start small businesses because they want to do something they love. Maybe they are great at a specific trade or industry and want to invest in themselves, and they are willing to take the risk.

My focus over the last 25 years has been on business finance. It has been my life's work trying to figure out why some business owners do the work and why some don't. Why some ask the right questions and why others don't. Why some love the numbers and why some don't. It's puzzling in a fascinating way to me because at the end of the day we all need the data.

I want to establish really quickly the differences between the financial structure of a large business vs a small business. This is critical to understand for the success of all small businesses.

A large business finance team will typically consist at minimum of a Bookkeeper, Controller, CFO and CPA.

A small business finance team will typically consist of a bookkeeper and the CPA.

You can see from the chart below the Gap in the financial side of things when you compare a large business vs small business.

I put a lot of emphasis on this diagram because I have witnessed profound failures in small business because of this Gap and I am determined to bring empowerment to small business owners. SBA

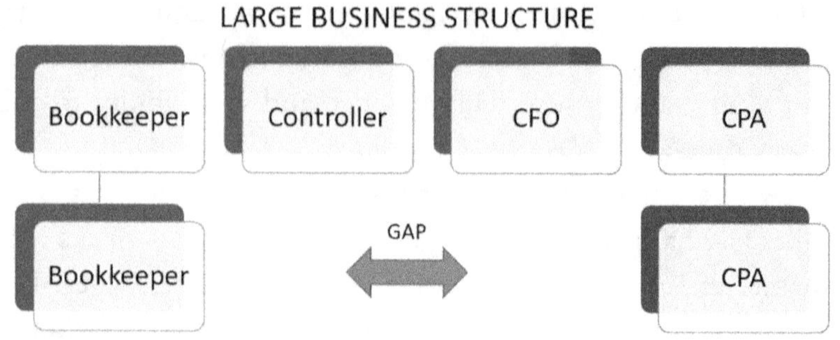

statistics show that 20% of small businesses fail in the 1st year, 30% fail by the 2nd year and 50% fail by the 5th year.

I believe most of these failures stem from the Gap and can be prevented with the right tools, the right amount of Grit and Mental Toughness. Let's dive a little deeper into some common things I see happen in Small Businesses.

Many small businesses choose to run on a small scale until they start making money and feel that they can start hiring staff to grow the business. They do this to control the financial output needed to start up a small business. There are three common methods I have seen small businesses use to navigate and monitor their success/failures. I call them the Cash in Cash out Method, the Bank Balance Method and Cash Flow Based Security Method.

The Cash in Cash out Method is just that, you get paid for a job or product and now you will pay the expenses directly related to the income you just received. The Bank Balance method which is by far the most commonly used, if your bank account is growing you can keep on spending. The Cash Flow Based Security Method is when owners use historical increases to project what they believe will happen again year after year and they use that data to make future investments or purchases.

The fact that business owners have developed these methods is honorable, creative and acceptable to most. The only problem is they are using these methods to make strategic business decisions.

Oftentimes, I see small business owners become complacent after they get comfortable with their method of choice. They start to base day to day operations on how they feel things are going in the business. The hard reality of what is actually happening in their business sometimes does not hit home for a couple of years.

A good example of these practices is when they spent the last couple of years investing their cash into more inventory so they can keep growing. More product equals more sales and more sales equals more profits. Here is an example of what can happen from this type of decision making.

It's time to get your taxes done and the CPA drops the bomb that they owe thousands of dollars in taxes. Their first thought is how is this possible we don't have that kind of money in the bank. I am not even taking a decent wage for my time spent there is no way I could owe this amount of money. This is the moment when it happens, they realize they are not actually in control of what is going on in their business.

The description above describes a high percentage of small business owners today. They are only talking to their CPA once a year for taxes, there really is no one providing oversight on a day to day, month to month, quarter to quarter basis to know what is really going on in their business. The reality is, even if you were talking with your CPA more frequently, their focus is on managing your tax situation, not how you run or manage the finances in your business.

This preventable circumstance is what I have obsessed about for the last 15 years. I call it bridging the gap between the bookkeeper and the CPA, serving in the role as a Controller/CFO.

As I mentioned, earlier I am determined to bring empowerment to small business owners, so that they can overcome what I believe is the top reason so many businesses fail today.

In order to bring empowerment to small business owners this required me to assess both the differences and common ground between small business owners. What they had, what they lacked, what they understood and what they did not. Out of this I created a model that I call the Bookkeeping Business Impact (BBI) for short. BBI is made up of 4 states that I use to identify the financial capacity in which your business is currently functioning

The first three states are the most common states I find small business owners operate in and the fourth state is what I work with them to achieve.

The First State I call the Primitive State – This means you are running your business with no financial structure, you are winging it, taking it day by day

The Second State I call the Utilitarian State – This means you are running your business using sensible, logical and practical thinking

The Third State I call the Responsive State – This means you are running your business based on what is happening around you. If you are making more money, then you are spending more money to try and sustain the growth that is happening from the demand in your industry.

The Fourth State I call Acumen State – This means you are running your business in complete control using plans. Measuring outcomes against those plans and making strategic business decisions based on the performance of the company overall.

The purpose of figuring out which state you fall in is so that we know where to begin. So we can meet you where you are, instead of being told you have to start over or there is no hope!

I am certain that you are thinking…..”what's next”?

What's next is that I have taken all of my knowledge and experience serving in the Controller/CFO Role, bridging the gap and developed from that the tools needed to teach and coach business owners, meeting them where they are and building on what they already know and have learned.

Here is where the magic happens; how we bridge the gap. There are 3 assets that must be mastered in order to bridge the gap. This is what I teach/coach/mentor at a customized pace individually or in a group setting.

- **Calculated Intentions** – This is where we get all of your ideas on paper and create a roadmap and define them into financial plans. We forecast, create goals, and manage the finances from a completely controlled and proactive position

- **Financial Framework** – This is where we develop the framework to measure and track how the company is performing against its intentions

- **Economic Intelligence** – This is where we develop your ability to interpret, understand, and communicate effectively about the financial health of your organization

Mastering all 3 of these aspects is what elevates a business owner to function at a higher level serving in their roles with the skillsets of a Controller/CFO. Mastering these skill sets will have you running your business in a completely different way. Growing and Profiting in a highly strategic manner and using tools to make strategic business decisions.

Remember earlier when I talked about business finance structure? That the roles served within the financial capacity of a business were the bookkeeper, Controller, CFO and CPA were the roles needed for the success of large businesses? The fact is that all businesses, whether large or small, need all of these skill sets within their organization to be successful.

Small businesses typically cannot afford to hire a full time Controller or CFO, not to mention they might not even understand what the different roles mean and this detail alone is why small businesses place so many demands on their bookkeepers.

When a small business owner does not have the right skill sets on their team to keep them informed, what do they do? They adapt, they create their own way of feeling their way through what they believe is going on in their business. This leaves them in a place making uninformed decisions about their business. It will also keep them from having controlled growth because they cannot track progress let alone performance.

While every small business has a bookkeeper, what they need is someone on the team with the skillsets of a Controller/CFO to ensure that their business has the Financial Framework it needs to track progress and performance, the Economic Intelligence to understand the financial health of the company, and Calculated Intentions to grow and manage in a controlled way.

It is my belief that we can teach, coach and mentor the Next Generation of Small Business Owners. I am living proof that with the desire to be better, understand more, and be in control of what is going on in your business we can lower the rate of small business failure.

I leave you with this.........

Believe in yourself, **you can achieve anything that you set your mind to**. Believe there are no limits out there, after all, the only limits are those that you impose upon yourself. Dream, believe and take action. Identify what you truly want and how you truly want to live your life and run your business.

For more information go to www.realizingeconomicgain.com and/or checkout our Podcast "Grit Equity"

Lorraine Wilson

Lorraine Wilson isn't just the operator of one successful company, she runs two every single day. The third and newest addition to the roster, Realizing Economic Gain, is a business catered towards the needs of modern-day small businesses and bookkeepers. Over her career, Lorraine has turned dozens of businesses into profitable ventures, and grown out her own portfolio of companies along the way.

Going back to her roots, Realizing Economic Gain (REG) is all about helping small businesses understand what they don't teach you in business school, when the numbers line up, but they don't translate to what's happening in the real world.

REG is built on years of experience from Lorraine's catalogue of knowledge, tools, and trade secrets that she can't wait to share with the world.

For more information go to, http://www.realizingeconomicgain.com/ and/or checkout our Podcast "Grit Equity".

23

EQ is the New IQ
– Margaret Boersma

Do your teams serve you?
Are you frustrated with employees who don't work well in teams? They seem stuck in their ways, not willing to contribute and display a general tone of negativity?

It doesn't have to be this way. There are specific things we can do to have teams that are fully productive with a direct result on the bottom line.

Picture yourself standing at the shore of an ocean. The waves build up a long way in the distance. Some waves are larger, and some are smaller. They crest as they come closer to shore.

Think of these waves as experiences in life. Something happens. We're activated and we react. Now consider that each wave is a lesson where we can get perspective on a situation. When our triggers engage, it's time to get curious. We can think of it as an offer to learn something new about ourselves. There will be small rollers along the way and some large breakers, but waves in life are certain.

What challenges dominate the workplace?

We are all on teams. We have teams at work consisting of leaders and employees, teams at school with teachers and students, teams at home in our families and in the community. Consider that every team member and every leader has waves in their lives. The wave is an invitation to work through something so we can move forward and become a better version of ourselves.

On teams, we are constantly navigating interpersonal dynamics which have the potential to totally interfere with the bottom line in business! It is well known that most people lose their jobs not because they lack the technical skills but because they don't have the people skills. If you are fed up with disconnected team members who need to develop their interpersonal skills, read on.

In more than 35 years of teaching and leading trainings locally and abroad, I have noticed many leaders really feel at a loss to empower people to handle team dynamics.

In this chapter, you will discover the productivity level of your team and the reasons for those results. You will also be introduced to a solution that promises to propel your teams to full productivity. When that happens your **impact** is transformed, your **time** is freed up, your **energy** increases and your **profits** jump.

Sink or swim?

Let me take you back a bit...

> *I am about 50 years old, doing well in my career. I love my work and have also served as a speaker in numerous conferences both near and far.*

It is early September, and I am sitting in a staff meeting with about 40 colleagues. My boss talks about two evening events we do every year and I suggest,

"Why don't we combine both nights into one?" The response from my boss was short, sharp and degrading. The tension in the air is thick. No one says a word for the rest of the meeting and most other meetings that follow.

My boss starts to target me, watching me every day and confronting me about what I "did wrong." He never asks my intention and displays a complete disrespect for my professional judgement.

No matter who is the perpetrator, the victim or the bystander, everyone is impacted. We all look for an "upstander," someone who will do the right thing and act. I feel absolutely no support and very alone in my struggle, yet I know everyone has an awareness of what is going on. There is a culture of fear.

I call the union several times to get advice asking, "What should I do in this situation?" I do what is suggested.

I decide to start keeping notes and for 18 months I record every incident as objectively as I can, and date the entries.

Action speaks

This is part of my story. It reminds me of my childhood when there were incidents of being bullied, waves to learn from. I wanted to be and do anything I put my mind to, to believe the world is filled with possibilities. I wanted to see how far I could go as a leader in my field.

I know you want your team members to be **open** to growth, to feel **calm**, **connected** and **inspired** as well as to **see future career possibilities**.

Emotional intelligence skills are key to success in any walk of life. Without them, people cannot achieve their goals, not students, employees, leaders, families or companies.

Reasons and excuses

I don't want to go through life feeling inferior. I know I am good at my work and want to fulfill my potential.

You don't want to deal with employees that **lash out** or **withdraw**, have **meltdowns** or **give up**. You don't want your employees to be **singled out** or to leave them in a state of **hijacked productivity**.

Consider this: At any given point in time, each of us does the best we can. It may not make sense to us when we think of what someone did or said, but that doesn't make it less true. We all have limiting beliefs that hinder or impede our productivity.

What I decide:

After about 17 months, a colleague comes into my office near the end of the workday. She says, "Margaret, you are not alone. There are eight of us. We all show leadership skills."

I decide to take things a step further. For myself and for me as a leader, I need to stop this nonsense. I need to deal with the waves.

A month later, things came to a head. I am sitting in my boss' office with my boss, the assistant manager and the new vice-president. As well, the union rep is there and says, "I am here in the role of mediator. This conversation is between you and your boss."

After some polite introductions, the vice-president says, "So, what seems to be the problem?" And the conversation begins. For two hours my boss brings things up and I say, "Actually, what happened was," and I read from my notes. When it is done, I am asked to leave the office while the others continue the meeting.

A few months later, my boss left the company.

As time went on, all eight of us went into leadership.

What I discover

That was a big wave! I had worked through many other situations, but this big swell had been coming from a distance. I was able to handle it because I had already worked out many smaller issues. And, I was prepared.

The incident with my boss was a steppingstone to claiming my power which enabled me to move forward and shine my light in the world.

Effects of an old model of schooling

Employees are a product of an outdated school system. The current public school system was created in the Industrial Era, where students learned to be **compliant** so they could be factory workers.

Now, in an era of innovation, we must develop our employees in **essential skills** such as the following:

Creativity	Coordinating with others
Critical thinking	Service orientation
Cognitive flexibility	Collaboration
Emotional intelligence	People management
Complex problem-solving	Judgement and decision-making

Let's do a little survey. We will identify four different states of **work productivity** based on the team leader/member relationship. Look at connections, goals and intentions for working together.

Think of your team. Consider the observable behaviors I define below as they pertain to your team members.

© Margaret Boersma, 2021

Diagram 1 – The Team Productivity Scale

Dysfunction:

The first state I call "Dysfunction," meaning there is a **very low potential** for productivity. You know you are in this state when your team members remain quiet even when asked and gossip happens outside of meetings. Team members ignore the unspoken issue in the room, causing stress and disharmony. There is an increase in negative feedback resulting in lack of trust and energy depletion. Decisions are usually made unilaterally and absenteeism increases.

Basically, team members lack "buy-in," accountability and are unproductive.

Struggle:

The second state I call "Struggle," meaning there is **limited potential** for productivity. You know you are in this state when your team members only do what is critical but are not achieving strategic goals. They complain to others, have excuses for behavior and blame circumstances. Members seek direction rather than take responsibility.

Basically, team members need nudging to do the minimum required.

Traction:

The third state I call "Traction," meaning there is **some potential** for productivity. You know you are in this state when your team members take responsibility to get work done in a reasonable time. Each person works independently. Problem-solving happens top down. There is reduced absenteeism and increased retention.

Basically, team members are getting work done but teamwork is missing.

Thriving:

The final state I call "Thriving," meaning there is **full potential** for productivity. You know you are in this state when your team members work as a tight-knit community and experience synergy while working toward strategic goals. There is a culture that encourages vulnerability and honest conversation. Members have a mindset of staying relevant, fresh and creative. Basically, collaboration is the norm, members express themselves freely inside a new model of communication and referrals from happy clients are abundant.

Your results?

Can you relate to any of these four states?

Is there a gap between where you see yourself and the state of thriving? Most people see themselves in one of the first three states.

Leaders are often at a loss to improve team productivity.

What is the cause of the problem?

When we hire employees, we want team players who can be instrumental in realizing the company mission. We want every employee to contribute to the state of "thriving" which is **full team productivity**, represented at the very top of our triangle (*diagram 2*).

© Margaret Boersma, 2021

Diagram 2 – The Cause Model

The base of the triangle is divided into three types of employee backgrounds which are foundational to their work. The first is **skills training,** meaning they must have the necessary technical, trade or academic skills for the job. They come with **knowledge**, whether it is street smarts, a diploma or a degree. And they bring life or work **experience**.

Our employees also have a perspective, or point of view. As humans, we are shaped by our upbringing, our culture, our schooling, and our beliefs. By the time we are working, we have well established perspectives. And **our perspective is our truth**™ or the point of view from which we operate. And this is the problem! Why?

Technical skills training, knowledge and experience does not give someone the skills needed to work together as a team, skills such as complex problem-solving, collaboration, people management, good judgement, and decision-making. We also have a point of view that can get in the way of growth. So, many of us are stuck, represented by the solid black line on diagram 2. We are simply not able to reach the top of the triangle, full team productivity!

There is a large gap between **our perspective is our truth**™ and **full team productivity**™ at the top. To get to a state of thriving, you need a foundation in emotional intelligence and social/emotional wisdom.

What is needed?

Creating an emotionally safe and supportive environment is key to a team that is thriving. Elevating everyone's leadership skills and implementing a new model of communication through training, mentoring, and coaching while simultaneously connecting the dots to specific company goals, is essential. Developing and implementing strategies in self-care, mindset and problem solving enables your teams to become fully productive.

Leadership Self-care Strategies™ enable you to be at your best. Leadership Mindset Strategies™ develops a mindset for success and Leadership Problem-Solving Strategies™ gives you practical tools for developing team interpersonal skills and teams that create synergy. This is your Leadership Cultural Impact™.

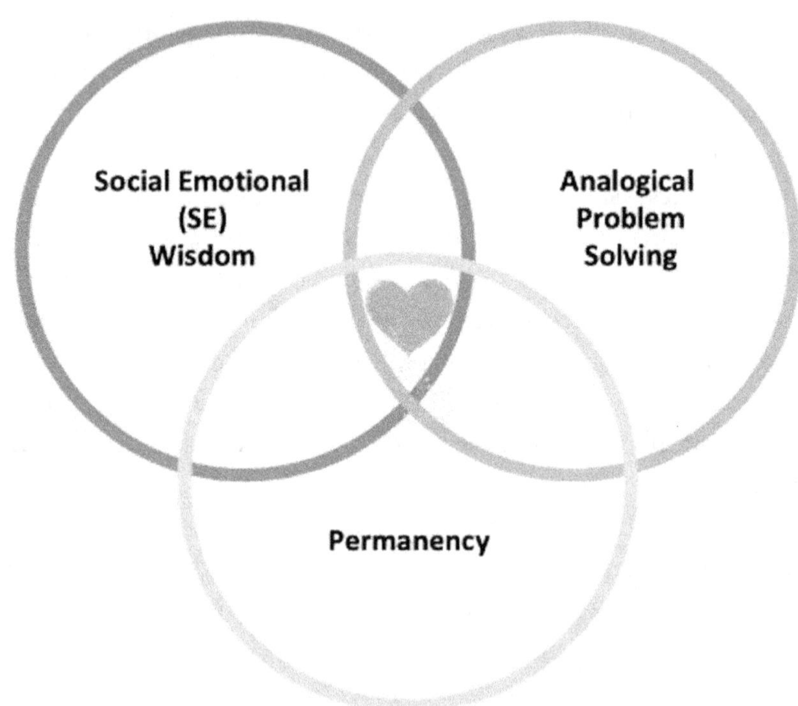

Diagram 3 – Team Transformation Program™

The **Team Transformation**™ program can give you your Leadership Cultural Impact™. It consists of three components. SE Wisdom™ which is social/emotional skills. Analogical

Problem-Solving™ is an engaging way to practice your strategies. This is like living inside a story or an analogy of life, a fun way of learning life lessons in simulations without real life consequences. The third component is Permanency™. This is an advanced mastermind group where we implement new learning with mentoring, coaching and participant support.

What if?

If I hadn't discovered I could stand up for myself and nurture relationships in general, I would have continued to think I wasn't good enough, get bullied and not be successful in my career and personal life. I learned not to give my power away and that my contributions are of value. As Jim Rohn, America's foremost business philosopher, said,

> **"You cannot change the circumstances, the seasons, or the wind, but you can change yourself."**
>
> *- Jim Rohn*

When I learned to stand up for myself, others noticed. It gave them power to stand up for themselves in their respective areas of life. Everyone is affected when one team member is either a victim, perpetrator or bystander. Morale goes down and productivity declines. When hard times come along, we have a choice, we can sink or swim, avoid or work through the waves.

What if you don't do something differently? You may continue to be in a state of dysfunction, struggle, or traction. Your teams will not reach their full potential and will actively contribute to the decline of the company. Your **costs** increase and your **profits** decrease.

What Lies Ahead?

What if you get the knowledge, you need and implement your new learning? You manage your team as a tight-knit community and experience synergy while achieving strategic goals. Your team members have a mindset of staying relevant, fresh, and creative. You are thrilled with the way your impact contributes to the company's success.

Imagine what is possible when we have and practice social/emotional wisdom skills. What would your team's productivity be like? How would it impact the company's growth? Career growth? Imagine the ripple effect when satisfied customers are impacted by your level of impeccable service. What about your family life? Community life?

Take the free questionnaire

Find out how your team is functioning now. Take a free five-minute survey then make an **appointment** to talk about next steps. Contact us at www.creativeeducationinaction.com for access to the survey. Make it happen now.

What now?

Unlike other trainers who don't go deep enough with emotional intelligence skill training, I guide you to have team members cultivate trust, develop a new model of communication, increase leadership skills and become fully productive. You learn practical skills such as how to de escalate a conflict, calm someone down, see things from multiple perspectives, deal with stress and make things right with others. And the learning is often through games and simulations because when we discover our learning for ourselves, it is retained and can cause a paradigm shift. These skills allow your teams to reach full potential.

Three choices:

1. **Team Transformation:** A comprehensive program that supports you with step-by-step practical tools you can implement right away. It includes SE Wisdom, Analogical Problem-Solving and Permanency.
2. **SE Wisdom:** Start with a 9-session program, virtual or in-person, to get a foundation in social/emotional intelligence skills.
3. **Lunch 'n Learn:** Discover your learning inside a fun simulation with your team.

Note: As a trainer, I qualify for the Canada Job Grant. If your company meets the criteria, much of the cost can be covered. Are you ready to learn from the waves coming your way? Waves that when dealt with can change everything for the better? Contact us today.

Margaret Boersma

Margaret Boersma is an educational consultant and speaker. Her varied career in more than 35 years of teaching, combined with her expertise in emotional intelligence (EQ), allows her to assimilate the affective domain (people skills) with your team goals. She has trained extensively in social and emotional learning, the arts, and with Dr. Eric Jensen in brain-compatible teaching methodology. Margaret's heart is to bring emotional intelligence to schools and workplaces so they can thrive. Her innovative training programs result in enhanced leadership and communication skills taking your team to a state of thriving and full potential. Margaret works with leaders in Canada, the U.S., the Netherlands, Brazil, India and New Zealand.

Website: creativeeducationinaction.com

24

The Unfair Advantage
– Nim Stant

Have you ever wondered why you always see your industry competitor on the cover of some magazine, on television, interviewing on the top podcast, writing that bestselling book and appearing on social media everywhere? These competitors aren't any smarter or better than you, so why are they more successful and make more money? This is a very common question that many entrepreneurs have, which is often accompanied by the question WHY NOT ME (especially if your competitors are less qualified or less established than you)! Don't give yourself a hard time. You are still doing fine, and you might still be on the right track. It's just your competitors know something that you don't: "The Unfair Advantage."

Building the relationship with the BIG NAME and getting yourself featured on multiple media platforms is the unfair advantage to get yourself known faster. Nowadays, you don't need to wait or take 10 to 20 years to build up your name and your business to be known everywhere. The world has changed, and you can become an authority in a short period of time if you know how to get media attention and exposure.

When I first moved to the United States, I had no money, spoke little English, and had no connections. I still remember it so clearly that every time I want to order food at the cafeteria, instead of ordering what I want to eat, I just copy the guy in front of me and order the same thing that he orders. I remember I was so scared that the worker was going to ask me a question about my food, and I wouldn't be able to understand what he said. I smiled and nodded my head a lot, not because I wanted to be nice to people or understand them but because I was in the moment of "pretending that I understand what people said." Life was good for a while, and I was working on learning English as fast as I could, while money in my wallet was getting less and less.

With no English and no connections, here comes...no money. I was working like most people here: 9 to 5, overtime and underpaid. I was a yoga teacher. I taught at 4-5 different yoga studios and gyms all over town and didn't have a chance to sit down and have dinner with my family because yoga classes were always in the evening. I made just enough to pay my bills and "get by." However, later on, I started my new gig hosting a yoga retreat in Thailand, my home country. I got clients from all over the US to go to Thailand for the retreat with me. My mind was blown by this change of events. I felt like I was living in a dream, having fun in the sun and making pretty good money at the same time.

This gig turned into a new career for a few years, until COVID-19 hit my world and our world. I was in total darkness because I had to refund money to the clients who had signed up for my yoga retreats in 2020 and 2021. My good friend suggested

I file bankruptcy. That was the moment when I said to myself: I am better than that, and I won't look back because I won't go that way...I will Go All In and get myself back up again.

I did! I found that the reason I didn't have high-ticket clients who would pay me ten thousand dollars to learn from me was because no one knew who I was, and I didn't have any social proof to show them. So I started to study and track the actions of successful entrepreneurs and really look into what they had done so I could mirror them.

Here is what I found…

1. They all write books...not one, not two, but many!
2. They have been featured and interviewed on television.
3. Their work and words have been published in magazines.
4. They speak on stage teaching what they wrote in their books.
5. They are visible and they are the authority!

That's it! I told myself. *It's time. It's my time to go all in, and the moment is NOW!* So, I started to map out my game plan and write down the action I needed to take and the date by which I wanted to accomplish these goals.

Today, I can say that I succeeded in those initial goals. Then, I kept going. I use the media to build my authority in my clients' eyes. Each day, new people will contact me and ask me to help them do the same and will pay me whatever I ask. This is "The Unfair Advantage" of being an authority in your ideal client's mind!

How can you become an authority and use unfair advantages to win your clients?

1. You need to be seen to sell.

If you have a business, it is your responsibility to make sure that people have heard of you. So many entrepreneurs make an excuse by saying they don't like social media, or they are not good at it. It is important that you study and understand the social media platform because social media is the place where your audiences hang out. You need to be in that room. Make yourself visible and deliver value to them. Not just showing up to fish new clients but to show up and be ready to serve them. Now, let me tell you this, social media is a great and important platform, but there's also a better way that can help you shorten the gap for your success.

Don't underestimate the power of television. This is gold, and you will grow very fast if you are interviewed by someone for their show or news on the big TV stations or shows. You may think that it is hard for you to get on TV. This idea is totally wrong! Remember, the producers need you as much as you need them. The TV producers need to produce their show every day, for seven days of the week, all day long. So, remember, they need to find people to be on their show, and they need interesting stories to keep viewers interested. You just need to know what they're looking for at that moment and be prepared to explain how your story and knowledge will fit well with what the producers are looking for. Those people that you see speak on TV, it isn't because they are any more special than you. They are on TV because they pitched the producers.

Every success isn't an accident. Success happens because you plan for it and you work on it. If you want to become an authority and gain more credibility for yourself and your business, you need to be seen and show up in front of more audiences. Remember, you'll never feel ready, but you need to make the decision that you are going to do it, at least once. To be featured on television equals instant credibility, and you shouldn't miss it if you are serious about becoming an unmistakable authority in your field.

2. Write your best-selling book

While everyone was worried and afraid of what would happen during the pandemic, I wrote my best-selling book "Go All In." At that time, I wrote the book because I wanted to keep myself focused on my work, and I was trying to get my message out to help people to live with faith and take action instead of living in fear. I didn't know that this book would turn into a new business and a new company that generates hundreds of thousands of dollars. My secret is simple: I don't worry about how many copies of the book I will sell; instead, I use the book as a gateway to attract my ideal client to discover me, trust me, and want to work with me. Since I became a bestseller, I have used this unfair advantage to speak to my audience as an authority and effectively help them succeed in their goals. There are so many different ways you can gain more revenue from your best-selling book. You can create an online course, teaching about the principles from your book. You also can create a workshop, seminar or live training.

A few months ago, I had an opportunity to interview the world-class thought leaders and New York Times Best Sellers. All of them didn't write just one or two books, but many of them; sometimes I even lost count of their books. Brian Tracy mentioned that he writes every day and publishes a new book every three months, which means four books per year. Dr. John Demartini said he writes and researches every day. He only slept for 4 hours each night for 32 years. Mark Victor Henson and Jack Canfield have been great examples of successful book sales of over a million copies around the world. They have inspired and impacted billions of lives. These are a few examples of what commitment to success looks like. These thought leaders didn't stop after writing only one book but continually wrote and published more than 80 books throughout their lifetimes. Have you ever wondered why they do that? For me, the answer is so clearly that they are doing it because they love it, they have fun with it and they are serious about being the authority in their field. Their determination and action bring them not only a great fortune but a whole new benefit in life and business. Dr. Joe Vitale told me during our interview that he was once homeless and basically lived inside the public library during the day and slept on the street during the night. However, he never gave up and really studied to help himself get out of poverty. Now, Dr. Joe Vitale has written books every year, established a million-dollar business and changed lives throughout the world.

We all are capable of doing the same, only we need to commit to taking action. There is no perfect time to write a book. Don't wait until you feel ready. It is an illusion. You will never feel ready. Life won't get any easier. Start now. Start wherever you are. Start with fear. Start with faith. Start even when you have doubt…but start. Soon enough, you will have your book in your hands and become the authority in your field. Take this advantage now.

3. Becoming an authority everywhere

I have mentioned the importance of being seen on television and becoming a bestseller already. Now, another way to become known as an authority is through publishing your article in a print or online magazine. This is an unfair advantage! When you publish your article in a magazine, you share your expertise and authority at the same time. You will also get to claim and use their company's logo as a way to show to your audience that you have been featured on that platform. It is social proof, and we can't deny that. Audiences will buy or sign up to work with you because they know you, trust you and have been impacted by you. You have the responsibility to show up and be in front of them so they can discover you. A lot of my clients that I mentor ask me which platform they should focus on. Here is my answer: "You should focus on everywhere that has an eyeball!" Have you seen Oprah Winfrey everywhere? YES! On television, in a magazine, on social media, authoring a book, etc. These are enough clues already for us to know that if you are serious about getting your business to the next level faster and staying in this "game" for a very long time, you need people to know you, trust you and be impacted by you. This unfair advantage of being seen everywhere will help you stay on this entrepreneurial journey for a long time.

Success tends to bless those who are most committed to giving it the attention it deserves. So, keep going all in and taking massive actions. Don't ever settle for taking an average amount of action or only going in 50%. The things that matter to you are worth all you've got.

One thing that I don't want to skip as I am sharing my message with you here is that getting yourself out there and being seen as an authority everywhere might make you feel uncomfortable. However, that is the right feeling. You're feeling uncomfortable because you are about to embrace something greater than you used to do, and you are brave enough to follow your gut, intuition or whatever you name it. Remember, commit first, figure it out later. The media needs you as much as you need them. The world behaves differently when you actually take action to go after what you want. If you are on the right path, you will start to see results from your actions. Your customers will start to show up, wanting to work with you, and you'll begin to have your starting breakthrough for your business. Being seen on multiple media platforms will give you the power to close sales effortlessly and scale your business to a completely different level.

Now it's time to enjoy the process and get yourself and your business seen everywhere. People are watching you and keeping their eyes on what you do, so why not take advantage of these opportunities to get visible, deliver value and make an amazing income! This unfair advantage formula will help you become the #1 recognized expert in your industry and elevate your business to the next level. You will have potential clients hitting you up wanting to work with you without you spending countless hours chasing them. This is the power of unfair advantage.

Nim Stant

Nim Stant, Founder of Go All In TV aired on abc15, Success Mentor, Bestselling Author, and Yoga Professional hailing from the third world country of Thailand, inspires hundreds of thousands of entrepreneurs to reinvent their businesses.

Coming from a broken middle-class family has taught Nim to become a purpose-driven entrepreneur who always seeks to live to the fullest potential. With 20 years of experience, she now dedicates her life to inspire others to unleash their limiting beliefs, commit to their dreams and goals and take real action.

In her Bestselling book, Go All In, Nim reveals the principles of Go All In to empower others to practice and step up toward lifelong results and has been featured in over 480 media as such CBS, abc, Fox, NBC, 3TV, International Business Times, Authority Magazine, Wall Street Select, NY Headline, LA Daily News, Success Profile Magazine, The Health Journal, Fitness Republic, and was interviewed by Kajabi, one of the most sophisticated solutions on the market for creating online course platforms.

25

In the Rapids:
A Leader's Journey
– Nina Penner

It was a beautiful Spring afternoon and my client Kira and I were relishing every moment of it. We were sitting at an outdoor café slowly sipping our coffee under a brilliant sun while a soft, warm breeze lightly caressed my cheek. I remember it so well because after a moment or two Kira broke the silence. Her eyes were shining as she told me about a recent breakthrough with her team and thanked me for my leadership; told me that she'd still be struggling if I hadn't shown her how to find and support the unique talents within her organization. I couldn't have been happier as I smiled and thanked her. I told her what a long road I had walked to meet that moment. She was interested in what I had to say and I confessed that I was fortunate and fulfilled by the rewarding and motivating career I had chosen.

I feel energized and enthused as I help leaders like Kira to discover and enhance their capabilities, perform at their best and create stand-out teams. After decades of supporting leaders worldwide and devoting myself to learning about strong leadership, I can now wholeheartedly support others to succeed.

It hasn't always been this way. Along my journey, I often wondered; Do we all need to travel this rough road for decades on the way to becoming great leaders? Is there a quicker route? Do we all need to be thrown into the rapids to sink or swim? Why do so many organizations do it this way when it's clearly so challenging?

My leadership journey began early. I was a quiet child, but I felt a deep desire to serve others and help them to succeed. When I was 8 years old, we had a new baby in the house, so my mother asked me to watch over my 5-year-old sister. I dragged her everywhere with me, but of course, she never listened to me and it gave me a glimpse of what was ahead!

I already knew that I would one day be on the stage and help others to get there too. I'd spend hours practicing on our clothesline stoop, which to me was a stage. When I was ready, I gathered a group of neighborhood kids and started my first "business," a theatre company! On show days, we'd hang hand-drawn posters and form a parade, marching down the street banging on pots and pans and yelling "Show today. Show today." Kids would race out to join the jaunt back to my house, where for 10 cents they'd sit on the grass and watch our show, played out on that clothesline stoop. One day, my friend Tommy and I counted the money while the other "actors" waited to collect their cut. Tommy suddenly said that he should get more money because he was the oldest and then other kids started complaining because I was the only girl playing lead roles. That day, I had played Dorothy in The Wizard of Oz. I felt betrayed and frustrated with Tommy for starting this whole thing. I bopped his head with my pencil and said he would get no extra money. As I stormed into the house crying, I yelled out that when we have a show in someone else's yard, that person could play the lead role. The following month, there was a show in my friend Tracy's yard and I was not included. I was hit by the sting of my own poor leadership for the first time in my life. I was devastated.

When I was 15, I was approached by Cindy from my school who asked if I'd be her friend. Cindy often skipped classes to go to the mall, smoke cigarettes and steal trinkets and she did not do well in school. The parents of most girls forbade them from befriending her, so she bullied them. Cindy told me that she'd decided to take school seriously and not to smoke, steal or provoke fights. She said I was the person to help her do that. I was speechless.

This time, unlike my smug 8-year-old experience, I felt the weight of responsibility and needed to think. Would my parents allow it? Could I help her? What would my other friends think? I decided to talk it over with my mother who told me that she and my dad had prepared me well and it was my decision. I laid awake in bed that night. I thought of how much easier it would be if my mother had just forbidden me to be Cindy's friend like the other moms did. I thought about what it was like to be Cindy. Ostracized by the other girls. Feeling like she needed to get into trouble for attention. A part of me empathized.

The next day, I told Cindy that I'd be her friend, with some ground rules and we quickly became inseparable. Cindy got a part-time job at a restaurant and was a model employee. She kept her commitment to work hard and get honors in school. She even got me through Grade 12 math where I struggled, and she excelled! Cindy and I became lifelong friends. Phew. That was a much better outcome than the 8-year-old theatre experience! I had learned about setting expectations, seeing others' points of view and engaging my empathy.

After completing school, I started my second business; a performing arts centre where I got to live my dream, but all the same challenges began to emerge. One company member felt she could decide which roles she played and that led to a whole series of upheavals including teachers, choreographers and directors who wanted to reframe the way I ran my business. All those old feelings of the 8-year-old me came rushing back. Why was this so hard? It was my business. Couldn't I run it my way? Clearly, I still had a lot of leadership lessons to learn!

Later, when I moved to the corporate world, I noticed other people with the same struggles. It wasn't difficult only for me! I saw it everywhere! Most leaders struggled to be effective. I worked with leaders from various industries and saw it universally; leaders were thrown into their roles with no support while struggling for success.

My own failures as a leader and the ineffectiveness of some of my own leaders along the way had a profound impact and led me to my most important realization: *Leaders lack the skills and support they need to lead their people to success.* This became the basis for the work I do today. I decided then to devote myself to helping leaders to lead with purpose, passion and complete confidence. I announced to my leader that I wanted to lead programs that do this. He quipped back "Good luck with that." He knew it would be an uphill battle. Five years later, there was indeed such a program, and I was leading it. I had immersed myself entirely in learning all that I could about leadership and creating rich support systems to develop strong, empowered leaders who built incredible teams. This was the work I was meant to do!

Today, after many years of having had the privilege of working with thousands of leaders worldwide, I listen while my clients tell me how they're supporting their leadership teams but they're still not thriving. Invariably, many of their efforts focus in three areas:

Top talent:

Organizations go to great lengths to attract the right talent and work to give them the right support. Efforts here focus on rigorous screening, supporting and promoting high achievers and high potentials, stretch assignments and job rotation programs.

Strong Results:

There is intense focus here, since organizations believe that nothing they do is more important than achieving results. Clearly defined targets, a solid focus on analytics and performance improvement measures are viewed as critical to success.

Cohesive Teams:

In an effort to empower and activate their teams, more and more organizations are focusing on providing opportunities for team building and flinging open the doors to allow more accessibility to their senior leadership teams.

The problem is that while developing top talent, focusing on strong results and team building are important, they are support activities, not the foundation on which to build your endeavors. Focusing in these areas without first building a foundation is like building your house on sand and we know what happens when we do that!

Leader Endorsement Effect.

In my experiences working in numerous countries, industries and roles, I've seen that organizations consistently struggle with one thing: Their leadership. I decided to find a way to help with that.

To assist businesses in taking a judicious look at their leadership, I have developed a framework that lays out four states that I've moved through over the years and have observed countless leaders moving through. I now watch my clients as we work together and they identify which state they're in.

I've developed what I call the **Leader Endorsement Effect™**, a framework that guides you to assess the intensity with which leaders provide the consistent, immersive and energizing support their people need to succeed. It allows you to step back and take a bird's eye view, objectively examining the state of your leadership and your business. Without judgement, justification, or blame, you dig deep and discover where there are tremendous opportunities. It empowers you to elevate how you support your own growth and that of your team, so you can all march as one towards your lofty goals.

The Four States of the Leader Endorsement Effect™
Dispiriting

The first state is what I call "Dispiriting." In this state, your business suffers because of a lack of direction by leaders who are unaware, ill-equipped, and overwhelmed.

You know you're in Dispiriting when:

- People don't know what to do
- Leaders are unaware of employee's needs
- There are complaints of overwhelm

- Work is piling up
- There is continual conflict
- There is a lack of communication at all levels
- Targets are repeatedly missed
- Blame is laid
- People hide their mistakes
- Your business loses money

When you're in a state of Dispiriting, you ask yourself these questions:

- Why don't people work together?
- Why does nobody take accountability?
- How can we start hitting our targets?
- How much longer can we go on losing business and money?

My client Syed found himself here when we started working together. He expressed that he felt lonely, demotivated and confused.

It's often difficult to find your way out, but over time, your business can't survive in this state.

Disengaging

The second state is what I call "Disengaging." In this state, your business gets by, but doesn't move ahead because of a lack of congruence between the support people need and what they get.

You know you're in Disengaging when:

- Decision making under pressure creates conflict

- People lack the grit and resilience to stay the course in tough times
- Solutions to performance gaps are ineffective
- People do only what is required
- People don't integrate change

When you're in a state of Disengaging, you ask yourself these questions:

- Why is there so much conflict when it's time for tough decisions?
- Why can't my team step up when the going gets tough?
- What will it take to get everyone performing?
- Why don't people challenge themselves to do more?
- How can we succeed when people don't embrace change?

Most organizations get stuck here. They're managing to get along, but don't know how to move beyond this point.

Contending:

The third state is what I call "Contending." In this state, leaders are aware of the support required for success, but lack the knowledge and skills to deliver it consistently. Your business is profitable, but not flourishing.

You know you're in Contending when:

- Most people solutions work for a while, then fade
- Problems are solved, but not mitigated before they happen
- Decision making quality is inconsistent
- People accept and implement change, but don't create it

- Professional development happens, but is unfocused and inconsistent

Many organizations don't make it this far and the ones who do get complacent until they start losing good talent, missing targets and losing money; effectively pushing them back to Disengaging or Dispiriting. This is the place that has spelled the demise of many industry leaders. It's a volatile state where organizations need to either invest time, resources and money to forge ahead or risk slipping back. My client Trish made that investment and has finally pushed through her limitations.

Elevating:

The fourth state is what I call "Elevating." In this state, your business has the highest level of Leader Endorsement Effect. Your leaders are fully engaged and consistently provide the proper support to generate superior business performance and lasting, measurable behavioral change.

You know you're in Elevating when:

- You are recognized amongst your industry peers as a thought leader
- Your people eagerly volunteer for extra assignments and stretch projects
- Targets are consistently surpassed
- Lasting, measurable change is embraced
- High quality decisions are the norm
- There is constant innovation
- People identify and mitigate issues before they arise
- Adversity leads to action, not demotivation

In this state, everyone works from a place of motivation, drive and mutual support. Innovation and creativity are the norm and the work becomes immersive and energizing. In my experience, this is where most organizations and their leaders strive to be.

In assessing your organization, do you know your level of Leader Endorsement Effect? Is it where you want it to be?

The **Leader Endorsement Effect**™ now guides all the work I do. It allows me to help leaders be their best, as they discover their current state and get clear about how they'll move to their desired state. Many choose to discover their **People Fueled Advantage**™, which uncovers their team's unique signature and acts as a true catalyst to the Elevating State. By developing in 3 interconnected facets; Agility Mobilizer, Culture Mobilizer and Performance Mobilizer, leaders overcome challenges in agility, resilience and performance and break through poor communication and ineffective people practices. When developed together, these 3 facets strengthen teams at the foundational level.

Working with me to identify his **Leader Endorsement Effect**™ state and develop his **People Fueled Advantage**™, my client Syed built a robust framework of deep connection and collaboration with his team, who have now crushed every goal they've set. My client Trish found clarity on how she'll reach the Elevating state which has been elusive for years. For Kira, it was the footing she needed to build her strategies and efforts on a solid foundation, not on sand. She got to her Elevating state by uncovering the hidden potential, talents, competencies and aspirations already inside her organization. It's what we're outside celebrating right now on this beautiful Spring day.

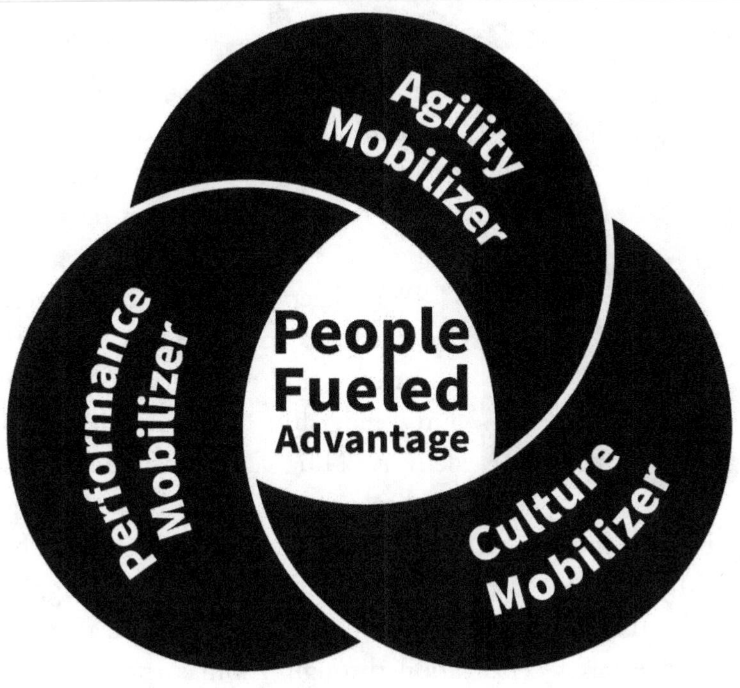

Would you like to explore your Leader Endorsement Effect™ and discover your People Fueled Advantage™? Please visit www.bluheliumconsulting.com or email info@blueheliumconsulting.com. I'd love to hear about your big aspirations!

Nina Penner

Nina is a highly successful coach, facilitator, consultant and speaker who has worked with over 2000 executives, leaders and entrepreneurs across the globe.

With deep knowledge in the areas of 360 feedback, psychometric consulting, executive and leadership coaching and leadership program design and delivery, Nina consistently helps clients to discover and enhance their unique capabilities, engage their passion and perform at their best. Nina is a Mental Fitness coach who holds her CTDP designation from the Institute for Performance and Learning and carries her Certified Analyst certification through Thomas International in the areas of emotional intelligence and behavioral styles.

Using her signature Leader Endorsement Effect™ and People Fueled Advantage™, Nina helps ambitious leaders to shift how they lead so they can fully engage their teams, lead sustainable, positive change and forge new paths to success and thriving. Nina's clients enjoy a deeper love of their work, consistently performing at their best and energetically attaining accelerated results for their organizations.

www.linkedin.com/in/ninapenner
www.blueheliumconsulting.com
info@blueheliumconsulting

26

Breaking Through
the Assumption Barrier
– Reg Charney

Assumptions

You make a lot of assumptions. But so do I. And that's OK when we are talking about basic stuff that you and I do every day. My assumption is that someone is reading this right now. But this assumption is not so basic, and it may not be true. It is my belief that assumptions are a hazard to your health and business when they do not match reality. I am assuming that you believe this too. The trick is identifying when an assumption is safe and when it is not. But there is one property of assumptions that is true – making assumptions about complex issues are most often unsafe. So, this chapter is all about recognizing assumptions, barriers and breaking through them to see reality more clearly, giving you a real chance at achieving your goals and becoming more successful.

Limiting Assumptions

Many of our assumptions limit what we think we can do in our business and professional lives. I call these limiting beliefs Assumption Barriers.

There is another especially important property of assumptions which limits us. We believe we are our assumptions. So, when someone expresses an opinion that is contrary to ours, we take it as a criticism of us personally. Then to justify our opinions, we use "facts" that we believe are true to support our point of view. And around these facts are other assumptions that we make. These assumptions are used to protect our ego.

In business, real life shows us the error of our ways by costing us time, money, and often damaging our image. If we are prepared to risk our ego, then we can break through the various assumption barriers that limit us.

How to Break Assumption Barriers to Develop a More Realistic World View

Assumption barriers exist in almost every direction. It's natural to want to be right. Our human tendency is towards confirmation bias, meaning we subconsciously seek out and easily accept information which confirms our assumptions as "proof" which validates our point of view, and thus ourselves.

Meanwhile, we often overlook the information which contradicts our assumptions that would force us to re-evaluate our worldview. By arbitrarily rejecting this added information, we put ourselves at a disadvantage because we often can't make truly informed business decisions.

To really break through the Assumption Barrier, we need to get feedback and advice from unbiased sources in the relevant fields.

Choosing the Right Expert

Before moving back to Toronto I worked in Silicon Valley. It was a terrific place to work since I am a system designer and serial entrepreneur. But after being away from Toronto for a long time, many of my former contacts here were gone. This left me at a loss for how to find the resources I needed to begin my next business venture.

Has this situation ever happened to you. If so, there were plenty of places you could go to find people. Nowadays, there is LinkedIn, forums, blogs, and networking events. There are all sorts of experts on these sites. But there is the question, of all the potential candidates, how can you find the right person for you. And when you do find them, how can you ensure that these experts are unbiased, with no hidden agenda?

My future business success, and I assume yours, depended on finding a way of differentiating between experts, because if I made a mistake, my budget would be blown, and I would not be able to continue.

Finding the right person often depended on their personality. All the people who claimed to be the experts I needed were able to provide good testimonials, but I was still left wondering, will their prior work apply to my situation and satisfy my needs?

After a lot of thought, I came to the conclusion that folks like you and me all faced the same problems with limited resources in terms of time, money, and resources. In particular, entrepreneurs and small businesses who have limited resources often face the same set of problems.

How Assumptions Affect Bringing Great Ideas to Market

Small businesses and entrepreneurs often have great ideas but have difficulty bringing them to market successfully. They need to find the right people who do the right thing, the right way, and in the right order. They also need to be unbiased and give you the unvarnished truth.

You probably have several great ideas, but you don't know if they are viable. Experts in relevant fields can help determine this for you. Then, if you decide to proceed, experts can help create an effective plan to bring the products or services to market.

To bring your idea successfully to market, you often need a business plan, marketing plan, pitch and many other marketing materials to help you access the financing, resources, and contacts you need to launch and grow your successful business.

Many people try to create these documents themselves and most of the time they don't work. We are emotionally and intellectually attached to our business ideas. In defending ourselves and our ideas, we use facts that we believe are true as arguments to support our point of view, but often are unproven assumptions.

These assumptions create the wrong mindset. To break the assumption barriers and bring your great idea to market, you will probably need help from experts in the field. When these independent experts help you produce your pitch, marketing plan, and/or business plan, your chances of succeeding are much higher than when you rely only on your assumptions.

EntreBahn Removes Assumptions and Helps Businesses Bring Great Ideas to Market

As I asked myself, what experts can I get? How do I know that Expert A is better than Expert B?

How to get the right advice from the right experts is a huge problem for entrepreneurs and small businesses who have limited resources. I discovered that no one was providing a solution to this problem.

That is why I designed EntreBahn, a unique software platform to help businesses bring their great ideas to market, by connecting them with the right people who do the right thing in the right way and in the right order.

It costs a lot less to review and revise documents and plans before launching, than to go to market and have the thing blow up in your face. Going to market with the wrong thing or in the wrong way is very costly in money spent, time taken, and opportunity lost.

A badly launched campaign or pitch that goes nowhere. Even worse, a bad pitch burns out the individual that you've given the pitch to. That person won't want to listen to you again. This can be especially damaging to entrepreneurs or small businesses who often have limited people they can pitch to or approach for information, or advice or funding.

Using Objective Criteria to Determine Readiness for Market

EntreBahn connects entrepreneurs with experts who can measure each plan or pitch submitted using objective criteria and get a weighted average which indicates a readiness (or not) for the market.

The expert can also provide unbiased feedback and advice on each submission. Feedback means experts will comment on what has already been done and how it was done (in the past). Advice is in regard to what to do next and how to do it (in the future).

EntreBahn provides a checklist of objective criteria to the experts. The checklist includes a rating of how well the entrepreneur did and comments on why they got the rating they did. Comments are optional to ensure that only helpful information is included and not just filler. The expert also has the ability to add a subjective opinion on the whole document. They may comment on overall flow and effectiveness.

For example, a sales pitch requires identification of audience pain points, who the target market is, what the solution is and the call to action.

The objective criteria vary by material submitted and the intended audience. A pitch, CV, and business plan will each have a different checklist which includes anywhere from ten to fifty items of criteria. A business plan will also have different objective criteria depending on whether it is intended for internal use, or application to a financial institution or pitch to angel investors or venture capitalists.

Each type of document has a series of one or more objective criteria to accomplish the entrepreneur's goal. These criteria are used to calculate a computed weighted objective average which represents how well the document achieves the goal. This objective average is independent of personal views.

Ensuring Objective Criteria from the Experts Meets EntreBahn's C.A.R.E. Criteria

EntreBahn's unique C.A.R.E. Criteria is an objective criterion used to measure the feedback provided to each client on each project from each expert. All expert feedback must fulfill the following requirements.

- **C**lear and understandable
  - Feedback will not include jargon or convoluted terminology
- **A**pplicable to the area about which we are talking
- **R**elevance to the submission provided to reviewer

- Executable by the client

  - Actionable, practical, and within the scope of what the client can do (e.g. don't tell me spend $100,000 on marketing if my budget is only $1,000)

Like all of the objective criteria, the C.A.R.E. criteria has a rating between 1 and 10. Why a rating is given may be explained in the form of comments. Every reviewer has a different point of view. This is both allowed for and given credence.

Each client can ask for multiple reviewers. I always suggest a client request three reviews. All reviewers use the same objective criteria. Each expert will give different advice and feedback. This allows the client to decide what feedback is most appropriate and which expert, if any, they may want to work with in future.

4 States of Readiness for Market

Your business is in one of the four states of readiness for the market. You need independent expert advice in the first three states to help you get to the fourth state.

1. Start-up State

In the start-up state, most entrepreneurs have no business background and no idea of how to bring their product or service to market. At this stage, you need a lot of help to create the material you need such as detailed instructions, how to's and templates.

2. Obscure State

In this state, your business may be up and running but you're not making any headway. You are still a small business who wants to grow. At this stage, you will benefit from the opportunity to have your material reviewed by one or more experts at the same time and compare the results.

3. Competitive State

In this state, you are raking in the money but not making headway against competition. You find it difficult to penetrate the market or innovate. You will benefit from specific guidance to leverage your business strengths and improve your weaknesses. Take advantage of the opportunity to revise your material and have the experts re-review it for additional feedback and advice.

4. Branded State

Your business is large and well known. People come to you regardless of what they do or don't know about you because of what they know about the brand. You are now branded as the expert in your field.

Let the Experts Do Their Thing

Your chance of success is much higher when you can access independent expert feedback and advice from multiple experts in the same subject and field. These experts operate within the structured process to quickly provide reviews, within 72 hours. The client picks which one is of value to them.

In order to ensure an unbiased environment, EntreBahn does not take advertising. Every reviewer has a different point of view, which the platform allows for and gives credence to. The expert's profile includes which industries they've served and their relevant experience.

When doing a review or revision, especially revision, the client knows, likes and trusts you. The relationship often leads into a long-term meaningful business relationship. EntreBahn hands ideal prospects to the expert free of charge. Those experts are in a position to do the work much more quickly because of the objective criteria checklist that EntreBahn provides. If the client is satisfied, the probability is high to get hired by that client for something else in the near future.

The EntreBahn platform is ideal for experts working from home or in transition. EntreBahn is well designed to help experts who are stuck at home with the pandemic or in transition to connect with clients and generate work.

Challenge What You Think You Know to Break Through the Assumption Barrier

When we start out with assumptions that we don't know are bad and we continue to work with those assumptions, and they don't match reality, then we're guaranteed to fail. Most businesses fail within the first year. Of the remaining number, half will be gone at the end of five years. After ten years, half again are gone.

When we base our business only on our own knowledge and assumptions, we may have a blind spot, or may not have thought of something. Different experts provide different world views which challenge your initial assumptions and may prove those assumptions wrong.

There is no other secure, opt-in platform with a structured review process that allows you to put material out for simultaneous reviews using the same set of criteria.

Leverage expert feedback and advice to get past the point where you don't know what you are doing, and your assumptions don't reflect reality. Objective advice from experts is risk avoidance which enables you to go to market with a higher degree of success.

Don't waste your very limited resources. Get expert help for your small business. Break the assumption barrier that's standing between you and your business success.

Reg Charney

CEO and Co-Founder, EntreBahn

Reg is a serial entrepreneur who thinks differently. He has developed products, often ahead of his time, and contributed to the business community in the innovative products he has designed, developed and sold worldwide.

27

Harmony in Leadership? – On Becoming an ECO Harmony Leader – Dr. Renata Buziak

There is an intrinsic relationship between nature, harmony, productivity and leadership.

Our connection with nature evokes positive emotions and governs our individual physical, emotional and mental wellbeing, resulting in feelings of peace and happiness. Whether the connection to nature is direct or indirect, the advantages to human health are extensive and provide us with 'cognitive, affective, and behavioral benefits' (Ballew & Omotto, 2018). There is a significant relationship between levels of engagement and productivity and feelings of fulfilment and satisfaction (Nekula, 2021). Consequently, emotional responses introduce passive associations towards a space or an occupation. *The potential for Harmony.*

This chapter is about human connection to nature and how you as a leader can create an environment that is connected to nature. Mark Miller, business leader and author of *Win the Heart: How to Create Culture with Full Engagement,* expands on supporting the cultivation of human wellbeing through prioritising our environment:

> As leaders, we have an opportunity to help people find meaning and purpose in their work. We can create a place where they can bring their best selves to work every day. The workplace we create determines, to a large extent, how engaged someone is at work. (Miller, 2019: 2)

In an environment that nurtures wellbeing, people can feel the positive and creative energy that gives them a sense of belonging and care. Therefore, providing this environment becomes a leadership obligation of great importance and priority. *Harmony via leadership.*

Further, Miller emphasises that the four cornerstones that foster effective leadership for engaging employees are connection, affirmation, responsibility, and environment. The philosophy behind this is that our 'Engagement = Level of Care.' The environment we create is a pillar that will support others. As Miller continues, "If we want people to genuinely care deeply" about their work, co-workers, the workplace and the natural environment, then "we have to create the right environment" (Miller, 2019: 6).

How can we create and provide environments that are engaging, that foster creativity and productivity, and that motivate deep care?

Biologist Edward O. Wilson proposed the *biophilia* hypothesis, which focuses on the love of nature and the inclusion of elements of nature within our environments for human wellbeing and creativity (Kellert & Wilson, 1993). Whether it is at home, in an office, home office or in an academic setting, nature influences our level of care and attention (Chowdury, 2021).

From prehistoric to contemporary times, the natural environment has provided a source of inspiration for human creative expression. This has been my direct experience; nature has been the fundamental source of inspiration for my life's work and research. In my early childhood in Poland, I was collecting medicinal plants with my mother and my grandmother from the meadows while enjoying the beauty of the colorful local wildflowers. We then used these plants to make home remedies, such as a strong, sweet cough syrup and very unpleasant herbal tinctures. This life in a harmonious environment—where my passion for nature and photography grew and where I felt creative, inspired and engaged—continued until my husband and I, a young, just married couple with a newborn, decided to emigrate from politically and economically torn Poland. As soon as we landed in Australia, the reality hit us: no language, no experience and no grandparents to help. The life as I knew it ceased to exist and I was lost. After too long, I went back to what I knew best: nature and photography. However, as the flora in my new country was foreign to me, this journey of connecting to a place was challenging. My deepest purpose always is to return to the root of all things—nature—and then to inspire this desire in others, along with encouraging them to further examine and get closer to their surrounding flora.

To this end, I developed a method of image-making called 'the biochrome process,' one that calls attention to the interrelationship between Science and Art. This process captures the beauty of plants during their transformative cycle of life. The method involves a fusion of organic and photographic materials, where I allow plants to lead my creative process, presenting the striking beauty of flora in its cyclic stages of decomposition as 'biochrome art' (Figure 1). In addition to the overall healing energy of the natural environment that surrounds us, the specific plants I work with often contain certain therapeutic properties, and discovering these encompasses a large part of my research into the different plant types according to their habitats. Over the years, I learned the language, how to research and network, I collaborated with communities, artists and scientists and helped others to reconnect with the natural environment. My work then culminates in the sharing of the healing power of nature across the many different environments, as discussed in my doctoral dissertation (Buziak, 2015).

Figure 1. Renata Buziak, *Centella asiatica… anti-inflammatory…*, Archival pigment print on paper, 66.7 x 95cm, 2015.

Since early 2005, I have contributed my expertise as an artist, researcher and educator to individuals and companies that are determined to rebuild their surroundings in an impactful way. This next section provides direct examples of how connection with nature can be enhanced through biochrome art.

Case studies

Cheryl's story

Cheryl Desha – End-user Coordinator, Griffith University

When I met Cheryl Desha at a function in 2018, she was already familiar with my biochrome artworks through mutual colleagues, and she asked if I would be interested to work with her on a new academic building she was overseeing the construction of—the Engineering Technology and Aviation building (N79) located at Griffith University's Nathan Campus in Brisbane. Inspired by the local Toohey Forest, familiarity with biophilic-inspired design and its benefits for the occupants, Cheryl wanted to bring aspects of nature indoors and connect to a local story. However, due to restrictions in planning and infrastructure, Cheryl was in search of a biophilic-inspired design without the integration of living plants.

As the building design was in its developing stages, Cheryl was faced with the problem of what to do with the multitudes of transparent glass walls that would surround the staff as they worked. It felt to her and her colleagues that they would be working in a fishbowl, experiencing an unpleasant atmosphere of feeling 'observed' from the outside. Another option, that of applying opaque frosting to cover all the glass panels, would result in a feeling of detachment from the space, other occupants, and nature outdoors. Cheryl was very familiar with both outcomes, and both were undesirable.

Her end goal was to provide a sense of safety and privacy for students and faculty members in the office and teaching spaces. We considered the functionality of the space and decided that without having to undergo any structural changes, the biochrome artwork could be installed onto the glass panels. This could be achieved easily with the use of affixed translucent elements, instead of framed pieces of art on walls. This concept incorporated the required sense of familiarity, safety, and privacy. Using biochrome art, we were successful in simulating a biophilic design without the drawback of needing ongoing maintenance (Figures 2 & 3). The relationship between art and science fused in the production of the biochrome art reflected the process of working together in the design of the harmonious environment of what became a space of innovation.

In Cheryl's words:

> *"The artwork provides inspiration for creativity …a similar feeling to when you are outside in the bush and you can see through trees, you can see through the foliage, but you don't experience full visibility of the other person or group. That really has helped us to create these open spaces that feel safe and welcoming."* (Cheryl Desha, 2019, https://youtu.be/hT_j61Pbstk)

Bradford's story

Bradford Lee Walton – writer and film director, Brisbane

I was first called on by Bradford in 2018 to enhance the production set of his short film *5 Moons of Pluto*. The lead character of the story is Piper, an 11-year-old girl who grapples with the recent loss of her mother. Overwhelmed by grief, Piper looks to the infinite possibilities of the cosmos in search for answers. Her

Figure 2. Renata Buziak, Engineering, Technology and Aviation building (N79), Level 3 Reception, Griffith University, Nathan Campus Brisbane, 2020

Figure 3. Renata Buziak, Engineering, Technology and Aviation building (N79), Level 3, Griffith University, Nathan Campus Brisbane, 2020

father, an artist, is the motivation behind the artisanal theme of this story.

Bradford's plan was to integrate an art form that could fully embody the tone of the film. Entrusted with this mission, I felt compelled to contribute to his vision with the utmost integrity. Working together, we created an environment that would unify the events in the story and enhance the film's thematic connection with the audience. The artwork vocalised the internal struggle of the main character, the burden of her loss and ultimately her reawakening. We introduced several formats and mediums of artwork throughout the film including paper, textiles (Figure 4) and 'work in progress' pieces, which can be seen in the film's darkroom scene. The artwork subtly and cohesively articulated the cycle of life, death, and harmony within the ever-expanding universe: a further example of the interrelationship of art and science.

The world premiere of *5 Moons of Pluto* by the Cleveland Film Company took place on 19 February 2021 in Cleveland, Queensland, Australia. Bradford was left with an appreciation of the emotional power of art beyond the lens.

"There is a complement between your art and the fabric of the cosmos. The fluidity and lucidity of your art just re-inspired that whole aspect of the film." (Bradford Walton, pers. comm., 2021)

Although over the years I have collaborated with artists from diverse disciplines, I had no prior experience in large-scale film production. By the end of production, I understood that the diversity that biochrome art had to offer this film was only a glimpse of the possibilities in which I could apply my techniques and guiding principles.

Through these and other projects, as well as my own journey, I have been able to study the relationship between a setting or workplace and the audience or inhabiting personnel, and how the contributions of biochrome art can deepen this connection. The

Figure 4. Renata Buziak, *Ecological Harmony,* Print on fabric,
50 x 180cm, 2019.

fusion of nature, art and interior design strengthens the underlying themes unique to each audience and place of work.

I analysed the process I had been navigating for decades and observed the methodical steps wherein these principles that I was applying could be universally applied. From these observations, I formulated the **ECO Harmony Blueprint**, an essential guide to developing intuitive leadership skills and fostering harmonious **ECO** environments in any setting or location.

The ECO Harmony Blueprint™

The ECO Harmony Blueprint is your guide for growth. It is a step-by-step tool designed to navigate you into exploration of the overall experience of occupants and audiences, working and participating in the spaces you provide for them, through art, science, and research. The ECO Harmony Blueprint includes evaluations, workshops, planning, resources and more, all within these four steps:

- Touchpoints
- Current environment
- Theme and premise
- Task management

Where to begin, though? How might you apply this method?

Prior to being guided through these steps, and to navigate the Blueprint with precision, you will first need to determine where you are on the ECO Harmony Compass (Figure 5).

What is the ECO Harmony Compass™?

The *ECO Harmony Compass* is a self-assessment tool which helps you identify your current stage in the journey to becoming an ECO Harmony Leader, who can create a harmonious environment with confidence, implementing biophilic design. By navigating the *ECO Harmony Compass*, you will gain insight as to how your employees, students, or visitors perceive their surroundings, and your ECO Harmony leadership.

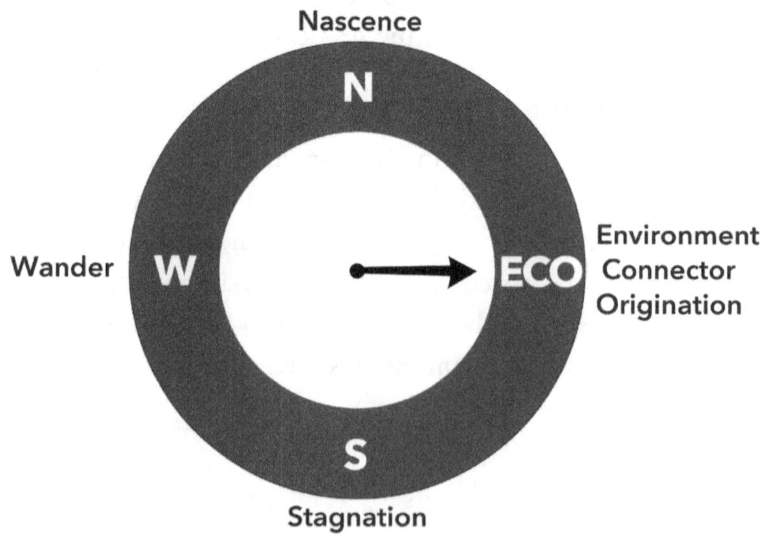

Figure 5. Renata Buziak, ECO Harmony Compass™.

The four stages of the ECO Harmony Compass:

Stagnation

In this first stage, you will notice feelings of resistance and disengagement by the occupants. The confines of your surroundings may be restricting you from moving your ideas forward. You don't know what to do, so you do nothing.

Wander

In this second stage, you are experimenting with multiple options to re-shape your environment. You sense a lack of purpose and direction, leading you and your employees/participants to unsettled feelings of frustration/distress and chaos.

Nascence

In this third stage, you are beginning to channel your focus in a direction with great potential, but you don't know how to apply your ideas on improving the environment and how long it might take to implement them.

ECO

In this fourth and final stage, you have recognised that the expansion of the human experience can occur in an inclusive re-energised environment. You have an appreciation of the symbiotic partnership between a space and its occupants, and have transformed it into an organisational ecosystem where harmony and cooperation flourish.

Bridging the gap

Many leaders find themselves trapped in an undesired stage on the ECO Harmony Compass. The driving motivators for change are surprisingly the same forces that are holding you back. The three culprits are:

1. *Personal experience* – A bad experience of an unhealthy and unproductive environment.
2. *Book-learned knowledge* – Theoretical education and experience on the impact of the work environment on wellbeing.
3. *Negative criticism* – Complaints about workplace conditions.

Can you relate to one or more of these? One immediate solution to break out of these unproductive cycles and to plan your next course of action is the *ECO Harmony Blueprint*. The Blueprint is a key component in the reassessment of your harmonious leadership strategy.

How can I grow my ECO Harmony status?

Simply put, you will grow your ECO Harmony status by adopting the ECO Harmony Blueprint. Through embracing the assets in this Blueprint, you will discover the critical areas of leadership that require your particular attention. Addressing these areas will elevate your ECO Harmony status as you move to the most ultimate stage of the Compass, the ECO stage.

As the ECO, you are the *Environment Connection Originator.* You will have the capabilities and preparedness to promote a harmonious environment in which your employees and audiences can thrive. Creativity, productivity, motivation, and engagement are all sustained through surroundings that nourish individual wellbeing.

Studies show that positive emotions can broaden one's sense of possibility, and directly influence comprehension abilities, judgement, behavior, and focus (Chowdhury, 2021). By associating emotions of joy and contentment within their professional lives, your employees, participants or clients will feel cared for, and will in turn be more thoughtful in their approach to their work, their workspaces, and their colleagues (Miller, 2019). Your visitors and audiences will be drawn to this environment; they will leave wanting to return and revisit your space.

The Challenge

I therefore challenge you to begin this journey by taking an open-minded tour through your own environment, noting the behavior and body language of those around you.

- What kind of emotions and sensations might they be feeling as a product of the environment?
- What emotions and sensations are you experiencing?

Finally, *how can you grow as an ECO Harmonious Leader?*

The answer is to pose these questions with clear intent to yourself and accept the valued feedback from your fellow supporters. Completing this challenge will sharpen your understanding of your working/learning environment, and help you assess which stage of the ECO Harmony Compass you are currently in.

Questions?

How might the ECO Harmony Blueprint benefit you and your organisation? To explore the possibilities, please visit ecoharmonycompass.com and download the ECO Harmony Compass self-assessment tool or email me at renata@ecoharmonycompass.com

References

Ballew MT & Omotto AM, (2018), Absorption: How Nature Experiences Promote Awe and Other Positive Emotions, *Ecopsychology* Vol. 10, No. 1., https://www.liebertpub.com/toc/eco/10/1

Buziak, R (2015) *Biochromes: Perceptions of Australian medicinal plants through experimental photography* (Doctoral dissertation). Queensland College of Art, Griffith University, Brisbane.

Chowdhury, M R (2021), *The Positive Effects of Nature on Your Mental Well-Being*, PositivePsychology.com. https://positivepsychology.com/positive-effects-of-nature/

Kellert, S R and Wilson, E O (eds) (1993) The Biophilia Hypothesis, Island Press, Washington, DC

Miller, M (2019) *Win the Heart: How to create culture with full engagement*, Barrett-Koehler Publishers.

Nekula P, Koob C (2021) Associations between culture of health and employee engagement in social enterprises: A cross-sectional study. PLoS ONE 16(1): e0245276. https://doi.org/10.1371/journal.pone.0245276

Dr. Renata Buziak

Dr. Renata Buziak, ECO Harmony Guide, is a biochrome artist, researcher and educator working at the nexus of art and science in close relationship with nature. Her research is based in plant life and photography, which she learned and taught at Griffith University and other institutions. By bending the rules of traditional photography where she let the photographic materials interact with organic matter Renata developed her process of creating art, which she calls the biochrome, that helps her, and others connect with nature. Renata's biochromes have been displayed in solo and group exhibitions, nationally and internationally. She has received a number of awards for her work, and it is featured in private and public collections. Renata's innovative process led her to work with homeowners, business owners and leaders to help enhance the experience of their spaces in Harmony with the natural world. Currently, as the ECO Harmony Guide, she takes her clients on a journey of becoming ECO Harmony Leaders.

Websites:
renatabuziak.com
ECOharmonycompass.com

28

Unleash your Genius
and Superpower Within
– Simone Hoa

Genius is 1% talent and 99% percent hard work.

Albert Einstein

We often hear people talking about popular genius minds like Alexander Graham Bell, Thomas Edison, the Wright Brothers, Albert Einstein, Walt Disney, Steve Jobs, just to name a few. But how about discovering ordinary people with ordinary genius minds like you and me! Is it possible that we can also have a Genius mind and some Superpower that can have a massive impact on people's lives and make a big difference in the world?

I definitely think and believe so, don't you?

For me, all human beings on this earth are born with these two super extraordinary powers inside of us, and yet, very few of us are even conscious of their existence, let alone exploit them to benefit others and ourselves.

What I would like to share here is my own interpretation of the human genius mind and superpower applied in the context of my own career as a personal and business development coach. I discovered by operating my business from my GSP, i.e., Genius and Superpower zone wisely and smartly, I can impact my ideal clients' life, career and/or business with fast concrete transformational results in sales and cash flow. Not only I can help them ease their financial stress, but also create a profitable growing business doing what they love.

My humble intention in this chapter is to show you, our readers, and hopefully your family and friends, how to find and benefit from these two superhuman powers that can absolutely change our life, career and/or business for the rest of our life without question.

"HOW TO FIND YOUR GENIUS AND SUPERPOWER"

To help you to understand and find these two super strengths in a human being, I have separated them into two vital elements with different faculties to simplify the process of their discovery as follows:

"The Genius thinks while the Superpower feels" Simone Hoa.

- Genius deals with the mind, i.e., the mental part, i.e., your brain. Its job is to create the Solution for your ideal client's pain.

- Superpower deals with the heart, i.e., the emotional part: what pain are you addressing to ease or even eliminate with the result of your solution that your client will pay for?

- Both Genius and Superpower are working together like a couple, they exist together, to help your ideal clients with their "children," which are information products, tools, programs, workshops, meditations, retreats, events, bootcamps … you offer to ease your client's pain.

FIND YOUR GENIUS

So, what is genius? What is the simplest definition of genius from a dictionary?

1. Definition of Genius

   - A person who is exceptionally intelligent or creative, either generally or in some particular respect.
   - Somebody with an "exceptional" natural capacity of:
     - Intellectuality
     - Creativity
     - Originality in a particular field
     - Innovation
     - Or with other natural abilities

A Genius is a very smart person with great intellectual capabilities who is also willing to challenge the status quo and prevalent thinking to come up with new ideas, concepts …

2. How to find your genius?

   - Analyze your background: personal & professional. It can even go back to childhood if applicable.
   - Look at your professional experience in what you are doing from when you started until now & identify the following:

- What comes natural to you as a talent, competence, or skill in what you do everyday?
- What are you also passionate about?
- What seems easy for you to talk about it, teach it & help other people with it?
- What don't you have to be motivated to do it: you just do it & can spend hours doing it without feeling the time passing by?
- What don't you need to focus on: you just do it?
- What is your most valuable competence/skill that allows you to charge premium prices?
- What makes you stand out as the brand in your field and the "Go To" expert that attracts your Ideal client?
- What massive results do you deliver to your clients?
- What generates repeat business for you?
- What makes clients look for you instead of you looking for clients?
- What makes your clients refer you to their friends, colleagues, and contacts?

3. Personal characteristics of a Genius:

8 Personality Traits of Highly Intelligent People (Backed by Science):

The scientific reasoning behind some of the personality traits that smart people share.

1. They are highly adaptable.

Intelligent people are flexible and able to thrive in different settings: they adapt by "showing what can be done regardless of the complications or restrictions placed upon them." Recent psychological research supports this idea. Intelligence depends on being able to change your own behaviors to cope more effectively with your environment, or make changes to the environment you are in. (I have watched a documentary film on Albert Einstein life, and he was a such a person.)

2. They understand how much they do not know.

The smartest folks can admit when they are not familiar with a particular concept. As Jim Winer writes, intelligent people "are not afraid to say: 'I don't know.' If they do not know it, they can learn it."

3. They have an insatiable curiosity.

Albert Einstein reportedly said, "I have no special talents, I am only passionately curious."

Or, as Keyzurbur Alas puts it, "Intelligent people let themselves become fascinated by things others take for granted."

Research published in 2016 suggests there is a link between childhood intelligence and openness to experience -- which encompasses intellectual curiosity -- in adulthood.

Scientists followed thousands of people born in the U.K. for 50 years and learned that 11-year-olds who had scored higher on an IQ test turned out to be more open to experience at 50.

4. They are open-minded.

Smart people don't close themselves off to new ideas or opportunities. Hammett writes that intelligent people are «willing to accept and consider other views with value and broad-mindedness,» and that they are "open to alternative solutions."

At the same time, smart people are careful about which ideas and perspectives they adopt.

5. They like their own company.

It has been observed that highly intelligent people tend to be "very individualistic."

Interestingly, recent research suggests smarter people tend to derive less satisfaction than most people do from socializing with friends.

6. They have high self-control.

Zoher Ali writes smart people are able to overcome impulsiveness by «planning, clarifying goals, exploring alternative strategies, and considering consequences before they begin.»

Scientists have found a link between self-control and intelligence. In one 2009 study, participants had to choose between two financial rewards: a smaller payout immediately or a larger payout at a later date.

Results showed that participants who chose the larger payout at a later date -- i.e., those who had more self-control -- generally scored higher on intelligence tests.

The researchers behind that study say one area of the brain -- the anterior prefrontal cortex -- might play a role in helping people solve tough problems and demonstrate self-control while working toward goals.

7. They're really funny.

Advita Bihani points out highly intelligent people tend to have a great sense of humor.

Scientists agree. One study found people who wrote funnier cartoon captions scored higher on measures of verbal intelligence.

Another study found professional comedians scored higher than average on measures of verbal intelligence.

8. They're sensitive to other people's experiences. Smart people can "almost feel what someone is thinking/feeling," says He.

Some psychologists argue that empathy, being attuned to the needs and feelings of others and acting in a way that is sensitive to those needs, is a core component of emotional intelligence. Emotionally intelligent individuals are typically very interested in talking to new people and learning more about them.

This material is quoted from Business Insider.

"FIND YOUR SUPERPOWER"

1. Definition of Superpower

This is my own simplified definition of Superpower for us to remember and use it in a normal situation rather than in a "super special" one: it is your dominant gift — an attribute, skill, or ability that is stronger than the rest.

I will also add that if exploited with a good intention and a significant purpose, Superpower is used to create Influence to achieve Impact: the more massive of an impact you can create with your Superpower, the more Power you have over your competitor and you can Dominate your target market effortlessly.

2. How to find your Superpower

Let me first remind you of One very important thing Not To Do: do not Copy somebody else's Superpower: find your Own based on what has been used successfully to you and your past Best accomplishment/s. This is where your advantage lies.

Ask yourself these important questions to uncover your dominant strengths.

1. What feels effortless?

Think about the activities in which you are completely focused, and it's easy to get to a place of peak performance. For some, this might be presenting. For others, it might be solving very complex analytical problems. Look for the **areas in which you excel without much effort**—what's the "gift" you continuously are using? Those are likely indicators of your strongest abilities.

Think of something that you get into the Flow Zone with–what they call peak performance zone, where you lose track of time, it just feels so good, you feel like you are One Entity with what you are doing. What sets your soul on fire? This is my own experience with my Flow zone to discover my superpower during the pandemic time. I like to suggest that you should create a Routine for yourself, whether it's a morning or evening routine. Mine is a morning one, to create this Flow zone for yourself to discover slowly but surely your superpower, guaranteed!

2. How do you amaze others?

What do people come to you for? Have you been told repeatedly that you are good at something? Do people seek you out to give advice or help them with certain projects? This type of feedback and request for assistance could indicate where your superpowers lie.

What is being said around you by other people? That includes everything from casual comments to performance reviews. Sometimes, it is helpful to ask trusted collaborators or mentors about where they see your most dominant strengths.

3. What makes you so willing to sacrifice?

Superpowers are a strong fusion of Passion and Mastery: Passion is not just in a way that makes you happy, but in a way that motivates you and makes you want to do more, even if it means hard work or other sacrifice.

For example, a nurse might say they love the clinical aspect of taking care of patients, even though it can be difficult, time-consuming work. But, instead, it makes them want to learn more and do their job better. Ask yourself: What are you doing when you have that deep interest that makes you want to do things better? This is a good indication of where your superpower lies.

I heard on the Radio Canada station last week women nurses in Brazil, a country that has been affected significantly by the pandemic, continue to work tirelessly, day & night without being paid as the country is in serious recession, because they simply cannot not continue to help and save their fellow country men and women from this deadly crisis.

4. When are you fearless?

Think back over your work and other experiences to where you were most confident. Are there times when you felt comfortable and confident enough to take measured risks and stretch your abilities? That comfort level is a sign that you have a true strength in that area. You believe in that true strength and continue to push hard to achieve something significant to help or contribute to a team, or to a cause: this is also an indicator to point you towards your superpower.

5. What can you see more clearly than others?

In any given situation where there is a challenge to overcome, the person who can see the situation beyond where it will be, is the one who can and will find a solution to the problem. How can a change in CEOs in a company that is losing its direction like a sinking ship save the ship from sinking? It is because the new CEO can see much beyond the actual state of the company and knows what to do to change the situation. Such CEOs are those like Jack Welsh who is a Genius with unique unrivalled superpowers.

I also like to use the word Insight for such situations: businesspeople with insight power are usually very successful people. Entrepreneurs with superpowers and insights are visionaries that become "Legends" in their achievements and leave lasting legacies for generations to come.

The strong message here for us all to learn is that getting Clarity about our strengths can make all the difference in our career, business, and life. The No. 1 thing you can do is determine your strengths, determine your superpowers. Because we are all individuals, and although we are all capable of accomplishing our goals, there is no predetermined way to do that.

Therefore, before we can set our objectives and goals to achieve our vision, self-awareness and understanding Who we are and what we Excel at is the No.1 step in anything we do.

In conclusion, I truly feel it is our duty to discover, unleash and activate our Genius and Superpower to first change our life, career and/or business, and then help other people do the same so that we can all live our best life with passion and purpose, making money doing what we love.

I don't think there is a better way to live a happy, fulfilled, abundant life serving humanity and leaving a legacy for generations to come at the same time.

Simone Hoa

In August 2012, I became a bestselling co-author of the book *"Cracking the Success Code"* with Brian Tracy, a multiple international bestseller author of over eighty books that have been translated into 42 languages. I have been wearing my Career Transition and Reinvention coaching hat since 2010 when I founded my company Passion 2Success Corporation. I have been guiding and supporting my unhappy frustrated clients how to transition smoothly and rapidly to a new happy, passionate, fulfilled life with full confidence and a clear vision, doing what they love. The techniques and strategies used were and still are simple, practical, effective, and work with ease and stress free for my clients.

This chapter you are reading is my second contribution to another book with Brian Tracy *"Emerge: Be the Unmistakable Authority in your field"* that makes me feel so honored and grateful. Since 2012, I have added another hat, a most complementary one to my core passion and mission of my coaching career: it's to help coaches, professionals and entrepreneurs … in the knowledge industry, to make an impact in millions of people's life to make a difference in this turbulent world we are currently living and beyond, by exploiting our highest human potential: our Genius and Superpower. I called these two superhuman powers our GSP, not GPS, which have only one supreme job to achieve: to connect human minds, hearts, and spirits to make the world a better place to live.

As a Transformational Personal and Business Development Coach, I empower ambitious mission driven self-employed professionals, entrepreneurs, and business owners shift their business to the next level with more sales and cash-flow, the two most important elements that keep companies alive, by operating their business only from their zone of Genius and Superpower. Then by using Authentic Selling from the heart to offer their services. The results delivered are transformational, fast and concrete to save their clients' time and money.

My services include public speaking, virtual experiential training with interactive workshops, group and personalized coaching, and retreats.

This chapter has a very deep, meaningful and utterly significant place in my heart as it birthed my long-awaited idea and business concept that will become my legacy I like to leave behind for generations to come: the creation of my "Genius Xcelpreneurs Business School" with my concept of "Entrepreneurship Re-imagined" in the Spring of 2023. Follow us on Facebook and/ or LinkedIn to enjoy our blog posts, and discover how you too can live your highest potential by Unleashing your Genius and Superpower and exploit them to live the life you Love!

For more information, go to https://simonehoa.com

My gift to you my readers: a complementary 60mns session of consulting with coaching addressing your current challenges that are blocking you from achieving your goals to live the life you love.

To contact me: simonehoa@passion2success.com

+1 (514) 777 9785

www.linkedin.com/in/simonehoa

29

Return on Influence
– Susan Luke Evans

"It was three o'clock in the morning," he said as he slowly leaned forward in his chair. He began his tale; the room was quiet. All eyes focused on this tall, handsome young man, new to the supervisory ranks of the chemical plant located in the sultry, low country on the southeastern coast of the USA.

He began in an almost hushed voice, "I was out at the back of the plant, hazmat suit and all, testing the level of the water quality in the ponds. I was alone, and it was very dark. As I stepped to the edge of the pond, I stretched my arm out over the edge to complete the test . . . when two glowing, reptile eyes popped up!"

To be continued . . .

What we know is that the goals of successful communication are to influence and persuade as the actual communicator, and to listen as the receiver.

Communication happens orally, visually, and kinesthetically. Those methodologies have common attributes in terms of how communication is given and received. There has been a great deal written, spoken, explained, researched, and repeated, to help us understand why communication is so important to our relationships, organizations, communities, and cultures.

The story is about *Little Timmy*, the infamous alligator that lived in the middle of the chemical plant's pond. Our soft-spoken young man continued: "I suddenly realized that it was just me, my flashlight, the testing material, and *Little Timmy* . . . alone, together, in the dark. I realized that *Little Timmy* wasn't a big alligator. Yet, realistically, I was well aware that even little 'gators have very big and very sharp teeth. Those eyes were sizing me up as his midnight snack. This was definitely not in my best interests," he said.

It was summertime, humid-hot in the interior, windowless room where the group was assembled. You could have heard a pin drop as the story continued. Every person in the room already knew about *Little Timmy*. Many of them could have told a similar story. They all knew that *Little Timmy* had been living in that pond for some time; it was not safe for anyone to be out there alone, especially in the middle of the night. Yet, the pond remained home to *Little Timmy* the alligator. Nothing had been done to remove *Little Timmy*, even after numerous notes in the daily log, and frequent conversations with management. Nothing had been done to change the procedure to ensure the safety of the person responsible for testing the water, especially at that time – during the graveyard shift. It was probably based on the fact there was not a staff member designated as "*Manager of Alligator Removal.*"

The story of *Little Timmy* had emerged as part of a management development program, illustrating a specific concept, chosen by the storyteller. In this instance, our tall, lanky storyteller wanted to illustrate that "the plant" should make changes in unsafe procedures before someone got hurt; "they" should be more proactive in preventing accidents and paying attention to details, rather than waiting for an accident to happen.

How did that story influence those in the training room that day? What was the return on its influence and how did it manifest itself?

Unbeknownst to me, during the break that day, several of the participants got together and took action. They knew there were laws dictating *Little Timmy* could not be killed, so they made a few calls and arranged for *Little Timmy* to go to a better place.

A few days later, sitting in my home office, I received four individual emails from four different participants. They all had the same photo attached, showing *Little Timmy* going to a better place . . .

We have not seen a lot about what the return on influence is, as communicators and leaders. This discussion is NOT "rocket science." It may, however, be a different perspective to help us look at the how and why of what we are doing, and reveal how we can focus that understanding to maximize our return on influence.

The return on a leader's influence is based on five levels. I developed a model, The Influence Pyramid™, based on my observations and experiences as a CEO, and on working with leaders at every level, across industry lines, for 30+ years, on six continents, and in over 50 countries, here's what I've learned:

A leader begins influencing others at the level I call **COMPLIANCE:** this is when employees change how they behave and what they do because you told them to change.

Understand that an employee may NOT exhibit all of these

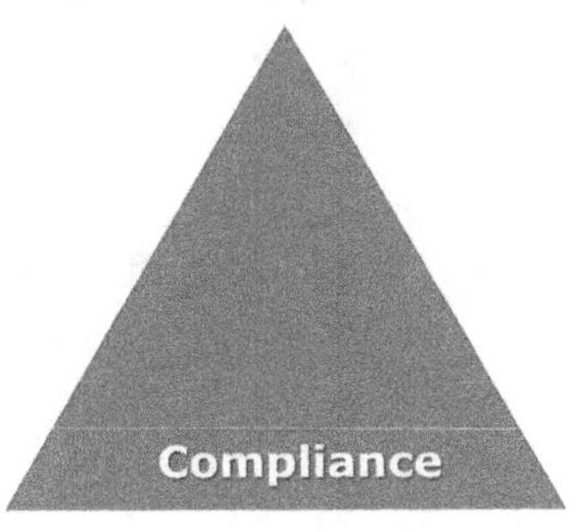

behaviors or characteristics; they usually demonstrate a majority of them.

You know you are influencing at the COMPLIANCE level when:

- People are doing what they should do.
- They're doing things correctly.
- They're punctual. They come to work on time, take breaks on time, for the required amount of time, and they leave on time.
- Typically, they do the bare minimum to get the job done.
- The leader is operating in a supervisory role.
- Looking deeper, we may see that there is little evidence of creative or independent thinking or problem solving.

Those at this level are complying as a BEHAVIORAL response. The important thing to remember is behaviors can change from day to day or sometimes, even minute to minute! Therefore, the influence the leader may provide is definitely good for that moment in time; tomorrow it may not work in the same way!

The second level is what I call the **PARTICIPATION** level: this is when changes are made selectively and_temporarily, based on the way the employee feels about_his/her work, which may change from day to day.

At this level, the leader observes:

- People appear to be more content with their work.
- They are happier and more approachable.

- They care about the outcome of the project or job, but only from the perspective of protecting themselves within the company or the team.

- There may be glimpses of initiative and creative input.

- Employees bring you problems and few, if any, options or solutions.

- Their enthusiasm for the project or the job is somewhat short-lived. Typically, they are great "starters", but often lack follow-through.

- When "stuff happens" they are easily frustrated, often dropping back to the COMPLIANCE level or sometimes below that into a DYSFUNCTIONAL level.

- They are less punctual: perhaps coming in late, leaving early, taking longer breaks and possibly more sick days.

- They are less productive. This happens because of the temporary nature of how they approach the project or job. When things do not happen in the way they should, or in the way they expect them to, they lose their enthusiasm.

- This is all about the NOW and how they feel. They function or participate in the moment.

The term "participation" used in this context refers to increased individual participation at this level; albeit possibly short-lived, there is some initiative taken by these employees.

Those at this level of influence are participating because of how they feel **EMOTIONALLY**. If it's a Good Day – they will typically be enthusiastic and more focused; if it's not, even because of things which may not have anything to do with work, productivity will be less, enthusiasm and cooperation may be non-existent.

The third level is what I call the **BUY-IN** level: This is when the employee contributes to the company because they have changed their mindset about the work they do.

You can recognize those at this level because:

- People's feelings of well-being for and about the project or the overall business are longer term and more sustainable.

- People come to you (the leader) with more options and solutions than problems.

- They have buy-in concerning the overall vision and mission of the organization.

- They understand this is all about getting the job done well and properly.

- They are more consistent and conscientious.

- You can rely on these folks; they rarely let you down.

- Often these are longer-term employees who have been in their position for years.

- They do not appear to have any interest in moving up the corporate ladder or expanding their role in any way.

- They are confident in their ability to do the job and do it well.

Typically, they are at this level of influence for one of two reasons:

1. They genuinely like what they do, they are good at it, and they do not like or want to change; or

2. they do not believe they are able to do more, or they are not confident in their ability to move forward.

- These folks are seen as the "diamonds in the rough" of the organization.
- They have both the skill and the ability to move forward and become leaders going forward.
- They need confidence, mentoring, etc.

We often ignore our "diamonds in the rough" because they always get the job done with little or no assistance. They need to be influenced to believe in their ability to do more and move to the next level.

Those at this level of influence are buying-in because they BELIEVE in the organization and in their ability to do the job as it is today.

The fourth level I call the **LEADERSHIP** level:

This is when the employees change their mindsets based on how they feel about themselves.

You can recognize when you are influencing at the LEADERSHIP level because it "feels" right. What that means is:

- These folks may have become your protegees.
- They may see themselves in your position, or in a similar position in another organization, in the future.

- They have original and creative ideas.
- They can expand on your ideas.
- They may be able to finish your sentences. (That's only creepy when it's "Alexa" completing your sentences ☺.)
- They are truly following in your footsteps (while NOT being underfoot).
- You may sometimes go to them for counsel or guidance.

Those at this level of influence are beginning to act like and be IDENTIFIED within the organization as leaders.

The highest level of influence is what I call the **VISIONARY** level: This is when the leader is influencing people to influence others.

At this level we realize that:

- These people are seen and accepted by others in the organization as leaders.
- Other employees turn to them for guidance.
- They actively work on building things that will outlive their tenure with the organization.
- Their focus is on a better, overall future for the organization.
- They may initiate programs: like community or environmental; not because it's part of their job, but because they're involved in building a LEGACY for the organization.
- They are building something much bigger than themselves.

Those who are at this level of influence are recognized as **LEGACY** builders, in building their individual legacies as well as contributing to the LEGACY of the organization.

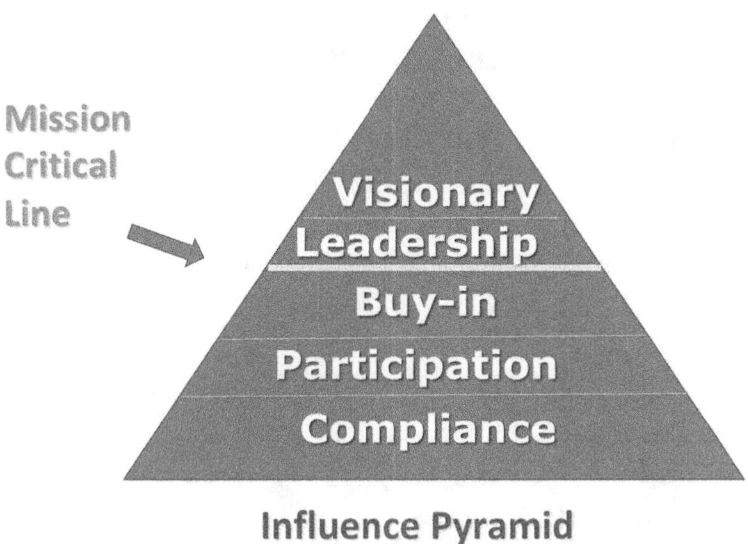

Influence Pyramid

- It defines the difference between the **TEMPORARY** and **SUSTAINABLE** Influence levels.

- Unless a leader is willing to share his/her own identity, his/her influence will always fall short of its potential.

Many leaders are either unaware of, or have not given much thought to, the Mission Critical Line – They:

- Influence to change behavior.
- Inspire to change how others feel.
- Convince others to "buy-in" to the mission and vision.

None of these things are BAD. However, they are considered TEMPORARY, and NOT SUSTAINABLE because the outcomes may not transfer from one project or day to another.

Influencing at the top two levels, **LEADERSHIP** and **VISIONARY**, requires each leader to share some of his/her own **PERSONAL EXPERIENCE** therefore, becoming more sustainable.

In my experience, the best, most powerful way to accomplish that is through living and sharing our own stories, our personal experiences.

There are many different types of "personal experience" stories; they must be personal to the teller's experience, either directly or indirectly.

The important thing to remember is, this is not about using storytelling to achieve a specific desired outcome.

It is about <u>leveraging</u> the <u>power</u> of stories to <u>elevate</u> one's message for <u>greater influence</u>.

Let's go back and set the stage for the *Little Timmy* story. What occurred before that young man raised his hand and told the story of *Little Timmy*?

The leadership team of the chemical manufacturing plant wanted to:

- empower their front-line managers.

- to make changes without having to ask permission or be afraid of retribution. They wanted

- to foster more direct action by the managers

- to have less "administrivia" for the senior leadership team.

- to ensure increased productivity while enhancing the bottom line.

Leadership decided to do this through helping them elevate their messages using stories. They asked me to conduct the session. Front-line managers from all areas of the plant attended the program, from research and development scientists to plant floor operators. It was an eclectic mix of ages, educational levels, ethnic groups, areas of expertise, and tenure within the organization.

The session began with me telling a story about when my son was three years old – not even remotely about business or leadership.

As is often the case when a story is well told, you could have heard a pin drop as everyone leaned forward, eager to hear the story.

Afterwards there was discussion.

- "What made it a good story?"
- "Why was it interesting?"
- "Why are stories important as a communication tool?"
- "What was the structure of the story?"

We debriefed my story to enhance their understanding of the process.

Next, I asked each participant to share one specific concept to be communicated to his/her team that week. I told them, especially the scientists in the room, I didn't necessarily need to understand the concept. Each concept needed to be important and specific for each individual team's respective areas of responsibility, immediately necessary and practical for their teams.

Each participant shared a brief sentence.

"You have 10 minutes to come up with a story to illustrate your point," I said. "It can be an experience from your childhood, about your kids, parents, or grandparents. It can be about sports, about something here at the plant, or a story from some other job you may have had. The frame for your story is only limited by your experience or imagination."

The groans were good-natured. They were used to me (after all, I had my own hard hat, hazmat suit, and size four, steel-toed boots -- which drove the purchasing department nuts). I was considered part of the team, and they were always willing to participate.

As I listened to the chatter in the room, there were a couple of participants who were quite sure they had no stories to tell. I asked them what they had done in the past 24 hours, and they were soon crafting wonderful stories about children's soccer games and an incident during the early shift at the plant. Suddenly they were focused on appropriate, anecdotal narratives, and the "buzz" in the room began to emerge with excitement and positive energy.

After 10 minutes I asked, "Who wants to volunteer first to share your story?"

The tall, handsome, young man with his "just chillin' attitude" -- who always sat in the far left-hand corner of the room, his lanky frame stretched out in his chair -- was the first to raise his hand. You could have knocked me over with a feather as he began in an almost hushed tone . . .

"It was three o'clock in the morning . . ."

Susan Luke Evan

CSP & Global Speaking Fellow. Author of *Return on Influence – the New Currency for Leaders* and *Log Cabin Logic*, she is a leadership consultant and communications expert. She is a dual citizen of the USA & Canada, and lives in Toronto.

Before starting her speaking business, Susan was CEO of a financial services support company.

Her business centers on assisting leaders who want to elevate their messages to create flexible, engaged, and agile workplaces while maximizing their ROI (Return on Influence). She serves clients in over 50 countries on six continents.

Website:	susanlukeevans.com
LinkedIn:	linkedin.com/in/susanlukeevans
Facebook:	facebook.com/susan.lukeevans
Twitter:	twitter.com/susanlukeevans
Instagram:	Instagram.com/susanlukeevans

30

Home Harmony Healing Advantage Nurtures, Balances and Enhances Your Life and Space – Tassia Keeng

Do you believe that your home can and should be a safe place where you can be at peace with yourself, in harmony with your family and in tune with your environment? A haven for rest and relaxation, a sanctuary for growth and healing. A space where you are free to be yourself without judgement, fear, or punishment.

Imagine the space where you live or work lovingly and beautifully designed to support complete wellness for you on every level. I truly believe that, "Home is where the heart is." Each of us has the power to build and create that for ourselves.

You might feel that right now something is missing from your home. Maybe it's a room or area that just doesn't resonate. Maybe you've had parents move in or kids move out and the way you use the space has changed. Maybe you've just made a purchase or renovation and you don't know where to go from here.

When you've experienced challenges in your home, you may not know how to reclaim the space and make it truly yours — to turn it into a space of positivity. You know what you don't want a house to feel like, but you may not be used to thinking about how you do want home to feel.

If that's you, I want you to know that I've been there. I understand. And I can help you reclaim your connection between heart and home.

No Heart in My Home

As a child of 10, my parents relocated the family from my much loved birthplace of England to Singapore. This change negatively impacted my life for at least the next 20 years.

My life was turned upside down into chaos. I now lived with grandparents and other family who were complete strangers to me and in a culture that was uncomfortable and foreign. Every action and movement was restricted. I shared a bedroom with my parents and brother which was a shock after having my own space and privacy. I was not allowed to touch anything, eat what was familiar or even watch TV. I felt like a prisoner on every level.

My parents were emotionally distant, and I often experienced abuse. When they eventually divorced, I had two 'homes.' My father was rarely home and I was miserable in a house with people who I didn't bond with. When he was home, he was abusive. I remember being terrified because I wasn't allowed to lock my door. My father wouldn't knock and would just barge in which was embarrassing for me as a teenager. If he found the door locked, for any reason, I would be severely beaten. This lack of safety, respect, and dignity within my home affected me for a long time afterward.

Things were better with my mother who lived with her family for years till she managed to gain her own apartment. But her trauma from life with my father made her unable to truly connect with me. Her cold, unsupportive apartment never felt like home either.

I yearned to find a place to call my own, without anger or fear. A place where I could feel loved and safe. But when I finally had my own space, I thought, "Now, what the hell do I do with it?" It took me a while but I found my home in Canada and it was here that I figured out how to transform my space into my safe haven.

I now journey with those who desire a happy, healthy home or workplace but have trouble fulfilling that wish. I found that many are unaware of the degree that our space impacts us which is why I created the Holistic Harmony Impact System. My system helps you to assess which one of the four states you are in to guide your next steps.

The first state: Maelstrom.

Your world is in utter chaos and you perceive everything to be going wrong for you. You experience high stress and anxiety from frequent relationship conflict, clutter, accidents, and lack of self care. You are plagued by financial strain, constant fatigue and little to no sense that you can get yourself out of the situation.

The second state: Insular.

You desire change but feel stuck. You feel uncomfortable and disconnected with your space, having tried to put strategies in place but without any positive effect. You need more privacy. Perhaps there is no clear design style or flow, you are financially getting by on a budget and it's okay if you are lacking energy. You live in a world of 'just okay' and you can't get to 'much better'.

The third state: Pedestrian.

You're in your comfort zone and you have convinced yourself that it's enough. You think you've reached good times because everything is acceptable. Your home makes sense and is pleasing enough to your family. Nothing can be perfect, right? You have decent finances, have created healthy living strategies and manage time for self care. But what is lacking is the feeling of joy.

Do you recognise yourself in any of these three states? I've lived in every one of them, sometimes at the same time. But I also realized that I did not want to settle for just 80%. What would living 100% look like?

The fourth state: Nirvana.

Your world is all that you could possibly desire, and more. You feel peace, harmony, and joy with family and colleagues. Your space is designed to fit you like a glove and everything delights you. All areas are utilized with optimal access; all senses are positively stimulated. You manifest abundant health and wealth. You feel complete.

Home Harmony Healing Advantage

Do you feel disconnected with your home? Have you gone through trauma? Or maybe you like your home well enough but there are spaces that are underutilized or just don't work for you. Feeling harmony in the space where you live is very important to your overall health and wellness. I truly believe that your home should delight you.

Which is why I created the Home Harmony Healing Advantage with its 4 intrinsic components. When these 4 elements are combined, they consistently achieve success in bringing about a joyful, healthy, prosperous and peaceful space in your home or professional location. You will move from Maelstrom, Insular, or Pedestrian to the state of Nirvana.

1. Intuitive Compositions
Freedom to dance with your space

I design to delight while creating freedom and flow through your space in harmony with your day, your family, and your life. Let's transform clutter and tripping hazards into safe, logical, intuitive pathways and help you build organizational structures designed around your daily routines and patterns. We create safe access for all, including disability access, without sacrificing design.

Client Story: On opening her new dental clinic, Dr. Salome's foremost concern was to create a space that would be accessible to all patients, many of whom have a physical or intellectual disability. I guided Dr. Salome to transform her clinic within the necessary parameters. For example, she needed physical access for wheelchairs in a very narrow turning space and she needed visual neutrality that didn't trigger anxiety for patients who are on the autism spectrum.

She is now the proud owner of a gorgeous, modern, professional dental clinic, which is also gentle, warm and comforting.

2. Affinity Accords
Energy flow that nourishes you

Applying a combination of math and science, Feng Shui and Energy Cleansing are two of the tools used in the Home Harmony Healing Process to alleviate energetic disruptions and shift the energy to a natural balance. I synergise the energy of each person in the home with the planet's natural energetic vibrations and chemical reactions to enhance personal energy and create a peaceful, restorative space.

Client Story: After his divorce, James moved to a new home where his young daughter stays with him part time. James is a very loving father. But he had suffered from insomnia for more than 10 years and in this new home his insomnia was no better. Based on my calculations, he eliminated EMF (electromagnetic frequency) devices from his bedroom and added the specific elements of metal and wood. He found a bedroom set that he loved which incorporated those two elements. Today, James happily sleeps 6 to 7 hours a day, which gives him bountiful energy and a new take on life. Happy dad, happy daughter.

3. Healthful Harmonizations

Care for your space, care from your space

Create a space that nurtures your physical, mental and emotional health in harmony with your brain and personality to create health, wellness, and self-worth for you and each member of your family. I use environmental psychology, sensory coding, and personality coding to ensure the sensory input in your space does not trigger or overstimulate using what your mind and body already tells you.

Client Story: Melody, busy mother of 4 young children, juggles career and family. With little time for herself, she needed an office space where she could go to focus on work as well as rest. Besides working and trying to look after the children, she was sleeping curled up on a tiny sofa in her old office. She had anxiety attacks because she felt overwhelmed by her space, the children, and no time for herself and her work. With my help, Melody reconfigured her office, breaking it up with white décor and open space.Her office now evokes a complete sense of peace and focus depending on what she needs and she feels like a much better mother who can completely love her children as she loves herself.

4. Prosperity Cultivators

Decrease unnecessary expenditure and increase financial value

Stop spending money on design elements and household items that don't work. Increase the financial value of your space and discover more time to focus on what's important to you, without that looming sense of overwhelm. My Home Harmony Healing Process empowers you to improve your focus and energy and spend your time more efficiently. As a result, your productivity is increased, and your finances are naturally enhanced.

Client Story: Emma had a beautiful, new home, with space for her three beautiful children and a home office, but after eight months, her income was declining. It did not make any sense. To make things more frustrating, her children were having a hard time becoming accustomed to the new home and they had toys and stuff everywhere.

Emma was exhausted and at her wits end! After I worked with her, Emma moved her office to a new area of the house that she had not considered before. By setting up her home office in a totally different way with a complete visual and organizational system that made sense, she managed to add on a desk for another teammate. Emma is now earning triple her previous income and her organization system allows both her and her colleague to move around her home office quickly.

Emma reorganized the play area for the children, with specific zones for toys and books. One child is a visual kinesthetic learner and needed a ton of coloured pens, paper and stuff around for her to learn. The fix? A chalk wall… where she could write and draw to her heart's content. Now, Emma spends less time picking up after her children. Learning to work with her children and respect their different personalities and learning styles enabled her to set up their personal spaces to each child's individual needs.

Home Wellness Design Expertise

I approach design very logically, drawing upon my experience and training in a variety of areas from art to medical science. But design is not just about logic; it's also about the heart. I design intuitively, finding what deeply resonates for you within your space and uncovering that which perhaps you may not even have been aware of.

With the gift of my intuition, I discern your optimal design by talking to all household members, with a respectful, compassionate and gentle approach. I find out how you feel and how you interact with the space, allowing me to speak to the kind of design you need. Through design, I can address whatever is going on underneath the surface of your life situation. If you or a family member who has diverse challenges or special needs, I can create an optimal space that is tailored toward these specific needs.

My intuitive insights and grounded scientific processes, empower my clients with information and choices about their home space. I coach them with tools and strategies to support themselves and achieve their goals independently. My clients experience results that create safe access for all residents, alleviate stress and reduce overstimulation, and transform the space into one which combines the best of logic and emotion, and brings joy to the entire household.

Start Living Well in a Home Harmony Healing Space

It doesn't matter what your background is as long as you desire to feel abundant and well in your home. Not just for you but also for your family.

Maybe you have a home that you don't like but you want it to be like some of the homes you visit, which feel really comfortable and beautiful, but you have no idea how to make it that way.

Maybe you are a parent who wants your family to be healthy and happy. Or you need help to tailor your environment around a family member with special needs or who requires access.

You may live on your own and want a place that is your own solitude, a place that you call your haven. Or you may have two or three generations living in the home with you, including seniors with different needs.

You may have been through trauma or abuse in your life, much as I did. Now that you have your own home, how do you ensure your home does not create triggers? Or like many others, you have gone through a death or divorce, and are now starting a new phase of your life. You may be grieving and find yourself coping alone for the first time in your life.

Perhaps you are neurodivergent or have special needs and struggle to make your space your own. You don't want to feel like you're a burden to somebody else but access is crucial. There is absolutely no reason that your space cannot be beautiful, accessible and trigger free.

No matter what your reasons, I am certain that we are all meant to live our lives happily, peacefully and feeling complete. Nothing else will do. There is always a path that you can travel to get you to that place. I warmly invite you to discover how you can change your life as you transform your space with the Home Harmony Healing process to resonate on every level in complete wellness. Because I believe you completely deserve it.

Tasia Keeng is the founder of Lovelight Home Design Inc., an interior design company that specializes in using Environmental Psychology, Feng Shui and diverse systems of sensory access to design residential and commercial spaces. She is the creator of the Holistic Harmony Impact System and Home Harmony Healing Advantage, plus host of the Inner & Outer Transformation Podcast. As an Interior Designer, Feng Shui practitioner and Intervenor for Deafblind Individuals, she has more than sixteen years' experience facilitating the interaction of people and their environment, be it social, sensory, medical and more. Tasia is the Diamond Winner of the Readers' Choice Awards in the city of Mississauga, Ontario, Canada for her work in interior design and home wellness design. www.lovelighthomedesign.com.

31

The Couples' Financial Intimacy and Pleasure Guide
– Betty-Anne Howard

Money, just like sex, can breed a lot of secrecy, insecurity, and fear. Past indiscretions can catch up with us in surprising ways in both worlds, and irresponsibility can follow us even after we form a lasting relationship.

But what if our money and finances could be a source of pleasure for us? Couples who understand financial intimacy have eliminated the confusion and frustration of planning for their future while living fully for today. For them, financial intimacy means making money decisions together to forge their way to a future that provides them with peace of mind and an enormous amount of pleasure.

Unfortunately, many of us grew up without having healthy attitudes about money or sex modeled for us, so we carry our flawed perspectives on these two essential topics into our relationships, which can take an enormous toll over time.

Even in our modern world, money continues to be treated as taboo, resulting in barriers to couples who want financial intimacy and pleasure. These barriers keep us mired in a conflict that prohibits us from experiencing intimacy in our relationships.

The 4 Barriers To Financial Intimacy and Pleasure

In my forty years of working with couples as a financial life planner, couples counselor, addictions specialist, and sex therapist, I've had extensive first-hand experience with how people communicate and fall in and out of love with each other. Unfortunately, in my work, I often encounter barriers that make it difficult for people to get closer to those they love.

Words Can Separate Us

Within our relationships, we speak different languages! A bold statement considering we likely both speak English, French or Spanish or whatever shared language we use. But our language differences come from our words having very different meanings, depending on our gender, family history, culture, social circle, and life experiences. These differences create challenging communication barriers between us. The meaning we give to the words we use has a profound impact on communicating with each other and understanding and sharing purpose.

Communication Problems

Have you ever heard that the message the receiver receives is rarely the message the sender is sending? This saying epitomizes and summarizes the challenges we face when trying to communicate with each other. In other words, I may be listening attentively to what you're saying; however, I'm also using my filters to interpret what you're telling me, and those filters skew my understanding.

Add to that the emotionally charged topic of money (or sex), and you can see where problems begin, grow, and become complicated.

Relationship Stages

Relationships go through different phases. These phases are a natural process in relationship development, and each stage has specific characteristics associated with that particular point in our relationships.

I'm sure we all remember fondly the attraction stage that kicks off the beginning of a relationship. In this first stage, we see and experience how we share common interests while basking in the glow of sexual experiences that are spontaneous, extremely enjoyable, and easy-going.

The same goes for how we deal with money in this stage; it all seems to work somehow because we're on our best behaviour. Rarely at this stage are we discussing our money mindset, money personalities, and the ways we spend, save, invest or donate the money we earn.

In the next natural stage of relationship development, we begin to see and experience how we're different. As a result, we start to focus more on our boundaries regarding what we talk about, how we talk about it, and what we are and aren't willing to do.

In our society and our families, sex and money are not topics we're comfortable with, so conflicts begin in our relationship. When disputes go to the extreme, a couple becomes more and more polarised in their views and corresponding behaviours. Their arguments about money may have resulted in mounting debts, virtually no savings, and a bleak perspective for their future together. At this point, in the worst-case scenario, they divorce.

In the next to worst-case scenario, couples want to stay together but feel stuck and unable to move forward in their relationship. In other words, they're still arguing about money. Their plans, hopes, and dreams for the future have all but disintegrated or diminished.

These couples are achieving some of their life and financial goals; however, they may still be debt financing lump-sum purchases like vacations and vehicle replacements, stopping them from saving towards longer-term goals. Ultimately they don't have a clear picture of how much money they have and how much money they'll need to send their kids to college or university or to retire.

When we are in the conflict stage of a relationship, we need specific tools and guidance to help us make our way to the mature relationship stage of relationship development.

The mature stage comes from working through our differences, creating an environment where we can grow as a couple and learn more about each other. This stage is where the notion of synergy comes into play - 1 plus 1 can now equal 5 or even 25 depending on how equipped you are to deal with the inevitable conflict in your relationship. The mature stage is the financial intimacy and pleasure stage of relationships.

Money Mindset and Money Personalities

We all have very different ways of looking at money, reflecting our money mindset and our money personality. In addition, individuals can come from the same family and background and yet have very different approaches to money.

Take my brother and me as an example - we were born only 18 months apart; however, our gender difference and how we responded to our family's relationship with money gave us very different money personalities.

We both grew up poor by Canadian standards; our Father and Mother's income combined were below the poverty line. My brother's way of dealing with our childhood experiences of being ashamed of the food we ate, the clothes we wore, the way we spoke, and the house we lived in was to live a fast and expensive lifestyle starting at a very early age. He took risks with money, lived way beyond his means, had fun doing it, and eventually went bankrupt.

On the other hand, I started working and saving my earnings at a very young age. I wanted to go to University to become a teacher, so I saved most of what I earned starting from the age of 14. After that, I continued to work and keep my earnings, living beneath my means for most of my adult life.

My money personality is a saver and security seeker. My mindset told me, "if I don't have money, I will never be able to get ahead in life." This mindset was printed indelibly in my mind (or so I thought), and those thoughts governed my spending and saving behaviours. Sounds perfect, right? Wrong!

What happens when a saver and security seeker partners up with a spender and risk-taker? First, of course, you're happy to have your new love spend lavishly on you during the relationship's attraction stage. But once you reach the conflict stage of relationship development, where you face your differences, arguments arise. These different mindsets and money personalities have the power to derail your relationship altogether.

It helps to have a specific set of tools and guiding principles that will enable you to constructively come through this stage of your relationship and out the other side to reach the mature stage of relationship development. The mature stage is where you can experience financial intimacy and pleasure in your relationship.

Guiding Principles to Growing Your Relationship Towards Financial Intimacy and Pleasure

Now that we understand the barriers that we face as a couple, the question becomes, how do we make changes and lean in towards intimacy and pleasure when it comes to money in our relationship?

The first step is to understand some guiding principles that act as a foundation for increasing intimacy and pleasure. We all have beliefs and values that we develop over the years, from our family upbringing and our experiences in our work. Guiding principles are a set of moral values that establish a framework for expected behaviour and decision-making.

Here are the guiding principles I believe are essential to embarking on this journey.

Behaviour Change Is A Dynamic Process

When working in addictions, I frequently heard people say that the person has to want to change their behaviour for change to occur. I disagree. There is an entire field of study in psychology, both cognitive-behavioural and positive psychology (the two are interconnected), based on the belief that it's possible to do things that can motivate someone to consider making a change.

There are stages of motivation, just like the stages in a relationship. When you're beginning, you haven't even thought about the impact your conflict about money is having on your relationship. Motivation starts with an approach that will help you begin connecting the dots by simply thinking about it.

The action then comes later - it's a process that, if rushed, can result in no action taken.

Self-Efficacy Leads The Way

Self-efficacy is our belief in our ability to do something. If your experience has shown you that no change is possible in your relationship, your self-efficacy is very low. The key is to start making small changes, taking that first step with your spouse or partner where you can experience a win.

With each small successful step in having exploratory and appreciative conversations with your spouse that lead to making small changes in how you approach and talk about money, your self-efficacy begins to take hold and grows. As your self-efficacy increases, you start to see and believe that it's possible to plan and dream for your future and be confident about how you are currently spending, saving, investing, and managing your money.

Our Brains Can Grow, Change, And Reorganize

As adults, our brains are not static and fixed; they can grow, change and reorganize themselves, a scientific concept known as the neuroplasticity of our brains. However, our brains are hardwired to focus on the negative, which is a protective mechanism built into our physiology to protect our species from hidden dangers - like a sabertooth tiger.

Even though these predatory threats are no longer part of our day-to-day lives, our brains are still programmed to be on the alert for danger. In other words, our brains are "velcro for the negative and Teflon for the positive."

I'm sure you can imagine how this predetermined predisposition towards the negative wrecks havoc in our relationships, especially when dealing with conflicts. But, the great news is that we can program our brains to start creating new neural pathways for the positive because of our brain's neuroplasticity.

Perfection in Relationships is a Myth

There will always be challenges for us to face in our lives. Part of our growth as individuals and as a couple means that there will be times when we experience less pleasure and intimacy in our lives and our relationships. It's a natural progression throughout our lives.

The key to dealing with any new obstacles you encounter as a couple is knowing and trusting that you can get through these times using the tools, communication capabilities, and skills that you have developed along the way. Perfection is a myth, conflict is a reality, but financial intimacy and pleasure are always possible when you utilize these guiding principles.

Pleasure Is A Motivator

It's easy to understand the immediate pleasure we get when we spend money in the moment - for example, a new car, a dinner out, or even a lottery ticket that we hope will give us the future we crave. But spontaneous spending gives us only momentary pleasure, not the lasting kind that comes from financial intimacy.

When we have the cash available to pay for vacations rather than debt financing them, a plan in place to pay off a mortgage, and the financial resources to retire and ensure our families will thrive and succeed, we experience a deeper pleasure.

The more profound pleasure of this financial intimacy is related to having our desires and dreams met. This kind of pleasure can entice us to continue along the path and motivate us to be financially responsible. It's an upward spiral.

Pleasure, after all, is profoundly reinforcing and keeps us motivated to continue on our journey towards thriving in our relationships. When seeking out joy in our relationships, we motivate ourselves to continue our journey to living our dreams and making our dreams a reality.

The Couple's Financial Intimacy
and Pleasure Guide

We all have our dreams for the future. Yours may include enjoying the fruits of your labour in retirement, or getting your kids launched by providing them with funds for their education, or being part of building and creating a world you can be proud of as part of your legacy.

As the hero of your own story, you'll encounter challenges and obstacles along the way to your ultimate goals. Every hero's journey involves finding a guide to provide you with the tools and support you need to address these inevitable challenges in your life. As a Philanthropic Financial Advisor, I guide my clients through a discovery process that I call The Couple's Financial Intimacy and Pleasure Guide.

The guide builds on the insights shared here to help couples respect each other's differences, understand each other, and find their own words and ways of communicating about money while creating a path forward that promotes harmony and pleasure.

The guide consists of 3 parts - The Dream Keys, The Pleasure Vault, and The Explorer's Trail Guide. In the Dream Keys, we create a vision for your future; with The Pleasure Vault, we look at the available tools and match them to your money personalities, and with the Explorer's Trail Guide, we put it all together with a path for your money, both now and in the future.

Finances can be a significant cause of stress in relationships. At the same time, money continues to be a taboo topic in North American culture. These factors make finances a complicated subject for couples to discuss openly and productively.

My purpose in sharing these insights with you is so you'll know that it's possible to experience pleasure in all parts of your relationship - including your finances! Understanding the barriers we all have and the stages of our relationships is a significant first step to more intimacy.

I hope that these insights will start to pave the way for you to experience financial intimacy and pleasure in your relationship. This synergy will help propel you to meet your financial goals together with your partner and to understand each other on a deeper level. Financial intimacy and pleasure is a worthy goal, and I wish you every success on your journey.

Betty-Anne Howard

Betty-Anne Howard, CFP, MFA-P, CLU, CHS, CEA is a Philanthropic Financial Planner, author, award-winning speaker, financial literacy advocate and charitable giving expert. For over 20 years, Betty-Anne has been guiding women, couples and families to realize their financial dreams and has shared her vision with audiences around the world. With her specialization in strategic philanthropic planning and charitable giving she has been able to direct millions of dollars to the charitable sector while dramatically reducing taxes for those individuals she has assisted. Betty-Anne lives with her life partner Maggie and their Goldendoodle, Phoenix, on beautiful Bass Lake between Kingston and Ottawa. They enjoy the great outdoors and spending time with their horses, Stella and Brooklyn.

With every donation, a voice will be given to
the creativity that lies within the hearts of
our children living with diverse challenges.

By making this difference, children that may
not have been given the opportunity to have their
Heart Heard will have the freedom to create
beautiful works of art and musical creations.

Donate by visiting

HeartstobeHeard.com

We thank you.

www.ingramcontent.com/pod-product-compliance
Lightning Source LLC
Chambersburg PA
CBHW071529030726
47598CB00001B/59

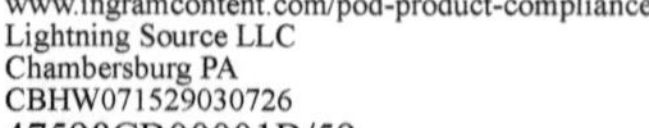